A VIEW FROM ABROAD

A View from Abroad

THE STORY OF

John and Abigail Adams

IN EUROPE

Jeanne E. Abrams

NEW YORK UNIVERSITY PRESS

New York

NEW YORK UNIVERSITY PRESS
New York
www.nyupress.org

References to Internet websites (URLs) were accurate at the time
of writing. Neither the author nor New York University Press is
responsible for URLs that may have expired or changed since the
manuscript was prepared.

Library of Congress Cataloging-in-Publication Data
Names: Abrams, Jeanne E., 1951– author.
Title: A view from abroad : the story of John and Abigail Adams in Europe /
Jeanne E. Abrams.
Other titles: Story of John and Abigail Adams in Europe
Description: New York : New York University Press, [2021] |
Includes bibliographical references and index.
Identifiers: LCCN 2020016509 (print) | LCCN 2020016510 (ebook) | ISBN
9781479802876 (cloth) | ISBN 9781479802883 (ebook) | ISBN 9781479802890
(ebook)
Subjects: LCSH: Adams, John, 1735–1826—Travel. | Adams, Abigail, 1744–1818—Travel. |
Adams family. | United States—Foreign relations—1775–1783. |
Ambassadors—United States—Biography. | Diplomats' spouses—United States—
Biography. | Paris (France)—Social life and customs—18th century. |
London (England)—Social life and customs—18th century.
Classification: LCC E322.1 .A23 2021 (print) | LCC E322.1 (ebook) | DDC 973.4/40922—dc23
LC record available at https://lccn.loc.gov/2020016509
LC ebook record available at https://lccn.loc.gov/2020016510

New York University Press books are printed on acid-free paper, and
their binding materials are chosen for strength and durability. We
strive to use environmentally responsible suppliers and materials to the
greatest extent possible in publishing our books.

Manufactured in the United States of America

10 9 8 7 6 5 4 3 2 1

Also available as an ebook

CONTENTS

CONTENTS

Introduction

An American Journey

But you must remember that my voyages and journeys are not for my private information, instruction, improvement, entertainment or pleasure; but laborious and hazardous enterprises of business [on behalf of my country]. I shall never be polished by travel.

John Adams to Nabby (Abigail) Adams Smith,
December 12, 1779

I would not exchange my country for the wealth of the Indies, or be any other than an American, though I might be queen or empress of any nation upon the globe.

Abigail Adams to John Adams, May 18, 1778

OCEAN TRAVEL IN THE EIGHTEENTH CENTURY WAS ALWAYS an uncertain undertaking, yet John Adams took it in stride. "This morning weighed the last anchor and came under sail before breakfast. . . . Thus I bid farewell to my native shore."[1] With that laconic notation written in his diary on February 15, 1778, while the Revolutionary War still raged, John Adams set out to launch his diplomatic career in Europe, directed by Congress to seek support for the American cause. John and Abigail Adams undertook—in John's case twice—lengthy physical journeys from Boston across the Atlantic, which included an often dangerous three-thousand-mile voyage, not to mention numerous trips overland by coach or carriage once they arrived abroad. By the time John returned permanently to the United States in 1788 after nearly ten years in Europe, he was a seasoned traveler who had covered nearly thirty thousand miles across land and sea in all kinds of weather on behalf of his fledgling nation.

The story of their trips abroad is fascinating on its own, but of more significance than their physical travels were the cultural, social, and political journeys John and Abigail experienced while in Europe, which expanded their formerly provincial worlds. Before they left America, they gleaned all they knew of Europe from what they had read and heard through the related experiences of others. On the eve of the American Revolution, Adams had fretted that he and his compatriots were unfit for the challenges of their times, and being "deficient" in "Travel" was one of his chief concerns.[2] Going to Europe would surely remedy that lack for the Adamses. Living in France and England influenced their opinions about American nationhood, the formation of an ideal American character, and what it meant to be American. Their time in Europe afforded them the firsthand opportunity to contrast the Old World with the New in regard to the manners of the people, the conditions of the respective societies, and the differing forms of government.

At the same time, their years abroad deepened their appreciation for being Americans and strengthened their nationalist commitment. In their travels through France, England, the Netherlands, and in John's case also Spain, they observed a variety of political structures and societal forms. Their time in Europe mirrored the challenges that many prominent American founders, including George and Martha Washington, Thomas Jefferson, Benjamin Franklin, and John and Sarah Jay experienced in the process of building a new national and personal identity after they separated from England. The Adamses struggled with how to elevate their status as civilized and cultured Americans who still appreciated many aspects of Old World refinement and culture. At the same time, they also grappled with how to carve out a unique American persona that was independent from British control and unfettered by centuries of English tradition. For years, the area along the American Eastern Seaboard was a colonial extension of England.

For this reason, seemingly inconsequential practices such as choosing what European fashions, china, and furniture to purchase and bring back home on their return voyage took on great significance. Despite the fact that Abigail often decried European luxury, the fine porcelain and other adornments she bought for their new house in Braintree, Massachusetts, became symbolic of the cultural refinement appropriate for American leaders. She understood that material possessions reflected genteel behavior. Similarly, John emphasized American simplicity and frugality, but his pride and joy became an intricately carved French desk he had acquired in Paris. As historian Kariann Akemi Yokota has observed, "Creating a national identity—unbecoming British—was a tricky business."[3] Indeed, the same could be said about shaping one's individual American identity in the wake of the revolution. Simultaneously, Europe allowed the Adamses to lay claim to a cosmopolitan exposure they deemed valuable for building knowledge and excellence in character. Living in Europe also enabled John and Abigail to examine and define what *separated* Americans from French, Dutch, and especially English citizens, and what in their eyes made Americans superior.

Past biographies of the Adamses have to varying degrees all touched on their time in Europe. However, *A View from Abroad: The Story of John and Abigail Adams in Europe* is the first full-length study that focuses exclusively on their residence in Europe to tell that story in detail and show its effect on their evolving American identity and their vision for the nation's future governance and development.[4] It aims to be a narrative history that presents a composite portrait of the Adamses as they navigated Europe. They were privileged but uncomfortable with privilege, engaged abroad yet missing home, dealing with changeable allies and an uneasy peace with a former enemy. *A View from Abroad* serves as a travelogue through time and place; it is an intimate portrayal of some of the most important people of their era and how they conducted themselves beyond America's borders. It is the story of a family, a marriage, and future presidents. The prolific letters and diaries of John and Abigail as well as of their children Nabby and John Quincy provide us with an intimate window into their hearts and minds and reveal the various ways they were influenced by a culture at once familiar and foreign.

Their writings also cast an illuminating lens on daily life in Europe during the late eighteenth century and the inner workings of the French and English courts. John and Abigail witnessed firsthand the height of royal excess as well as the deep social and economic divides in Europe during the era. The two met the absolutist French rulers Louis XVI and Marie-Antoinette at the Palace of Versailles and the staid but still imposing British monarchs, King George III and Queen Charlotte, at St. James's Palace. Abigail looked with disdain upon the elite opulence she encountered in France and in England. She was even more appalled by the number of Parisian women who were driven into prostitution by dire poverty. Equally disturbing was the sight of countless beggars in tattered clothing in London, as well as farm laborers who toiled in the bucolic English countryside in order to eke out a bare living.

Although the Adamses came to admire much about the storied culture and venerable history of France, England, and the Netherlands, they viewed life in America as morally, politically, and socially superior to the Old World. By the time they left Europe in 1788, however, one of their greatest fears was that Americans would be corrupted by European mores and soon aspire to the same level of luxury and opulence, which would threaten moral and civic virtue. This was by no means an entirely new concern for John.[5] In a letter written to Abigail in April 1776, less than three months before the Declaration of Independence, John warned of the pitfalls of meaningless extravagance. He declared, "Whenever Vanity and Gaiety, a Love of Pomp and Dress, Furniture, Equipage, Buildings, great company, expensive diversions, and elegant Entertainments get the better of the Principles and Judgments of Men or Women there is no knowing where they will stop, nor into what Evils, natural, moral, or political, they will lead us."[6]

Abigail had always exhibited a fundamentally optimistic personality, but John was more skeptical about human nature. His political thought had evolved over time, yet his worries about the rise of a new American aristocracy, composed of wealthy citizens, prominent merchants, and influential grand landowners who focused on self-aggrandizement instead of the public good, stretched back to the 1770s. That view only became more pronounced in the 1780s as he and Abigail surveyed their fellow Americans from their European vantage point.[7]

As Adams put it in *A Defence of the Constitutions of Government of the United States of America*, the political tract he authored between 1785 and 1786 while living in England, there was "no special providence for Americans, and their nature is the same with that of others."[8] In his eyes, human nature throughout the world remained constant over time. Only a well-ordered republic that featured a balanced, three-branch government and was based on the rule of law, not men, could control the serious threat of the rise of an oligarchy and help shape a citizenry committed to public virtue and civic responsibility. It was a political model that he hoped Americans would adopt. He believed that such a form of government would mitigate the inherent dangers that all nations faced, and it was an outlook he advocated until the end of his days.

The Adamses shared a vision of the ideal American future. Indeed, John and Abigail were deeply committed to the view that an effective republic required a robust system for curbing the quest for excessive power, especially among ambitious politicians and oligarchs. Yet they acknowledged that leaders required some level of strength to be effective. The challenge would be to maintain the delicate balance between liberty and authority. For the Adamses, unbridled power *and* too much democracy were both to be feared. As historians Nancy Isenberg and Andrew Burstein have observed, this was not a popular notion among some Americans, including Thomas Jefferson, who espoused a vision of American exceptionalism and maintained an abiding faith in the judgment of "the people." Adams has often been criticized for offering too conservative and cautious an approach to contain the "undemocratic self-aggrandizement" that he believed operated at the expense of broad liberty. He worried that "the people" would easily be misled by charismatic leaders.[9]

Both the Adamses departed for Europe with preconceived notions. In the American imagination at the time, Europe was viewed as the site of monarchial and aristocratic displays of power while America was, by contrast, regarded by its citizens as an exemplar of virtue and egalitarianism. Use of the word "Europe" for many Americans became a code for everything that needed to be eradicated in the quest to become an independent American nation: rank, status, elaborate ceremonies, excessive luxury, corruption, ostentatious fashions, and profligate lifestyles.[10] Despite their reservations about interacting in such a European society, John and Abigail were motivated to make the journey to the Old World not because of their desire to tour the globe or acquire a European polish, but because of their intense patriotism and underlying commitment to the public good.

Ironically, it was the Adamses' encounters with fellow *Americans* in Europe as well as correspondence with relatives back home, such as Abigail's uncle Cotton Tufts, her sister Mary Cranch, and John's political colleagues in Congress like the powerful Robert Livingston, rather than their interactions with Europeans that convinced them that public virtue had declined precipitously in their homeland. They feared that a rising oligarchy posed a serious threat to the viability of the new republic. After Abigail joined John in Europe, she too became increasingly worried about the fate of America and what she perceived to be the erosion of standards in her home country.

Still, despite their concerns, they remained in Europe longer than they had planned or wished for in order to continue to press for stronger financial support and favorable commercial treaties with France, England, the Netherlands, and other European powers. For John, his sense of duty to America often trumped personal responsibilities. On behalf of his country, he had left his family behind for years, first while serving in Congress, and later as an American emissary working abroad to secure treaties of peace, amity, and commerce. At the same time, he yearned for distinction and was clearly flattered at being named a foreign minister. He welcomed the opportunity to play an active role in history. Despite his deep and genuine affection for his wife and children, he often ended up privileging public service over his family. Adams himself recognized his ambition, vanity, and need for recognition as a character flaw. Yet he was gratified that his compatriots thought enough of him to confer the appointment, indicating, John believed, that his colleagues understood that he had been essential to securing American independence and that he would conscientiously further America's economic and political interests in Europe.

Abigail cared far less about fame than John. In 1778 she declared, "My soul is unambitious of pomp or power."[11] If we take Abigail at her word, she harbored little desire for advancing her personal status. Despite their collaborative relationship, it appears that in this regard she primarily supported her husband's diplomatic service in Europe out of a strong sense of patriotic duty, familial affection, and loyalty, as well as for the sake of holding her marriage together. She understood how important the assignment was to John's self-esteem and sense of worth.

Still, Abigail was reluctant for him to remain in Europe after his first posting. In 1783, while John was in the Netherlands, she wrote passionately, "If Congress should think proper to make you an other appointment, [I] beg you not to accept it. Call me not to any further trials of your long absence from your family."[12] Despite her heartfelt plea, John *did* accept another diplomatic post, and finally, a resigned Abigail joined him in Europe, despite her initial reluctance. Resilience was one of her most notable qualities, and once Abigail set sail for Europe, she made the best of her circumstances and availed herself of every possible cultural opportunity.

John's first journey abroad at the age of forty-two was not to be the typical leisurely grand tour of Europe that so many elite, affluent men had undertaken before him. For example, wealthy Philadelphian William Bingham, who later became John's political ally, had visited Europe in 1773, when he was in his early twenties, to combine pleasure and business. Earlier George Washington's well-to-do Virginia planter father sent George's older half-brothers to England to be polished by a British education. John sailed to Europe because he regarded his diplomatic duties as essential to the well-being of the new nation. Nevertheless, he often struggled as an absent husband and father to retain his cherished family ties and to balance them with his public calling. Not only his wife but also their offspring suffered from the repeated and lengthy separations, and all four of the Adams children endured troubled lives as adults.

Abigail was often lonely and sometimes resentful while John was away. In strongly worded letters like the one above, she urged him to return home. Yet, because she felt that her husband was essential to the success of the American cause, she relented and supported John's diplomatic role. It was a path that her mentor and fellow patriot Mercy Otis Warren was unable to sustain in relation to her own husband. As Warren's biographer Rosemarie Zagarri noted, Mercy was unable to keep "acting the part of the Republican Wife who was willing to sacrifice her own happiness for the good of the country."[13]

From youth, Abigail had been taught by her parents and her religious tenets to meet personal challenges with acceptance and fortitude. These factors served as her succor when separated from her husband for long periods, and they helped her endure personal illness and the loss of several of her children. Ultimately, she stood behind John in his political undertakings because of her deep-rooted sense of moral and civic responsibility and her religious faith, which emphasized America's special destiny and her belief that Providence guided her family. As she put it dramatically in the summer of 1780, she was convinced that "the welfare and happiness of this wide-extended country, ages yet unborn, depend on their happiness and security upon the able and skillful, the honest and upright, discharge of the important trust committed to him [John]."[14]

John and Abigail spent several years together in Europe, but John's residence stretched nearly a full decade. He embarked on his first trip to Europe in 1778 after he was appointed an American emissary to France to develop critically needed support. Many years later, he recalled how hard it had been to leave a "dearly beloved Wife and four young Children" and that he had been cognizant of his "Want of qualifications for the Office [of foreign minister]." Yet he claimed to have weighed the pull of family ties against the dire situation because "my Country was in deep distress and in great danger. Her dearest Interest would be involved in the relations she might form with foreign nations."[15]

In many ways, Adams was the American founder most suited to promoting the country's interests abroad. Even before he arrived in Paris in 1778, John had understood that the establishment of political *and* economic ties with European countries was crucial to the future success of the nascent American nation. As several historians have argued, American leaders from colonial days to the American Revolution and the early years of the republic saw commerce as the cornerstone of American diplomacy. Few understood the centrality of commerce better than Adams. In 1776 he had been instrumental in creating the American Plan of Treaties, which aimed at establishing reciprocal economic agreements with France. Inspired by Enlightenment thought, many American leaders, including Adams, had hoped to substitute the principles of free trade for the old mercantilist philosophy that had long reigned in Europe. However, as they attempted to promote equitable commercial treaties, Adams and his fellow American diplomats in France and then in England found themselves stymied at every turn by European leaders who jockeyed to secure their nations' hegemony in the transatlantic world.[16]

Adams was among the most economically and politically astute of the revolutionary leaders, but he did not boast an aristocratic background like many of the leading patriots from Virginia and New York. Despite his own modest beginnings and middling social status, Adams learned to negotiate the proper royal etiquette in Europe, even as he detested empty civility and hypocrisy. Still, he was never a natural diplomat like Benjamin Franklin. John's detractors viewed him as vain, ambitious, and irascible. His family, friends, and other supporters saw him as a man of unshakable integrity.

John Adams was all of the above: brilliant, learned, fiercely independent, honest to a fault, as well as prickly and impetuous at times, but he also could be warm, loyal, affectionate, and congenial and possessed a wry sense of humor. Moreover, to some degree he learned to temper his own personal vanity and quest for recognition as well as his frequent frustration with official protocol. While in Europe, his unshakable commitment to the public good of his country often allowed him to control his considerable ambition and swallow his pride, at least in public. It is these contradictory traits that make Adams a complex and fascinating figure, and the story of his and Abigail's European sojourn so compelling.

Nevertheless, John Adams has often been overshadowed by other more charismatic American founders, such as Franklin, George Washington, Thomas Jefferson, and, more recently, Alexander Hamilton. As historian Joseph J. Ellis observed, Adams has been the "most misconstrued and unappreciated" among the great men in American history, arguably the most "fully human member of his remarkable generation of American statesmen."[17] Although in recent years a number of writers have paid more attention to Abigail than to John, both Adamses have often been derided as uninspiring, backward-looking, pessimistic conservatives who had little faith in democracy. For example, eminent historian Gordon S. Wood maintains that Adams "became the representative of a crusty conservatism that emphasized the inequality and vice-ridden nature of American society."[18] Yet even Wood seems to have fallen victim to the very cult of personality that Adams warned of. At times Wood mistakes charisma, which other American founders such as Jefferson exuded, for integrity and substance. Guaranteeing *liberty* rather than equality for his fellow Americans was Adams's fundamental goal.

John's service in Congress had launched his national political career, and it was his time in distant Europe that marked a turning point for the fragile American nation. Before he sailed for Europe, the furthest John had ventured from New England was about five hundred miles, during a harrowing winter trip south to Baltimore on horseback in 1777 during the war. In Paris, he served as one of the American representatives to the glittering French court of Louis XVI. He played a pivotal role in the signing of the 1783 Treaty of Paris, which formally ended the Revolutionary War, and he afterwards became America's first envoy to the London Court of St. James's, which was a far cry from his provincial milieu in Massachusetts.

Adams was certainly no country bumpkin. Before we examine his stay in Europe and that of Abigail in the coming chapters, it will be helpful to explore their early lives in order to put their time abroad in context. John was the son of a respected Massachusetts Congregationalist deacon. He was descended from a long line of modestly successful middle-class yeoman farmers who had long resided in the agricultural hamlet of Braintree, about fourteen miles from Boston. He was well educated, and the colony of Massachusetts boasted the highest rate of male literacy in America. Still, fewer than 1 percent of New England males received a college education; Adams was one of the privileged few. He graduated from Harvard College, which enlarged his intellectual horizons and placed him among elite Massachusetts society. He quickly became one of the busiest and most respected lawyers in Massachusetts. John also possessed a keen insight into economics and the intricacies of commercial trade that served him well. Indeed, it was a combination of good fortune, stubborn persistence, and financial acumen that enabled him to later secure much-needed loans from the Dutch to help pay off debts that had accrued during the war.

Adams could also be an articulate and volcanic speaker, and a persuasive, albeit somewhat ponderous writer. He launched the first of his political tracts in the early 1760s with an article in the *Boston Evening Post*. In the 1770s, during the days leading up to the American Revolution, he penned a series of influential pieces in the *Boston Gazette*, known as the *Letters of Novanglus*, in which he argued for colonial autonomy. Later, he authored the seminal *Thoughts on Government*, a publication that helped convince his fellow Americans to support the revolution and also served as a guide for several state constitutions.

Fortunately, he was vivid, candid, and engaging in his private correspondence and diary entries, which make his complicated personality come alive. John was also one of the most well-read men in America during his era. Thomas Jefferson rivaled and perhaps exceeded Adams as an inveterate reader, yet for all his breadth of knowledge, Jefferson had not read as deeply as Adams. Adams delved into law, history, theology, political philosophy, and literature, and he was an accomplished political scientist. Although fine art, drama, and music were far from his main focus, he appreciated their aesthetic value, even if he lacked sophistication. In short, he was what today we would term a dedicated lifelong learner if not a Renaissance man on the level of Jefferson.[19]

Yet Europe was an ocean apart, both literally and figuratively. Although he had at times rubbed elbows with the colonial elite, John had never before witnessed the levels of wealth and privilege he would encounter in France and England. The Old World stood in stark contrast to the simpler, relatively egalitarian way of life he so admired in his hometown of Braintree and in the Massachusetts colony as a whole. Adams began his European voyage with virtually no command of spoken French and little firsthand knowledge of contemporary European political intrigue or the customs of foreign diplomacy. His knowledge of Europe came from books, and most of those had been published long before he embarked on his transatlantic journey. Certainly, he had never come face to face with real-life monarchs or the splendor that characterized the French and English courts and the lifestyles of the nobility.

Yet it is important to recognize that royalism and reverence for the British king had a long history in the American colonies. Until at least 1774, even emerging committed revolutionaries such as the Adamses and George Washington had celebrated the English monarchy and regarded King George III as a benevolent father figure. Indeed, elements of the imperial past were often interwoven into the early republic, and the quest to form a new national character reflected struggles over opposing worldviews among Americans. As historian Brendan McConville has argued, the fundamental battle was between those who "viewed the world as new, tabula rasa, and believed human nature . . . moldable and remakeable" and those like Adams who were attempting to rework past institutions in a new form.[20] When he later met with the king as the American minister to England, John developed an ambivalent but respectful relationship with George III, and he saw much to emulate in the British form of a constitutional monarchy. As Yokota has pointed out, "The process of 'becominge American' . . . did not necessarily entail a categorical rejection of British culture."[21] Many upwardly mobile Americans still aspired to acquire a "mother-country polish."[22]

When he first departed for Europe, Adams moved forward with determination and unremitting diligence, and worked relentlessly to rectify the omissions in his life experience. He arrived in Paris on April 8, 1778, full of hope that the efforts of the joint group of three commissioners, which included Benjamin Franklin and Arthur Lee, would be productive. Ultimately, John did play an important role in securing critical French naval support for the American forces. Although many of his diplomatic efforts abroad would be unsuccessful, Adams's most pivotal accomplishment turned out to be the significant loans he secured in the Netherlands for the struggling American nation. His dogged single-mindedness and often unconventional diplomatic undertakings, pursued largely on his own in isolation, helped convince the Dutch to invest in the economic promise of the fragile American republic.

John's wife did not join him in Europe for several years, but even from afar, Abigail remained his supportive if sometimes reluctant partner, and she continued to play an influential role in his life. Fourteen years before he set sail for Europe, on October 25, 1764, John Adams had married Abigail Smith, daughter of a prominent Weymouth liberal Congregationalist minister, William Smith, and Elizabeth Quincy Smith, who stemmed from a well-known Boston political merchant family. It was a union initially opposed by her parents, especially by Abigail's mother, who did not care much for the brash young lawyer whose status and prospects she deemed beneath her daughter's social station. When Abigail and John wed, Massachusetts was still a loyal English colony in the far-flung British Empire, and Elizabeth Smith could never have dreamed that one day her daughter would later become the wife of a leading political figure in the newly created United States and become the nation's second First Lady.

Despite her parents' opposition, the strong-minded Abigail stood fast in her desire to marry John. From the beginning, Abigail kept the brilliant and principled but sometimes vain and erratic John grounded, and her natural serenity and optimism helped tame his often-mercurial temperament. Her influence became particularly important after she joined John in Europe, where the need for skilled diplomacy was crucial. As historian Joseph J. Ellis put it, Abigail provided John's "ballast."[23]

Like most women in early America, Abigail Adams never formally attended school. Her voracious appetite for knowledge was fed by relatives and especially by her soul mate and husband. Abigail read deeply and widely, from Shakespeare and novels to philosophy, history, and political theory. Reading would have been possible only after working demanding days overseeing the household and the family farm once her children were asleep. In 1780, not long after John and their eldest son had departed for Europe, she wrote to advise John Quincy, himself a future president, "Learning is not attained by chance. It must be sought with ardor and attended with diligence."[24] It was a maxim she followed her entire life. In regard to the question of widespread education, she and John were of one mind. Although advanced knowledge could not cure all political and social ills, education helped build character and could produce the enlightened citizenry they believed was indispensable to successful self-government and the future of the American experiment.

From the first days of her marriage, Abigail became part of a politically minded family. In the days leading up to the American Revolution, the Adamses were incensed with what they perceived to be Great Britain's encroachment on liberty in the colonies and the loss of their rights as English subjects. John became a leading member of the Continental Congress, and his stint as a Massachusetts representative in Philadelphia gained him valuable political experience and the opportunity to test his philosophy and world outlook while honing his speaking and writing skills. Although Abigail remained behind at home, caring for their four children, supervising the family farm and finances, her unwavering support of John and the revolutionary cause enabled him to play a pivotal role on the American road to independence.

In many ways Adams was out of his element in the more sophisticated social circles he moved in once he arrived in Europe. From the moment he stepped onto French soil, however, he was determined to conduct himself with dignity, exhibiting the diligence he applied to all his endeavors. Moreover, John adjusted surprisingly well to life on the Continent. He began his European service by studying French aboard ship. Unlike Franklin, Adams became a competent speaker and writer in the language, even composing sections of his diary in French. At times, these jottings included his growing critical attitude toward Franklin and suspicion of the French foreign minister, Comte de Vergennes, as well as his ambivalent feelings toward Louis XVI and Marie-Antoinette.

There was much that John found to be of value in the civilized culture of the Old World. As he wrote to Abigail, "There is everything here that can inform understanding, or refine the taste, and indeed one would think that could purify the heart." At the same time he saw serious flaws in French society that he believed were antithetical to American values, especially the Yankee ideals of honesty, fiscal and community responsibility, and the Puritan-inspired moral code he had absorbed from childhood, which played a central role in shaping his thought and behavior throughout his life.[25] John was neither a strict Calvinist, a Puritan, nor a prude, but he was a man of moral integrity, one who set high ethical standards. Above all, he rejected extremes and valued balance, both in how individuals conducted their personal lives and in their form of government.

John took self-reflection and self-improvement seriously, and he combined select segments of the religious values of his youth with some of the Enlightenment-inspired progressive ideals about religion and political philosophy he had incorporated in his education at Harvard, which moved him toward a more liberal world outlook.[26] Still, it is important to recognize that religious faith underpinned the lives of the Adamses. American identity in the postrevolutionary and early national period was shaped by both republicanism *and* Protestantism. It was in Paris that John penned the oft-quoted philosophical dictum that drove his public service to the American nation during and after the American Revolution: "I must study politics and war that my sons may have the liberty to study mathematics and philosophy. My sons ought to study mathematics and philosophy, geography, natural history, naval architecture, navigation, commerce, and agriculture in order to give their children a right to study paintings, poetry, music, architecture, statuary, tapestry, and porcelain."[27] John remained a lifelong advocate of the study of political science as a tool for understanding and improving the human condition. Indeed, one of the driving forces that shaped his character was the overarching desire to help create an American nation that would ensure the well-being of *all* its citizens, regardless of their social or economic status.

Before her voyage to join John in Europe, Abigail had never been more than fifty miles from home. She too admired the social and political structure of the close-knit community in which she had grown up and hoped that it would be replicated on a wider scale as the American nation matured. Indeed, John and Abigail believed that New England should serve as the model for the creation of a new national identity.[28] Abigail may initially have had reservations about traveling to Europe and leaving her accustomed life, but from the beginning, she was determined to conduct her time there with dignity and propriety. Despite her distaste for the dictates of high fashion, she understood the role comportment and stylish clothing played in projecting one's social image. She worked diligently to serve as an able representative of the nascent American nation and endeavored to earn the respect of French and English leaders and members of the upper crust.

Despite the centuries-old history and cultural sophistication she encountered in Europe, Abigail remained convinced that life in America provided significantly more opportunity for citizens from all walks of life. The time she spent near Paris and then in London reinforced Abigail's view that Americans were blessed in comparison to those living in the Old World, even in England, which she considered the most enlightened and progressive of the European nations. "How little cause of complaint have the inhabitants of the United States, when they compare their situation, not with despotic monarchies, but with this land [Great Britain] of freedom," she declared. Moreover, Abigail looked askance at Americans who overtly criticized their homeland (even though she would often do so herself). "The ease with which honest industry may acquire property in America, the equal distribution of justice to the poor as well as the rich, and the personal liberty they enjoy," she argued, "all call upon them to support their government and laws to respect their rulers and gratefully acknowledge their superior blessings."[29]

Abigail's patriotic zeal would only become stronger over time. She would later insist that her beloved country was a sovereign nation, one that should always remain independent of European influence. As she declared to her sister Mary Cranch years later when John served as president and when war with France appeared to be a distinct possibility, "As an independent Nation [the United States], no other has a Right to complain, or dictate to us, with whom we shall form connections."[30] Moreover, John and Abigail came to believe that America should set the standard for the world as a well-ordered society and that the American nation, if it adopted the proper form of government, would serve as an example of virtuous civic responsibility. In short, the Adamses exhibited an appreciation and reverence for human excellence in all aspects of life, which they hoped would characterize their new nation.

Shortly before Abigail and her daughter were due to sail for Europe in 1784, John provided Nabby with some fatherly advice. "I hope that your journeys in Europe, and your returning voyage to your own country, will be equally prosperous. . . . I need to say to you, that the end of travel, as well as study, is not the simple gratification of curiosity, or to enable one to shine in conversation, but to make us wiser and better."[31]

It was certainly a philosophy that John and Abigail took to heart. The Adamses' travels in Europe provided them with a firsthand framework of comparison and an opportunity that allowed them to judge for themselves and to inform their fellow citizens about the potential superiority of America. At the same time, they viewed their life abroad as an opportunity to expand their life experience.

By the time Abigail set sail for their return to America, she had significant concerns about the future of the United States. Still, she left Europe even more convinced of America's potential. Although John was optimistic about America's long-term success, he maintained serious reservations. He feared that the luxury, dissipation, and inequality he had witnessed in Europe would soon affect his fellow Americans, and that the potential for deep divisions between social classes, if left unchecked, would increase over time. Because of his advocacy for a strong (and virtuous) executive, whom he believed could help counteract those forces by lending a wise, impartial, and steadying hand, John was often criticized as being a monarchist. Even his former close friend, the Boston writer and staunch revolutionary patriot Mercy Otis Warren, later offered such a harsh opinion. In her history of the American Revolution, she charged that John had abandoned his earlier revolutionary principles under the corrupting influence of the French and English royal courts.[32]

Nothing could have been further from the truth. John may have found elements to admire personally in both Louis XVI and George III, and particularly in the benefits of a constitutional monarchy with a balanced government, which he had experienced firsthand in England. However, their time in France and England only made the Adamses more fervently nationalistic Americans, and they believed that political leaders should govern, not rule. Their European residence was an experience that was filtered through their American background and upbringing and their evolving perspectives. From their perch across the Atlantic, it allowed them to identify more clearly the flaws in American society that they had seen developing for some time.

Living near Paris and then in London played a role in shaping John and Abigail's thinking about the ideal American character, one that would emphasize public and personal virtue, restraint, and frugality. With the notable exception of Thomas Paine, whose fiery pamphlet *Common Sense* helped spark the American Revolution and who disdained mixed government, most American leaders supported a bicameral legislature. Yet the Adamses sincerely believed that support of John's *particular* vision of a balanced government would protect property, religious freedom, the rule of law, and liberty and would at the same time foster an exemplary spirit in the emerging United States. In 1786 John wrote the French aristocrat Comte de Sarsfield that he hoped "to see rising in America an Empire of Liberty & a Prospect of two or three hundred Millions of freemen, without one noble or one King."[33]

John was neither a reactionary conservative nor a monarchist. What he advocated was an executive with sufficient power and authority who could play a central role in steering an American republic on the right path by counterbalancing the negative influences of aristocratic forces, what he termed "the few," on the one hand, and the unchecked democratic influences of "the people," or "the many," on the other.[34] Indeed, John believed that it was human nature to amass power, and what he feared most was a rising American oligarchy composed of wealthy or charismatic aristocrats who would prevail over those citizens who possessed genuine virtue and talent, a situation that he believed would put the future of his native land in serious jeopardy.[35]

As beliefs about the American character and nationhood evolved among newly independent Americans like Abigail and John as well as some of their revolutionary comrades, such as Thomas Jefferson and John Jay, they were all forced to reevaluate their place in the transatlantic world. The Adamses reflected *one* important strain of thought regarding an American identity, but they were not representative of all Americans. Their outlook was based on a distinct New England sensibility and was also shaped in reaction to their experiences abroad. Their views served as a counterpoint, for example, to those espoused by many prominent southerners. As historian Brian Steele has pointed out, not only did Jefferson believe that "his generation had made the world anew," but he also believed that Americans were exceptional and peculiarly fit for democracy.[36] While both the Adamses agreed that geography, abundant natural resources, and land offered Americans unprecedented opportunities to prosper and live in peaceful contentment, they held the deep-seated belief that human nature was fundamentally the same all over the globe.

John and Abigail crossed paths with many Americans abroad, but not all of them shared their outlook. Like the Adamses and Jefferson, New York revolutionary and American diplomat John Jay and his wife, Sarah Livingston Jay, and wealthy Philadelphians William Bingham and his young wife, the cultured Anne Willing Bingham, had also spent time in Europe. Jay and Adams had first met when they served in Philadelphia as delegates to the First Continental Congress, and both men had played a pivotal role in writing their own state constitutions in the 1770s. Jay even served as president of the Continental Congress for a time, where he first met European diplomats who had been dispatched from Spain and France. Along with Benjamin Franklin, Jay and Adams later worked together while stationed in Europe to negotiate the Treaty of Paris to end the Revolutionary War in 1783.

In the 1790s Bingham, a prominent merchant and patriot, became an ardent Federalist and supporter of Adams during his presidency. He also became an influential politician, who served as a United States senator from 1795 to 1801. Anne Bingham became one of the leaders of Philadelphia society when they returned to America in 1786. Abigail and John crossed paths with the Binghams frequently in both France and England. Abigail never developed the admiration for European society and the cultured female French *salonniéres* exhibited by Anne, but the two women became well acquainted in Paris, a connection that developed further in London and when the Adamses later lived in Philadelphia, the temporary capital of the United States. Nonetheless, Abigail looked askance at Anne's admiration of French customs and manners and her extravagant style of dress.

The political outlook of both Bingham and Jay, whom one biographer called the "most conservative of the leading founders," included strong skepticism about the desirability of widespread popular democracy and firm support for a bicameral legislature. In fact, Jay and Bingham would align more closely in later years with Adams's political philosophy than with that of Thomas Jefferson.[37] Despite his great wealth, Bingham exhibited a dedication to the public good that Adams admired. In 1780 Bingham expressed a sentiment that mirrored Adams's concerns about the decline of American public virtue, when he observed that "they were no longer governed by that pure, disinterested patriotism, which distinguished the Infancy of the contest [the American Revolution]."[38] The three men regarded the concept of American exceptionalism in much narrower terms than Jefferson. Perhaps most importantly, they did not share his level of faith in the ability of Americans to govern themselves wisely. As Steele has argued, "Jefferson's confidence in the American people was rooted in his sense that they were exceptional,"[39] but Adams never regarded Americans as unique examples of humankind.

John Adams espoused what many have considered a rather dour view of the human capacity for improvement, but it was an outlook he would have likely defended as mere prudent pragmatism. Wood has contended that it was the optimistic, enlightened worldview of Thomas Jefferson that has most strongly resonated with American citizens over time, and not that of John Adams, whom Wood has labeled "uninspiring." Nor, by extension, does Wood praise the outlook of Abigail Adams. In light of today's political and social American landscape, however, the Adamses' concerns seem far more prescient and reflective of reality. Wood's portrayal of John Adams exaggerates the challenging aspects of his character and unfairly suggests that John's political views were more driven by "long-simmering . . . jealousies and resentments . . . that sprang from his tormented soul" than his integrity and deeply reasoned concerns about America's long-term future. Similarly, Wood contends that Abigail became bitter as she aged.[40]

It is far more accurate to assert that Adams was an unflinching realist rather than a pessimist, and historian Edith B. Gelles, who has
probably provided the most sensitive and nuanced picture of Abigail,
has observed that she possessed "uncanny optimism," which survived
intact into her last years.[41] As John entered his old age, he mellowed
and became more hopeful about the American future. He believed that
by coupling a more realistic appraisal of human nature with a firm commitment to human rights, the new American republic could succeed in
guaranteeing liberty, unlike other republican experiments that had failed
in the past. John and Abigail's years abroad reinforced many of their earlier views about the relationship between human nature and governance
as they continued to refine their world outlook.

At the same time, however, their stay in Europe cemented their bond
with their native land and kept them strong patriotic Americans, ones
who had to reconcile their love of country with their realistic concerns.
When Abigail and John Adams returned to America in 1788, like many
of their fellow American who had toured overseas, they had enjoyed
many aspects of their stay and acquired a more sophisticated cultural
veneer and a wider life experience, but at heart, they remained fervent
Americans. Even while the Adamses resided abroad, their center of
gravity always remained in America.

ONE

John Adams

An American in Paris

Tis a little more than three weeks since the dearest of friends and tenderest of husbands left his solitary partner, and quitted all the fond endearments of domestic felicity for the dangers of the sea, exposed, perhaps, to the attack of a hostile foe.

Abigail Adams to John Adams, March 8, 1778

Europe, thou great theater of arts, sciences, commerce, war, am I at last permitted to visit thy territories.

Diary of John Adams, March 30, 1778

I am wearied to death with gazing wherever I go, at a Profusion of unmeaning Wealth and Magnificence.

Diary of John Adams, May 20, 1778

JOHN ADAMS RODE HIS HORSE THE LAST MILES FROM PHILADELPHIA back to his home in Braintree, Massachusetts, in November 1777, surrounded by the brilliant fall foliage, which made the New England countryside so famously beautiful. John and Abigail, as well as their four children, were overjoyed when he returned to his beloved farm that autumn after so many prolonged separations. He had promised to reunite with his family, restore his health, and resume his law career in order to earn a good living. And now he was coming home, but his retreat to private life was short-lived.

Even after his four grueling years as a member of the Continental Congress, and the untold personal sacrifices that had been made by both Adamses on behalf of their country, their patriotic resolve was to be tested yet again. To Abigail's chagrin, just a month after he returned, the couple received notice from the new president of Congress, Henry Laurens, of John's official election as a joint commissioner to the court of Louis XVI at Versailles to help forge an alliance with France. When the news arrived in Braintree, John was in Portsmouth, Maine, arguing a case before the Admiralty Court. Abigail, instructed to open all John's correspondence in his absence, was the first to receive what was for her most unwelcome news.

Adams was to replace the recalled American diplomat Silas Deane, who had been sent to France in 1776 as a special agent of a three-man American commission. Now John was instructed to travel to Paris to join the other two remaining American envoys, Benjamin Franklin and Arthur Lee. The latter had sparked Deane's recall by accusing him of financial irregularities. Adams's maiden journey to France would provide him with a firsthand opportunity to define with more clarity what separated America from European nations and to develop his ideal view of the emerging individual and national American identity. While abroad, in addition to his diplomatic duties, John would grapple with the pressing issue of how to balance European inherited traditions with new American cultural models.

Although John had known that a formal invitation from Congress might be forthcoming, he initially had been poised to decline the post in order to remain near his family, whom he had often neglected during his lengthy stints in Philadelphia. His youngest child, five-year-old Thomas, barely knew his father, and when Abigail had given birth in the summer of 1777 to a stillborn daughter, John had not been by her side to share their grief. Although he had been grateful that Abigail's life had been spared, the loss of the baby was a cruel blow to John, who commented to his wife poignantly, "Is it not unaccountable, that one should feel so strong an Affection for an Infant, that one has never seen, nor shall see?"[1] Not only had John pined for Abigail while away, but he also understood that he had missed many seminal events in his children's lives.

John had long been an ambitious man, and he undoubtedly felt that his European service would secure a place for him in the annals of history. Just the previous year he had told Mercy Warren that he felt unsuited for foreign diplomacy because he lacked "Complaisance and Ductility of Temper."[2] Unlike Benjamin Franklin, Adams had never set foot before in Europe, but he was well-read and more familiar with the subject of foreign affairs than most of the members of the Continental Congress. Soon he, along with his eldest son, John Quincy, would embark on a lengthy grand tour abroad.

A distraught Abigail met the prospect of their setting sail with justified trepidation. At first Abigail insisted that she and all their children journey to Europe, but she reluctantly gave in when John decided that embarking on such a voyage would be "too hazardous and imprudent," and that the cost of housing the family abroad was too prohibitive. Many years later John recalled that his wife had always supported him in "all antecedent dangers and perplexities."[3] Although the Adamses experienced a strong and loving union, in the eighteenth-century world, women were legally and economically subordinate to their husbands, and the Adams marriage was no different. Once again, out of a strong sense of domestic and civic responsibility, Abigail deferred to her husband. She would remain in Braintree on her own, tasked with supervising the family farm, managing the finances, and overseeing the education and upbringing of the three children left behind.

She carried out these demanding undertakings admirably despite separation from her "dearest friend" for years at a time. Now she would lose the company of John Quincy as well. Her eldest son, then only a boy, had stood beside her on the Adamses' doorstep watching the momentous and terrifying Battle of Bunker Hill during the early days of the Revolutionary War while John was away serving in the Continental Congress. Abigail appreciated his keen intellect and precocious maturity, and now he too would leave her.

The saltbox house on the left served as the Braintree home of John and Abigail after their marriage. Courtesy National Park Service, Adams National Historic Park.

As historian Woody Holton has demonstrated, while her son and husband were abroad, Abigail also became a successful businesswoman in her own right, selling luxury goods that John sent her from Europe. These items included fine handkerchiefs, gauze fabric, ribbons, decorative feathers, and artificial flowers, as well as intricate lace from Holland, all popular in New England with fashionable women. Abigail even peddled some of her wares through a Tufts cousin and her friend Mercy Otis Warren, who lived in Plymouth. Not only did that income help to pay their Massachusetts taxes and living expenses, but it also allowed her to make investments and land purchases. On at least one occasion she instructed her uncle Cotton Tufts to purchase bonds for her and use the "money which I call mine"—an unusual request in a time when a married woman's property legally belonged to her husband under the law of coverture. Somehow, Abigail and John were able to reconcile their distaste for excessive luxury with their sale of such goods to fellow

Americans, fueling the excessive American consumption of the "fripper-ies" they both disparaged.[4]

John's official appointment to serve as an emissary to France would usher in a ten-year period of diplomatic service abroad on behalf of his country and mark his initial experience with imperial power. Still, like other revolutionary era leaders, Adams had incorporated classi-cal eighteenth-century European political thought about the balance of power and state interests into his outlook, and he viewed America's role within that framework. John later told a Dutch acquaintance that he had "been educated from my Cradle" in the "Balance of Power in Europe."[5]

In February 1778, accompanied by ten-year-old John Quincy, John Adams set sail on the American-built *Boston* for a hazardous six-week and four-day voyage to France to help negotiate the terms of the Franco-American Alliance. Abigail and John had good reason to worry about the upcoming journey. Winter was the most dangerous season in which to cross the North Atlantic, and the prospect of John's intercep-tion and capture by English forces and possible execution was a real risk. In later recalling his journey to Europe, Abigail eloquently described what challenges her husband had faced, which included "encountering the dangers of the ocean; risking Captivity, and a dungeon; contending with wickedness in high places; jeoparding his Life, endangerd by the intrigues, revenge, and malice, of a potent; tho defeated Nation [Great Britain]."[6]

As he prepared to sail, John recorded in his diary entry of Friday, February 13, that the "Wind was very high, and the Sea very rough." The Adams party met the ship surreptitiously at Hough's Neck near Braintree instead of the more common port of Boston to ensure that British spies were not aware of their departure. John and his son, along with a hired servant from Braintree, Joseph Stephens, a former seaman and soldier, boarded the ship on Saturday. The Adamses slept comfort-ably that night on cots that held double mattresses. Tucked into their own familiar home-sewn sheets, which they had brought aboard, and sufficient blankets, they were snug though outside nature did not co-operate. It snowed heavily, howling winds sent icy crystals swirling, and the ship was buffeted by fierce gusts as the passengers endured frigid temperatures.

On Sunday, February 15, their departure seemed imminent as they "weigh'd the last Anchor, and came under Sail, before breakfast. A fine wind, and a pleasant Sun, but a sharp cold Air," John observed. But the hope of departure was premature. After stopping at Marblehead to bring additional crew aboard, the ship was stalled again. John became impatient as winds reached gale strength later in the day. On Monday, he noted that the young commander, Samuel Tucker, whom John came to admire, decided that due to increasingly strong winds followed by more heavy snow, they could not "go to sea." John pronounced himself "anxious at these Delays," and fretted, "We shall never have another Wind so good as We have lost."[7] It was not until Tuesday, four days after John had bid farewell to Abigail, that he and John Quincy were finally underway.

Although John found the ship and the young crew to be in a state of disorganization, he did not fault their thirty-year-old captain, who had already amassed years of sailing experience and accorded Adams all due respect as a pivotal American emissary. John was pleased with the company of several of the ship's passengers. Dr. Nicholas Noel, a French doctor returning to France after serving in the Continental Army, became a favorite and graciously tutored John Quincy in French. The boy would soon become fluent and later, while only a teenager, he served as a translator and secretary to Richard Dana, the American emissary to the Russian court of Catherine the Great.

John was pleased to have been asked to supervise the voyage of two young men on their way to France. One was William Vernon, a recent graduate from Princeton College; the other was eleven-year-old Jesse Deane, the only son of the very man John was to replace. Jesse would later attend a private boarding school with John Quincy in France. Supervision was a task that John undertook with relish and what he termed a "kind of guardianship." As he recorded, "Few Things have ever given me greater Pleasure than the Tuition of Youth at the Bar, and the Advancement of Merit."[8] The latter had always been important to John, who saw future American success as predicated on widespread education, which he believed would build character and eliminate hereditary rank by substituting merit, industriousness, and diligence as the avenues to personal advancement. Indeed, it was the very path Adams had pursued, and which had thrust him onto the national stage.

Despite the threat of belligerent British warships, potential capture, the possible presence of spies, and the added dangers of a treacherous winter crossing, forty-two-year-old John Adams and young Johnny, as he was nicknamed, braved the North Atlantic. Abigail's fears turned out to be prophetic, however, when the *Boston* came under British fire. Still, Abigail took heart from what she considered John's essential value to the American cause. Letters served as the link to connect the Adamses. As historian Edith B. Gelles has pointed out, writing served as a form of therapy for Abigail, a way of processing her thoughts, rationalizing her husband's choices, and keeping her emotionally balanced.[9] The parting had been painful, but she accepted it with both resignation and courage as part of her patriotic responsibility and wifely duty. Although it might have been self-rationalization, Abigail assured John, "Though I have been called to sacrifice to my country, I can glory in my sacrifice and derive pleasure from my intimate connexion with one [John], who is esteemed worthy of the important trust devolved on him."[10]

Plagued by stormy seas, cramped and dirty quarters, the uncouth behavior of many of the sailors, and the dreary scenery, even the stoic Adams was frequently uncomfortable. He noted in his diary that once they sailed into the open sea the passengers were assailed by "constant Rolling and Rocking. . . . Last night made Us all sick—half the Sailors were so." John Quincy and Jesse also became seasick, and John himself was "seized with it."[11] By the next day, however, the ocean had calmed, and the "Mal de Mer" put behind them until they encountered an even stronger storm in the Gulf Stream, which inflicted serious damage to their vessel. As John recorded, "To describe the Ocean, the Waves, the Winds, the Ship, her Motions, Rollings, Wringing and Agonies. . . . No Man could keep upon his Legs, and nothing could be kept in its Place." John remained determined to carry out his mission, but he feared he had perhaps made a mistake by exposing his son to such danger. However, John was heartened at the boy's visible resolve and "manly Patience."[12]

Adams and John Quincy were well supplied on board with items that John considered essential to his existence, such as his beloved books, paper, ink, pens, and tobacco and clay pipes. They also brought along a variety of animals to keep them well fed, including chickens, hogs, and sheep. Wine, spices, condiments, and even a tin of chocolate were all stowed away for the voyage. John appears to have been especially fond of chocolate. Years later, after Abigail had joined her husband abroad, she thanked her sister Mary for arranging to replenish the Adams supply of chocolate in London as "Mr. Adams was just mourning over his last pound."[13]

Congress was footing the bill for John's supplies, but the always thrifty Abigail worked industriously to gather the best items at the least cost. John valued his culinary comforts, but he was forced to make the best of the ship's cuisine, which was indifferent at best and unpalatable at worst. The Adamses and their manservant shared the often malodorous, crowded ship with nearly 170 fellow passengers, most of them members of the crew. A good number of those aboard were French officers, returning home after stints in the American Continental Army. John admired these men for their military prowess and willingness to aid the American cause.

During the arduous voyage, John displayed formidable determination and even courage when the ship was under direct threat, whether by the forces of nature, including a damaging lightning strike, or the British navy. As John put it, "This Day Six Weeks We sailed from Nantaskett Road. How many Dangers, Distresses and Hairbreadth Scrapes have we seen?"[14] The *Boston* was a brand-new, imposing twenty-four-gun frigate, which was especially fortuitous when they crossed paths with three enemy British vessels, one of which opened fire. To John's satisfaction, the American ship prevailed in the ensuing skirmish, and the *Boston*'s captain and crew ended up capturing the English frigate merchant ship *Martha*, which was carrying a wealth of supplies to the British in New York. Later, the vessel was recovered by British forces.

At one point when the *Boston* was under fire, John stayed on deck to offer his assistance, and a shot whizzed directly over his head. Another time he helped steady one of the vessel's officers, when the young man underwent a leg amputation as the result of the accidental discharge of a cannon. That shipman later died of his wounds and was buried at sea. Influenced by his Revolutionary War experience and the toll disease had taken on American soldiers, Adams became an early advocate for good sanitation. He did not hesitate—indeed, he likely considered it his duty—to share advice (probably often unappreciated) with Captain Tucker about improving conditions aboard ship. "I am constantly giving Hints to the Captain concerning Order, Economy and Regularity, and he seems to be sensible of the Necessity of them, and exerts himself to introduce them," Adams recorded with satisfaction in his diary.[15]

Several weeks into the voyage, John complained of boredom and wrote that life was dull aboard ship, with "No Business; No Pleasure; No Study." As for the scenery, he insisted, "We see nothing but Sky, Clouds and Sea, and then Seas, Clouds and Sky."[16] Despite the formidable challenges and monotony, John developed a measure of fondness for life at sea. Adams may never have been a sailor, but he always craved the sight, sounds, and smells of a nearby ocean. As early as 1769, his admiration for seamen and interest in their welfare led to his honorary induction into the Boston Marine Society. Admission was generally limited to men who had served as ships' masters, but even then, when John was only in his mid-thirties, he was recognized as a shrewd lawyer and a rising political force. John had long appreciated that seamen played a pivotal role in successful commerce and nation building.[17]

By March 7, John reported that good wind and weather enabled his ship to have successfully "passed all the Dangers of the American

Coast." They were proceeding on course, at about two hundred miles each day. Less than two weeks later, they were once more assailed by violent gales. Adams had to hold fast to secured furniture and railings to remain upright.[18] Five days after John sighted the verdant Spanish coast through a spyglass, the *Boston* finally docked in Bordeaux, France, at the beginning of April 1778. In Bordeaux, John received his initial taste of European life. He attended his first opera, enjoyed a play, and was a guest at a sumptuous dinner hosted by local dignitaries. Adams was gratified to have been cheered by a large crowd while cannons were fired in his honor. Just days after reaching Bordeaux, the American travelers proceeded to Paris. They arrived there on April 8 after a strenuous five-hundred-mile trek by coach. John couldn't help proudly noting that John Quincy had endured the "fatiguing and dangerous Voyage" with "Utmost Firmness."[19]

Shortly after he reached Europe, John had been astonished to learn that agreements between France and America, described as treaties of amity, commerce, and an armed alliance, had been executed the previous month following the Battle of Saratoga, which had resulted in a significant victory for the American forces against the British. Diplomatic historian Jonathan R. Dull suggests that it was not Saratoga but instead worsening French relations with England and the completion of French rearmament that propelled France's entry into the war.[20] In any case, the three American envoys then in Paris, Franklin, Deane, and Lee, had indeed concluded initial agreements with France before Adams's arrival, and England had even sent out signals that it was interested in peace. With French sentiment toward its American ally highly favorable, Adams was greeted in Paris as a hero, but John's role was now unclear as his mission had largely been accomplished before he had even arrived.

Soon after he came to Paris, Adams met with Franklin. The elder statesman, whom the French idolized, confirmed that he and his fellow envoys had already secured a diplomatic milestone, including a most-favored-nation status along with a military alliance. Even in the face of reservations about aligning France with a republican nation, the young and often politically naïve Louis XVI had assured Franklin of his support for America. Despite the diplomatic progress achieved, John understood that much still remained to be done. Moreover, he was convinced that his presence was necessary to serve as a buffer between Franklin and Lee, whose growing discord threatened the mission.

Adams arrived in Paris as a confirmed republican, who viewed public and private virtue as life's central goal, and as a strict moralist committed to basic tenets of the faith that had brought his Puritan forebears to Massachusetts. For Adams, in an ideal republic, elected officials, instead of a hereditary monarch, served as the representatives of its citizenry, and they were governed by the rule of law. Faith in God's sovereignty and the centrality of religion remained a constant in his life, and he looked on Catholicism with disapproval. Moreover, most Americans, including Adams, had been taught from a young age to look down upon Catholic France and its absolutist government.[21]

John was shocked by his first encounter with the observance of traditional French Catholic precepts on the one hand and liberal deism, even atheism, among many members of the aristocracy on the other. When he joined Franklin, Adams may have distrusted the French almost as much as he did the British. In some aspects, it was a collision of cultures. After attending one Parisian salon, John was moved to criticize French mores, and even at the beginning of his time in France, he worried about the negative effects European manners might have on American society. "What Absurdities, Inconsistencies, Distractions and Horrors would these Manners introduce into our Republican Governments in America; No kind of Republican Government can exist with such national manners as these," he insisted.[22] Still, Adams was above all a realist, and he appreciated the critical need for French support if America was to prevail in the conflict with Great Britain. Schooled from his youth as a citizen of the British Empire, Adams certainly understood the necessity of powerful allies in the struggle for a favorable balance of power.[23]

Despite his critical attitude toward European dissipation and frivolity, John found much that captivated him in France. Yet he never became a man of the world like Franklin. Venerated in Europe as an Enlightenment-inspired scientist and intellectual and a symbol of republican America, Franklin counted the most famous of the French Enlightenment *philosophes*, Voltaire, as a friend. In part, Franklin's social and diplomatic success was a result of his chameleon-like personality. As historian Claude-Anne Lopez astutely observed, Franklin was "immensely adaptable, knowing how to bend his personality to each time and place." He was far more appreciative of French manners than Adams and was able to adeptly and profitably mix business, friendship, and pleasure.[24] Indeed, Franklin came to love France so much that at one point he had even contemplated settling there.[25]

Dissembling was a trait Adams rarely exhibited. His sense of rectitude inspired frankness and unbending determination. Still, if Adams never developed the adoration for everything French that characterized Franklin, John appreciated the storied history of Europe and the opportunity to access its rich cultural offerings. He took long walks to explore his surroundings. Adams was amazed by the sights and sounds of Paris: the incessant rattling of carriage traffic along the crowded thoroughfares, the shouts of street merchants hawking their wares, the ringing of church bells. The court of Versailles was widely acknowledged at the time as the most opulent in all of Europe. Paris was then the sophisticated hub of Europe, and diplomats from most countries were stationed there. The city, with a robust population of about 650,000, buzzed with cutting-edge trends in art, music, literature, science, and medicine. In short, French culture dominated European taste.

Within days of his arrival, Adams traveled to Benjamin Franklin's garden apartments in the Hôtel de Valentinois in Passy. The magnificent residence was located in the outskirts of the bustling Paris metropolis and conveniently situated on the road to Versailles. Part of the huge edifice, which included beautiful formal gardens and even a sparkling lake, had first been loaned and then rented to Franklin by Jacques-Donatien

Le Ray de Chaumont, a wealthy shipping magnate, favored by the Crown. Franklin was particularly popular with the French ladies, who in turn were popular with him. His lengthy stays in Europe on behalf of the American government—a total of eight years in France and sixteen in England—had made him much more familiar than Adams with European culture, customs, and etiquette.

Still, at the age of seventy, Franklin had risked his comfortable lifestyle to join an uncertain revolution with his fellow American patriots. The self-made civic and business leader was the eldest of the revolutionary group, which included Thomas Jefferson, thirty-seven years his junior, and Adams, twenty-nine years younger than Franklin. Although Franklin had been a staunch supporter of the British Empire through the early 1760s, his "Americanization," as historian Gordon S. Wood has described it, moved him quickly toward the Patriot cause.[26]

From 1752 to 1762, Franklin was stationed in London as a colonial agent with the goal of limiting the proprietary power of the Penn family in Pennsylvania. He returned to America in 1762, but in 1764 he again sailed to England to promote Pennsylvania's interests. He witnessed the dangers of royal government and eventually opposed the Stamp Act of 1765, which the British imposed on the American colonies. In 1775 his service in England came to an unhappy end when he was chastised by the British government for what it considered his traitorous intrigues. Upon his return to America, an outraged Franklin became a leading member of the Philadelphia Continental Congress and a pivotal force in the drafting of the Declaration of Independence.

In late 1776, Franklin was named the first American minister to France, where he advanced support for the new American nation. He remained there until he returned to America in 1785. In France, Franklin was venerated as a philosopher and man of science, famous for his experiments with electricity. That adulation often irritated the sober Adams. John also worried that Franklin's popularity made him highly susceptible to French influence to the detriment of American affairs. Adams even began to question Franklin's patriotism.

Engraving of Benjamin Franklin in fur hat in France by
Johann Elias Haid. Courtesy Library of Congress.

Adams's envy of Franklin's widespread reputation in contrast to
John's own relative obscurity may have colored his opinion of his fellow
envoy. He would come to think of Franklin as lazy, frivolous, and even
duplicitous—"a conjuror," as he famously termed him. At one point,
Adams claimed in a humorous tone that Franklin's friends were "all
atheists, deists, and libertines as well as the Philosophes and Ladies . . .
in his Train."[27] At the same time, John appreciated, at least grudgingly,
that Franklin's skilled diplomatic efforts and maneuverings had helped
secure much-needed French loans and gifts worth about $40 million

today. After defeat by Britain in the Seven Years' War, the French were receptive to the American cause. France had been the first nation to recognize American independence, and more importantly, it provided both financial and military aid, which allowed the cash-strapped American government to function in its early days.

Despite some friction, Adams and Franklin had been relatively amiable comrades in Congress, and the two men got along well at the beginning of their time together in France. Along with Arthur Lee, Franklin and Adams co-authored a missive to the Dutch government, an initiative they hoped would foster a commercial relationship between the Netherlands and America. Moreover, Franklin served as John's entrée into the dazzling Parisian social life and its influential salons governed by strict rules of protocol. The friendship between Franklin and Adams must have been sufficiently robust at first, since the elderly envoy graciously invited John to come live at his quarters at the Hôtel de Valentinois.

Adams moved into the small, furnished garden apartment formerly occupied by Deane. John didn't have to pay rent, which must have pleased the frugal New England Yankee, although he likely found the estate too grand for professed American republicans. Adams remained there for ten months, until February 1779. On weekdays, John Quincy attended a private French boarding school in Passy along with Franklin's grandson Benjamin Franklin Bache, further cementing the connection between the two American envoys. John Quincy joined his father on weekends, and the two became inveterate sightseers. Father and son especially enjoyed attending the theater together and browsing the enticing Parisian bookshops. Franklin became very fond of the younger Adams, and when the boy later left France, Johnny received an affectionate letter from Franklin.

Before long the relationship between John and Franklin began to deteriorate. Adams now found himself surrounded by a world of privilege and wealth, class distinctions that were far less apparent in America at the time. On his first full day in Paris, he and Franklin dined with the still powerful former French minister of finance Anne-Robert-Jacques Turgot at his grand home. After visiting Turgot's mansion, John gushed that "it is in Vain to Attempt a Description of the House, Gardens, Library, Furniture, or the Entertainment of the Table." John's visit with Turgot was followed the next day by supper at the luxurious residence of the aristocratic Brillion family.[28]

Because he understood that France's support was so crucial, Adams was predisposed to form a favorable opinion of the French. Indeed, in the early days of his commission John was optimistic about his work. He reported in his diary, "The Attention to me, which has been shewn, from my first Landing in France at Bourdeaux, by the People in Authority of all Ranks and by the principal merchants, and since my Arrival in Paris by the Ministers of State, and others of the first Consideration has been very remarkable, and bodes well to our Country. It shews in what Estimation the new Alliance with America is held."[29] Many members of the nobility whom Adams encountered in Paris were decked out in glittering jewelry and exquisitely decorated ensembles, far more elaborate than John had ever seen. The magnificent estates, attractively designed buildings, and cultural works were equally impressive. Although John had crossed paths with the wealthy and elegant in Boston, it had never been on the grand scale that he witnessed in Europe. He reacted with mixed feelings of appreciation and disgust, which he often conveyed to Abigail back home.

John and Abigail each experienced periods of profound loneliness while separated. Correspondence had long been the bond that kept John and Abigail tethered during their frequent separations. When letters from John were infrequent, Abigail alternately became anxious that either he or their son was ill or in danger or that her husband was perhaps enjoying his temporary "bachelorhood" too much and had forgotten about her, although she knew she never had any cause to suspect him of infidelity. "How lonely are my days. How solitary are my nights," she wrote plaintively to John during one hard winter evening when she felt she was as isolated as if she "lived in Greenland."[30] Overseas mail could take months to reach its destination. It was also notoriously unreliable,

and undoubtedly some letters were lost or John was simply too preoccupied to write as often as he had during his time in Philadelphia. Still,
Abigail felt neglected and sometimes angrily expressed her resentment
to John, who was often left helpless and irritated. At one point, she
insisted that "I cannot reconcile myself to the Idea of living in the cruel
States of Seperation."[31]

John began moving in exalted circles, although he always preferred
the company of those people who were more similar to his own middle-
class background. Indeed, he consciously led a modest lifestyle during all
his years in Europe. He proudly reported to Abigail that he even denied
himself the customary personal conveyance that his fellow diplomats
sported: "I am told I am the first public Minister that ever lived without
a Carriage."[32] Soon he was exposed to the swirl of palace intrigue and
was wined and dined regularly in the homes of members of the influential elite. Franklin introduced Adams to a host of well-educated, wealthy
aristocratic men and women, including the city's leading Enlightenment
intellectuals and philosophes, such as the elderly Voltaire and the Marquis de Condorcet.

He also met many of the famed Parisian *salonniéres*, such as Madame
Helvetius, widow of a well-known French philosopher, the politically
astute Duchess de La Rochefoucauld, and Madame Brillion, Franklin's
attractive young neighbor. The cultured Brillion was an accomplished
pianist and referred to Franklin familiarly as "mon cher papa," undoubtedly shocking Adams's sense of propriety.[33] At the same time, the stark
contrast that John encountered in the French capital between the rich
and the poor was in evidence daily, and he was appalled at the many
beggars, who struggled to acquire even rough bread.

Adams's time in France provided him with the opportunity to learn
more about the liberal ideas circulating among the French *philosophes*
and refine his own political thinking. He often parted ways with many
Enlightenment thinkers and categorically rejected what he considered
their naïve and romantic view that the world was set firmly on a progressive trajectory and that the application of human reason could eradicate

all social ills. Adams thought it impossible that economic equity could be achieved through social engineering. He believed that humans across the world and throughout history had been driven by the same underlying universal desire for prestige, no matter their social class. Hardheaded New Englander that he was and influenced by his Puritan Protestant religious heritage, Adams maintained that human nature would never change, and utopian visions never held any attraction for him.[34]

In Paris, Adams encountered leading diplomats and political figures, including probably the most influential individual in the ongoing negotiations with France, the astute Charles Gravier, Comte de Vergennes, who served as Louis XVI's foreign minister. John and his fellow revolutionary statesmen had imbibed from youth the European idea that the level of a nation's power played a central role in diplomacy.[35] In France, he was exposed to its inner workings in real time. French support for the American cause was largely driven by the desire to degrade the position of England, France's longtime primary rival both in Europe and in the New World. Vergennes was an industrious and ruthless though cautious diplomat whose most pressing aim was to tilt the balance of power toward his country and isolate Great Britain from its European neighbors and potential allies. Providing support for American independence likely attracted Vergennes because of its potential to accomplish these overarching goals. In retrospect, it was a shortsighted policy, for France's involvement in the American war was ultimately a significant factor in its financial crisis and derailed attempts at internal reform that might have avoided the French Revolution and the overthrow of the monarchy, which Vergennes revered.[36]

Adams first met Vergennes in April 1778, when Franklin and Lee accompanied Adams to his first visit to Versailles. The magnificent French palace had been built under the direction of the absolute monarch Louis XIV, who became king in 1643 at the age of four and reigned for over seventy years. Located about twelve miles from Paris, it took almost twenty years and around thirty-six thousand workers to construct the baroque-styled royal residence located at the end of a grand boulevard that linked the castle to Paris. Louis XIV had consciously chosen the location to distance his palace from the city, which he viewed as a fertile ground for rebellion. The huge edifice, which was emblematic of French grandeur, was set among attractive parks, lakes, and forested areas. It housed not only the royal family but also members of the French nobility whom the king wished to keep under scrutiny, but who had found favor in the monarch's eyes and adhered to the rigid protocols of rank that the "Sun King" had mandated. Inside, glittering chande-liers, sparkling china, crystal, and silver vied for attention with luxurious tapestries, striking paintings, rare *objets d'art*, ornate silk and brocaded furniture, and massive statues.[37]

Adams had his first glimpse of the current French monarch, Louis XIV's great-grandson, as he toured the magnificent palace, which John pronounced "sublime." As Louis XVI subsequently passed through his sumptuous apartments on his way to the Council, he bestowed a polite smile on Adams and the rest of the group without stopping to speak to any of them.[38] John must have been awed at his first glance of a king but at the same time chagrined at the sight of all the conspicuous consump-tion and the monarch's evident air of entitlement.

Louis XIV had introduced the lavish entertainments that continued in his great-grandson's reign, including impressive theatrical produc-tions and fireworks displays. After attending one of Louis XVI's reviews of his guards, Adams was moved to remark, "The Shew was splendid, as all other Shews are, in this Country."[39] Yet, during his future visits to the palace, John realized that if one looked beyond the glittering façade, it was rundown in some sections. Versailles suffered from neglect, and broken windows and peeling paint were in evidence. Louis XIV's sti-fling control of the nobility, whom he excluded from governance, as well as his extravagant spending, had long-term effects on his successors that left French coffers seriously depleted and contributed to the unrest that later stoked the French Revolution.

Little more than a month after he arrived in Paris, Adams received an invitation for his first official audience with the king. Before the meeting, John recorded in his diary that he was open-minded about the philosophical question of monarchy. Although he maintained that American society was best suited to a republican form of government, headed by a strong executive, balanced by a bicameral legislature, he believed that in some European nations a king was a necessary ingredient for stability. He contended that a monarch could broadly fulfill the role of executive and insisted that kings were not necessarily inferior in virtue to other men, nor more corrupt or attached to a love of power.[40]

John was formally presented to King Louis XVI on May 8, 1778. For this encounter with the king, who was only in his mid-twenties at the time, Adams donned the requisite ceremonial sword, purchased new French-tailored fine clothing, and made sure his powdered wig had been styled and refreshed. American officials in Paris, including Adams and later his fellow revolutionary comrade Thomas Jefferson, understood that dress conveyed privilege and rank, so even if their personal preference would have been for simpler "republican" attire, they acquiesced to what was expected of their positions as gentlemanly statesmen. Only Franklin clung to the rustic dress he had decided to don in Europe, but this eccentricity seemed to contribute to his popularity as a symbol of American republicanism. Unlike Franklin and Adams, Jefferson, raised as a Virginia aristocrat, appears to have appreciated stylish clothing. He purchased the finest fashions and art while later serving as an American minister to France. When Abigail later joined John in Paris in 1784, she noted caustically to her sister that although the wearing of extravagant clothing chafed against her more spartan tastes, "Fashion is the Deity everyone worships in this country and from the highest to the lowest you must submit."[41]

Along with his two fellow American commissioners, Franklin and Lee, Adams was ushered into the king's ornate private bedchamber, where he was in the process of being dressed by his servants. Unlike Franklin, who never mastered French grammar or became a proficient French speaker, John grew comfortable in conversational French. However, at his first audience with Louis XVI it was the multilingual Comte de Vergennes who facilitated the brief exchange of words. Adams was impressed with the "Character of Mildness, Goodness and Innocence in his [the king's] face," and he noted the monarch's devotion to Catholic rituals and daily prayers, during which he knelt for hours on hard marble floors. John noted with approval that he was encouraged that the king's reign was already distinguished by his agreement to sign the Franco-American Alliance treaty, and he described the young king vividly in his diary, observing that he appeared to have a strong constitution that boded well for longevity. Adams could not have predicted then that Louis XVI was destined to die at the hands of French radical insurgents. Though Adams would witness the deep emerging cracks in the French regime, he did not foresee the violent overthrow of the monarchy.[42]

In part, John held a favorable opinion of Louis XVI because, unlike Jefferson, he did not reject the institution of monarchy per se; rather, Adams opposed absolutist rule. Still, John noted critically that the alliance between the two countries was not sufficiently appreciated by French leaders, including Louis XVI. Perhaps more significantly, Adams understood that France was riven by competing factions. The growing political power of the French nation, John later maintained, had not only resulted in political danger for France, but also put all of Europe in a precarious position.[43]

John liked the king, whom he found to be kind, well read, and well intentioned, if naïve, but it was Queen Marie-Antoinette, dressed in an ornate gown with her hair swept up in an elaborate powdered coif, who captured his attention. He later rapturously described her beauty, fine dress, and grace. Although time may have burnished John's memory, he recalled the queen as "an object to[o] sublime and beautiful for my dull pen to describe." It is interesting to note, however, that although he found the queen to be a handsome woman, with a fine complexion, he later insisted that he had met many women in America, France, and England who were far more beautiful than the king's consort. John astutely understood that part of Marie-Antoinette's attraction revolved around the magnificent jewelry and costumes she wore at state occasions. At one event, the queen was reported to have worn sparkling diamonds worth millions.[44]

Despite his developing regard for the French, particularly his enjoyment of their cuisine and exuberant sociability, Adams was never enamored of the opulent Parisian high society, which he considered largely dissolute and immoral. He also looked down upon the constant focus by the elite on frivolous amusements. John noted that virtually every genteel French house he had visited boasted a stage for play performances, billiard and backgammon tables, chess and checker sets, and a host of card games. Adams also tired of incessant social events and elaborate palace ceremonies, and by early May confided in his diary, "Am to dine at home—a great Rarity and a great Blessing!"[45]

In early June 1778, John had the opportunity to visit the summer court of the French monarchs at Marli. He considered it the "most curious and beautiful place I have seen yet." He wrote, "In point of Magnificence it was not equal to Versailles," but Adams judged it to be superior in "elegance and Taste."[46] Less than a week later, along with Lee and Ralph Izard, the meddling American ambassador to Tuscany, Adams returned to Versailles for an intimate view of Louis XVI and Marie-Antoinette at their "grand Couvert" and, after paying a fee, "watched the King, Queen, and Royal Family at Supper." John recorded that he "Had a fine Seat and Situation close by the Royal Family," so he was able to observe the monarchs' behavior. Although that evening John was well dressed, it was still on a very modest scale compared to the glitter of the fashionable women and men surrounding him, who were decked out in glittering diamonds, sumptuous gold jewelry, and exquisitely embroidered costumes.[47] John found the pomp impressive but vacuous and without any signs of the republican ideals of simple American elegance he had long admired.

There were other social occasions that John found more to his liking. The next month, on July 4, Adams and Franklin invited a group of American nationals and a few local Frenchmen to a dinner at Passy to celebrate the anniversary of the Declaration of Independence, and the day passed "joyously."[48] By the fall, John had had enough of French grandeur and longed for his simpler life at home in Massachusetts. After he visited the richly appointed apartments of the Prince of Conde at the Palace of Bourbon, he maintained with apparent sincerity that "I had rather live in this Room at Passy than in that Palace, and in my Cottage at Braintree than in this Hotel at Passy."[49]

One aspect of French society that John clearly *did* admire was the accomplished, educated women whom he met in Paris, although he often felt gauche among sophisticated females. Abigail was not wholly pleased by the admiration of such women, and from Braintree, she took the opportunity to lament the general state of female education in America. In response to the praise (often unwelcome) she heard from John about the "brilliant accomplishments" of Parisian women, Abigail shared her strong views. She especially regretted "the trifling, narrow, contracted education of the females in my own country. . . . In this country, you need not be told how much female education is neglected, nor how fashionable it has been to ridicule female learning; though I acknowledge it my happiness to be connected with a person [John] of a more generous mind and liberal sentiments."[50] Indeed, John and Abigail felt that education, for both men and women, albeit focusing on different subjects, was essential to a viable republic. Their daughter Nabby was sent to a respected female academy in Boston. The Adamses believed that America required a virtuous, educated citizenry to succeed, as knowledge built character, enlarged wisdom, and developed leadership qualities. They remained lifelong advocates of the study of history, political science, philosophy, and literature.

Living in Paris brought the differences between Adams's native land and France into sharp relief. Soon after he settled in Paris, John wrote Abigail that he found the French people deficient in morality, but at the same time they were welcoming, charmingly polite, and surprisingly charitable. As he put it, "The Delights of France are innumerable. The Politeness, the Elegance, the Softness, the Delicacy, is extreme." He confided reluctantly to Abigail, "In short stern and hauty Republican as

I am, I cannot help loving; these People, for their earnest Desire, and Assiduity to please." The architecture of France, which featured exquisite cathedrals and churches, stately mansions, sculpted gardens, and the grand Palace of Versailles, was dazzling. He summarized his impressions by declaring succinctly, "The richness, the magnificence, and splendor is beyond all description."[51] Still, despite its outward grandeur, the Palace of Versailles, like the broader French society, had hidden faults lurking beneath its glittering surface, which Adams observed with dismay.

Although John appreciated the civility of the French and admired much about the culture and physical beauty of the country, his Yankee background and lifelong belief that moral and civic virtue were the only sound foundation for good government led him to be cautious. As early as 1776, John had maintained to Massachusetts patriot and writer Mercy Warren that "Public Virtue is the only Foundation of Republics," and he hoped that a thoughtfully designed government would ensure its continuance in America.[52] From France, he warned Abigail about the splendid trappings that veiled underlying corruption, dissipation, and decadence and which were merely "in Exchange for the great Qualities and hardy many Virtues of the human Heart. I cannot help suspecting that the more Elegance, the less Virtue in all Times and countries." It was a situation he hoped would never develop in his "own dear country." Sometimes in his more pessimistic moments, he feared that the love of extravagance might even infect America in the future, if it had not already done so. John ended his missive to Abigail with the declaration that "All the Luxury I desire in this World is the Company of my dearest Friend [Abigail] and my Children."[53]

The longer Adams remained in Passy, the more strained became his relationship with Franklin. Their temperaments could not have been more dissimilar. John confided petulantly in his diary, "On Dr. F. the Eyes of all Europe are fixed, as the most important Character in American Affairs in Europe. Neither L[ee] Nor myself are looked upon of much Consequence. The Attend of the Court seems most to F. and no Wonder. His long and great Rep[utation] to which L's and mine are in their infancy, are enough to Account for this." John reiterated that Franklin's age, his tendency toward indolence, and his sociability often made him oblivious to keeping exacting records and combined to "render it impossible for him to search every Thing to the Bottom." Adams took up most of the mundane but necessary work of the American legation, including writing urgent business letters. Yet Adams also acknowledged the respect Franklin received from the French, a circumstance that John well understood made the elder statesman essential to American diplomatic efforts.[54]

The reality was that although Franklin was crucial in raising French funds for the American cause and holding the alliance between France and America together, neither he nor Lee had been methodical about keeping records or reining in their sometimes extravagant expenditure. Moreover, the two disliked one another and were often distracted by their feud. John had worked hard to bring order to the commission's chaotic finances while at the same time keeping Congress updated on foreign affairs. These were the types of task at which he excelled. As John asserted years earlier in his diary, "I was born for business; for both Activity and Study."[55]

Adams was by nature organized, hardworking, exacting, and often blunt; Franklin, who as he aged was visited by a number of irritating illnesses, grew careless, unfocused, and at times content to merely sit back and work behind the scenes to charm his many French admirers, especially the ladies. With stern disapproval Adams noted Franklin's inclination for incessant socializing; he recorded how Franklin dined out almost daily, often not returning home until late in the evening, sometimes even at midnight, making it difficult for Adams to consult with him.[56] John seemed naïvely unappreciative of the way that Franklin successfully combined business and pleasure.

John still respected Franklin, but was increasingly resentful of the unqualified admiration the "doctor" enjoyed, and he tired of Franklin's complaints about his fellow ministers. By April 1778, Adams recorded the bitter discord among the American emissaries and wrote of his "Grief and Concern" over their disputes. He declared himself "untainted with these Prejudices" and maintained that "Parties and Divisions" would have only "pernicious Effects."[57] Clearly, Adams had subtly altered his view of Franklin, whom he admitted was a genius and a great politician, but perhaps lacking in morality and statesmanship. In John's opinion, Franklin was too deferential to the French and easily manipulated by the sophisticated Vergennes. Moreover, it appeared that Franklin had been duped by several of his so-called English friends. It was later revealed that British secret agents had insinuated themselves into the American mission, raising suspicion between the French and American diplomats. John often felt himself awkwardly caught between his colleagues and tried to steer a tactful course as "an Umpire between two bitter and inveterate Parties." Yet John still felt compelled to publicly defend Franklin's reputation because of the importance of the office he held and the favor he found at the French court.[58]

By the end of 1778, Franklin and Adams diverged in their opinion about how strongly to urge France to make greater military commitments to the American cause, but the two men still agreed on most substantive issues. However, as John became less optimistic about the prospect of an American victory over England and peace seemed increasingly distant, he became more suspicious of French intentions. The result was that Adams and Franklin moved farther apart. John astutely understood the central role naval power played in the American conflict with Great Britain, and he continued to press Franklin and Vergennes for increased French aid. John often forgot or ignored the fact that discretion, tact, and even outright dissimulation were frequently the most effective tools of diplomacy.

Vergennes was often unwilling to meet John's relentless demands because his primary goal was understandably to weaken English power, not to bolster the American war effort. Moreover, he was offended by John's dogged and single-minded persistence in a manner that did not view French interests as primary. It resulted in uneasy relations between the two men. Yet Adams was right to remain resolute in urging French military intervention. The deployment of the French navy, backed by Spain and the Netherlands and secured through alliances brokered by Vergennes, later proved essential. Indeed, France's intervention played a decisive role in the American victory. Historian John Ferling posits that John's concern about the course of the war and his differences of opinion with Franklin over how much pressure to apply for additional French military support were central factors in John's decreasing confidence in Franklin's diplomacy and their growing discord.[59] Adams would have probably been wiser to have made an ally of Franklin. A strong partnership might have allowed them to work in concert together to influence Vergennes. Without Abigail by his side to smooth over his tendency to become irritable when frustrated, however, John easily slipped into suspicion and anger, which clouded his judgment.

John often felt like a third wheel in the American commission, overshadowed by Franklin and Lee, burdened by mere clerical tasks, and wounded by his perception that he was underappreciated by French diplomats as well as his countrymen back home. The mounting discord between Franklin and Lee, as well as their friction with Izard and Deane, frustrated John. He considered Lee and Deane men of integrity but too hot-tempered, and he tartly observed, "I had found more Intrigue and finesse among my own Countrymen, at Paris, than among the French."[60] For the sake of efficiency, John recommended that Congress reduce the number of French emissaries to one.

All of John's colleagues agreed that he had the best interests of his country at heart but that he sometimes blundered in his frank style. The exchange of correspondence between Congress and the American emissaries in France was excruciatingly slow. It made it a challenge for the diplomats to ascertain their instructions and, in turn, to provide updated information to members of Congress. One of John's most valuable contributions was keeping Congress abreast of developments in Europe with his frequent reports. As he put it succinctly, if immodestly, "I found that the Business of our Commission would never be done, unless I did it."[61]

Even more distressing to John was what he perceived as ongoing British folly regarding a peace settlement. He lamented to his friend Elbridge Gerry, then a member of Congress, that "Great Britain is really a Melancholly Spectacle, . . . Destitute of Wisdom and Virtue to make Peace; burning with malice and revenge; yet affrighted and confounded at the Prospect of War. . . . An Idea of a fair and honourable Treat with Congress, never enters their Minds." Adams informed Gerry that to his displeasure, Franklin had agreed that they would not proceed in peace negotiations without first consulting the French court for advice. He also confided that he thought that Franklin was responsible for some of the challenges that the Americans encountered with England. He noted that Franklin harbored personal "severe Resentment" against England's King George, which impeded American efforts. Certainly, Franklin seems to have never overcome his sense of injustice at the hands of British politicians and the English court that had occurred back in the 1760s.[62]

Despite diplomatic frustrations, the bright spot in John's sojourn in Paris was the company of his eldest son. Even in the face of inherent danger, John and Abigail had been united in their resolve to broaden the life experiences of their precocious child. They believed that the opportunity to accompany his father to Europe was an exceptional avenue to expose Johnny to the culture and venerable educational institutions in the Old World. Despite his youth, the Adamses were already imposing high standards on John Quincy and grooming him for greatness and service to his country. The close ties that developed between father and son were visible throughout their lifetimes. Years later, after John Quincy returned to America for college, Abigail's sister observed that "His Father is his (*Delphic*) Oracle. There never was a Son who had greater veneration for a Father."[63]

By the time John Quincy became the seventh president of the United States in 1825, arguably he was better prepared for conducting foreign policy than any of his predecessors or many of those who followed him. After father and son first arrived in Europe in 1778, Abigail offered her

Johnny prescriptive advice, frequently echoing John's philosophy about the necessity of public duty. She instructed her son to harness his talents to "Improve your understanding for acquiring useful knowledge and virtue, such as will render you an ornament to society, and honor to your country, and a blessing to your parents."[64] John later emphasized that the goal of John Quincy's education was to become "a good Man and useful Citizen."[65] Thus, deep respect for the duty owed to their homeland was ingrained in the next Adams generation.

The Adamses were nothing if not industrious, and they were able to impart that trait to their eldest son. From youth, John and Abigail had developed a strong Protestant work ethic. Naturally studious and highly intelligent, John Quincy scrupulously followed his parents' example. The elder Adams's first months in France were characterized by unrelenting effort as well as the opportunity to immerse himself in culture firsthand. His son followed his own arduous schedule during the week at a rigorous boarding school. Classes began at 6:00 a.m. and ended at 8:00 p.m., punctuated by time for meals and exercise. John Quincy's course of study included French and Latin as well as music and drawing, but he spent convivial weekends with his father, who found him a delightful companion. The elder Adams relished his temporary role as a single father, one who had the opportunity to focus his parental attention on just one child at a time. Father and son conversed freely about a wide variety of subjects, and John delighted in his son's fine mind. In the face of his often frustrating diplomatic work in France, Adams sometimes became melancholy, but the time spent with Johnny was a balm. He told Abigail that while abroad, John Quincy had proved "the Joy of my Heart."[66]

As the months passed, John worked relentlessly to improve his fluency and command of French grammar, and by the beginning of 1779, he declared that he "could talk as fast as I pleased."[67] He and John Quincy applied themselves to reading French textbooks and literary works. Father and son also attended meetings of the Academy of Sciences, where the proceedings were conducted entirely in French. The two often enjoyed plays and operas together. Even those entertaining productions served as a vehicle for education, a way to perfect their French and soak up the local culture. To hone their skills, for example, John made it a habit to take his French language book to the theater to improve his pronunciation by mimicking the actors. This was no mere frivolous exercise, however. French reigned as the diplomatic language par excellence in eighteenth-century Europe.

Ironically, the members of the American delegation seemed unable to solve their own disagreements diplomatically. At times, Adams was out of his depth in the complex world of foreign diplomacy, sometimes misreading situations and mishandling sensitive diplomatic interactions. For example, he often underestimated Vergennes's power and the French minister's strong preference for Franklin's conciliatory style. After he criticized Deane and then defended Lee to Vergennes, John soon found that he was to be relieved of his joint commission by Congress. His worst fears were confirmed when Franklin was named the sole minister to the court of Louis XVI in September 1778, although the decision did not reach Paris until February of the following year.

Despite the fact that it was Adams himself who had recommended a reduction in the number of American diplomats in France, he was still taken aback by the abrupt end of his commission. It is likely that he hoped that he would be the one chosen as the solitary American minister. Yet he tried to cast the decision in a positive light, and he recorded matter-of-factly, "It appears that Dr. Franklin is sole Plenipotentiary, and of Consequence that I am displaced." Somewhat disingenuously, he added that it was "the greatest Relief to my Mind."[68] Later in his diary, John blandly noted, "The Pleasure of returning home is very great, but I confess it is a Mortification to leave France. I have just acquired enough of the Language to understand a Conversation."[69] Lee was to go to Spain, and Adams, who was left in limbo without any instructions, made the decision to return home. He likely longed to return to Braintree and be soothed by his family and familiar surroundings.

In early March 1779, Adams visited Versailles to take formal leave of the French court and his ministry and to bid adieu to Vergennes. John was proud of the dispatch he received from Louis XVI tendered by Vergennes. The letter singled out "the wise conduct that you have held to throughout the tenure of your commission [and] . . . the zeal with which you have constantly furthered the cause of your nation, while strengthening the alliance that ties it to his Majesty."[70] Surely, the words must have bolstered John's ego and allowed him to feel that his sojourn in France had not been in vain.

John again pretended to Abigail to be happy with the congressional decision. He wrote that he would soon join her back in Braintree as he was "reduced to a private Citizen which gives me more Pleasure, than you can imagine."[71] Inwardly, however, he still seethed. Adams fretted that the members of Congress, almost all men of wealth and position, had become a partisan oligarchy, with all sides putting their personal interests first. He had hoped to have been dispatched on a second mission to another European country such as Holland. In a later letter he complained to Abigail that Congress had instead left him in a state of "total Neglect and Contempt."[72]

Determined to leave Europe quickly, he and John Quincy made a five-day journey to Nantes, which included the opportunity to visit Bordeaux, Brest, and other French towns as they searched for an available ship for their return voyage. While he awaited passage, John enjoyed dinners with locals and caught up on his reading. He also helped arrange an exchange of prisoners of war and the release of captured seamen, and he crossed paths with the famous American naval officer John Paul Jones. After numerous delays, he and John Quincy ended up sailing from Lorient to Philadelphia on June 17 on the French frigate *La Sensible*.

It was the same vessel that carried the new French minister to America, the Chevalier de La Luzerne. In fact, Luzerne's ship quarters were directly across from John's, and according to Adams the two men shared many engaging conversations about American affairs and literature. Adams recorded that he was discreet about American politics, and John Quincy tutored the charming Luzerne in English.[73] Adams later recorded with satisfaction that in all his talks with Luzerne, "no unguarded Word has escaped me. I have conversed with that Frankness that makes a part of my Character, but have said nothing I did not mean to say."[74] Adams had at least learned to be diplomatic when he wanted to be.

After a year and a half of separation from their family, father and son arrived home in early August 1779. Their return came as a shock to Abigail, who had little advance warning. Though she had heard rumors that John and their son intended to sail home, she had received no details. Their arrival in Braintree ended nearly two years of anxiety for Abigail. Letters from John in Europe had only arrived sporadically, and Abigail, worried about her loved ones, had often complained to her husband about his prolonged absence. Back in the fall of 1778 she had declared to her friend and relative John Thaxter, "I wish a thousand times I had gone with him."[75]

Little did Abigail know that she and John would soon be parted again as he undertook a second voyage to Europe on behalf of his country. Nor could she predict that she would join her husband across the Atlantic Ocean and visit the Old World to learn firsthand the opportunities and challenges that beckoned as she and her fellow Americans continued to build their nation and a distinctly American identity.

Two

Second Journey to Europe

Those who Envy him [John Adams], his situation [as an American emissary] see not with my Eyes, nor feel with my Heart.

Abigail Adams to Mercy Warren, February 28, 1780

Let us [Americans] have ambition enough to keep our simplicity, our frugality, and our integrity and transmit these virtues as the fairest of inheritance to our children.

John Adams to Abigail Adams, post May 12, 1780

[America] is a Temple of Liberty, set open to all the World. . . . I never had thro my whole life any other Ambition than to cherish, promote and protect it and never will have any other for myself nor my Children.

John Adams to James Warren, April 16, 1783

FOLLOWING THEIR LONG SEPARATION, ABIGAIL WAS OVERJOYED to have her husband and eldest son back from Europe in the summer of 1779, safely beside her again in their Braintree home. Their snug, two-floor slanted cottage, constructed in the typical New England "saltbox" style, featured a parlor, office, and large welcoming kitchen with a massive fireplace on the first floor and the family bedrooms on the second story.[1] The adjoining farm, on which they raised corn, wheat, and oats, encompassed more than 180 acres. John was always most content when surrounded by his family on his beloved farm and at the same time fruitfully engaged in his legal work and civic pursuits. He quickly moved back into the public sphere, and his life resumed its customary hectic pace. Shortly after he returned to Massachusetts, John laid the groundwork for the founding of the Boston American Academy of Arts and Sciences, which was formally incorporated in May 1780. Of more consequence, Adams refocused his considerable talents on local politics.

As the elected representative from Braintree, John began writing a constitution for the "Commonwealth of Massachusetts," modeled, in part, on the British constitution but which also drew on his earlier views expressed in 1776 in his *Thoughts on Government*. It was adopted in October 1780 with only minor revisions and, remarkably, remains in effect to this day. Adams was immensely proud of the project, which reflected what he considered to be the essential ingredients for ideal governance based on the rule of law: a "mixed" political structure that effectively balanced executive, legislative, and judicial powers, and encouraged the growth of a virtuous citizenry, so essential for its success. Adams advocated for a strong executive, whether on the local or the national level, for he believed that a powerful leader was necessary to counteract the self-serving impulses of an oligarchy, on the one hand, and the unchecked masses of "the people" on the other. Although he was disappointed that his recommendation for absolute veto power for the governor of Massachusetts was not incorporated into the final version, he was satisfied that a bicameral legislature met his fundamental goal of guaranteeing liberty.

Yet barely two months after John returned from Europe, his plan for the resumption of normal life was upended. To his astonishment, on September 27, 1779, Congress elected Adams to again serve on behalf of the American government, and he was redeployed to Europe as minister plenipotentiary to France. In early November, John penned a heartfelt letter of appreciation to Henry Laurens, the new president of Congress. As the course of the Revolutionary War tilted toward the prospect of a conclusion, his charge was to negotiate peace and commerce with England and to be at the ready whenever the British finally agreed to proceed with talks. Laurens and John's other supporters in Congress likely believed that Adams's past European experience, firmness, and robust legal skills would serve America well in potential negotiations.

John was well aware that he would first have to negotiate with the French. The 1778 Franco-American Alliance had required France and America to concur before any peace agreement could be concluded with England. Adams understood the serious diplomatic challenges that lay before him. "Peace is an Object of such vast importance; the Interests to be adjusted, in the Negotiations to obtain it, are so complicated and so delicate; and the difficulty of giving even general Satisfaction is [so] great," John declared to Laurens, that "I feel myself more distressed at the prospect of executing the Trust, than at the Thoughts of leaving my family and Country; and again encountering the danger of the Seas and of Enemies."[2] Apprehensive as he might have been, Adams was flattered by the appointment, which he believed was one of the most important commissions Congress had ever bestowed.

Before John departed for France, he had engaged in a different set of negotiations at home. Once more, a conflicted and disheartened Abigail was left behind, for John again deemed an overseas voyage for women and a young boy too risky. Soon after her family sailed, Abigail lamented that "my hopes and fears rise alternately. . . . My dear sons I can not think of them without a tear. . . . God almighty bless and protect my dearest Friend."[3] The woman who had already braved so many terrors of war later admitted to John that she now felt "alone in the wide world, without anyone to care for me, or lend me an assisting hand through the difficulties that surround me."[4] John may have been of two minds about parting from his wife and children, but as Edith B. Gelles has observed, in the final analysis, he was likely "more committed to public service than family life."[5] At the age of ninety, John regretfully recalled to a granddaughter, "At this time it seems to me to have been wicked to have left such a wife and such a family as I did."[6]

With mixed emotions, on November 13, 1779, John took leave of his wife, his daughter Nabby, and his youngest child, Thomas. Just two days later Adams sailed back to Europe from Boston harbor on the *Sensible*, the same French frigate that had brought him home in the summer. It was a sizable ship, crowded with paying passengers and sailors, bringing the total number on board to 350. On John's second transatlantic trip, he was accompanied by his eldest son, John Quincy, and Charles, who was only nine. Also joining the party were John's faithful servant Joseph Stephens; John Thaxter, now hired as Adams's private secretary and sometime tutor to the boys; and Francis Dana, a Boston lawyer, who would serve as secretary to the American delegation and as Adams's personal assistant; as well as Dana's servant. John and Charles shared one tiny cabin on the *Sensible*, and Thaxter and John Quincy occupied another small room. To his satisfaction, Adams would receive a guaranteed salary from Congress of 2,500 pounds to enable him to carry out his duties.[7]

John had been right to worry about the physical challenges that he and his fellow voyagers would encounter. Though he had become a seasoned traveler, none of the Adamses could have anticipated that this second trip would turn out to be such a fraught journey. In the end, the combination of the ocean passage to Spain and the subsequent overland trip to France lasted a challenging three months. The *Sensible* turned out to be a dangerously leaky ship, one that would have been unable to overcome stormy seas. Even working full-time, the ship's pumps proved inadequate to stem incoming waters. The passengers were forced to dock at El Ferrol on the rocky western coast of Spain because the captain deemed it too hazardous to proceed to France.[8]

The Adams party was left stranded in El Ferrol, a thousand miles from Paris. Unwilling to delay his critical mission to France until another vessel became available or the *Sensible* was repaired, John took the advice of a local resident who recommended an alternative means of travel. He decided that his group would make the overland journey to France across a wide expanse of northern Spain. They traveled on muleback and hired small-wheeled carriages, popularly known as calashes. The old worn-down wagons were uncomfortable conveyances at best and proved to be just one of many inconveniences in what became one of the most challenging trips of John's life.

In his diary entry of December 9, 1779, John recorded going ashore at El Ferrol with his family to secure lodging. The Spanish court did not recognize American independence at the time and had not supported the American cause as hoped, but Adams found the Spanish to be cordial if not as enthusiastically welcoming as the French. In Corunna, he reported with relief that the governor had informed him that "he had orders from Court to treat all Americans as their best friends."[9]

The unplanned stop in Spain offered Adams the opportunity to compare yet another European country with his native land, and the trip through the hinterland revealed much about everyday Spanish life. Although some of his later critics accused John of acquiring a taste for European values and venerating the institution of monarchy, that perspective is unsupported by his writings while abroad. He particularly denigrated political and social life in Spain, although there were a few aspects he appreciated. John, who always enjoyed good food, praised the local produce, especially "the Bread, the Cabbages, the Colliflowers, Apples, Pears." Ever loyal to his New England ties, however, he found that the "Oysters were tolerable, but not equal to ours in America." To his consternation, he discovered that there was "little Appearance of Commerce or Industry" in Corunna, which offended his Protestant work ethic, but he recorded that the building of a number of new stone houses there reflected at least some indication of modest prosperity.[10] John's interest in horticulture led him to observe that despite the winter season, local fields and gardens were still verdant. He wrote his daughter Nabby that he would have been delighted if he had been able to send her some of the tasty watermelons that were plentiful in Spain.[11]

By mid-December, the Adams party trekked across the rugged country by plodding pack mule, loaded down with foodstuffs, utensils, and bedding. They crossed treacherous roads and climbed dauntingly high mountains, sometimes against the backdrop of splendid groves of orange and lemon trees. As time passed, John found much to complain about, and he often regretted his decision to make their way to France overland. He especially criticized the inferior lodgings and lack of cleanliness he encountered in Spain. Adams and his fellow travelers were forced to sleep in dirt-encrusted, filthy inns, and they encountered bedding infested with lice, which tormented John's sleep. He disdainfully observed at one stop that "the floor has never been washed nor swept for an hundred Years."[12]

The calashes were in disrepair, and they offered no relief from the rutted paths. Mud flew in all directions as the carriage wheels churned up the uncertain roads. After one uncomfortable ride, he declared in frustration, "This Country is an hundred Years behind the Massachusetts Bay, in the Repair of Roads and in all Conveniences for travelling." More pointedly, Adams was moved to despair over Spanish governance and the terrible depredations that he felt were visited on the hapless population: "All three together, Church, State and Nobility exhaust the People to such a degree, I have no idea of the Possibility of deeper Wretchedness. Ignorance more than Wickedness has produced this deplorable State of Things. Ignorance of the true Policy which encourages Agriculture, Manufactures and Commerce."[13]

The situation John witnessed in Spain only served to increase his admiration for life in America and his hope for the future of his new nation, if it could only remain on an ideal trajectory that connected moral virtue with economic progress and fulfilled his high ideals for a government that fostered liberty and a comfortable lifestyle for its citizens. It has been suggested that Adams's dour view of Spain was colored by his anti-Catholic bent.[14] Although bias was certainly a factor, John's irritation was likely fueled by the backward governmental system he witnessed, the formidable physical challenges he and his sons faced, and his mounting frustration over the delay in beginning his diplomatic duties.

In mid-January 1780, Adams summed up the perilous trip across northern Spain and over the Pyrenees. He and his fellow travelers had endured heavy rain and snow as they traveled rough terrain, and it was one of the most draining physical experiences of his life. He wrote that although for a quarter of a century he had been almost continually engaged in "journeying and voyaging, and I have often undergone severe Tryals and great Hardships, cold, wet, heat, fatigue, bad rest, want of sleep, bad nourishment, &c., &c., &c. But I never experienced any Thing like this Journey." John also grumbled that almost everyone in his party, including his two sons and Thaxter, were violently ill with colds, wearing themselves out in "barking [coughing] and sneezing," and that the Spanish servants he had engaged were "dull, discouraged and inactive." He concluded morosely, "In short I was in a deplorable situation, indeed—I know not what to do.—I know not nor where to go. In my Whole Life my Patience was never so near being totally exhausted as at Present."[15] It would be another tedious month before they concluded their trip and John's spirits lifted.

The Adams party commenced the last leg of their laborious trek by post chaise on February 2 and reached Paris on February 8, 1780, having covered the last five hundred miles in just five days. Once in Paris, John was relieved to find rooms available at the elegant Hôtel de Valois on the rue de Richelieu, near the famed Tuileries Gardens, which he had so admired during his previous visit. This time he was determined not to live alongside Franklin. Historian James H. Hutson has suggested that John had developed an unfounded paranoia about Franklin, believing that the elder statesman was bent on sabotaging his diplomatic mission.[16] More likely, John wished to distance himself from Franklin's influence and remain scrupulously independent. Once settled, Adams enrolled his sons in the same school that John Quincy had attended during their first stay in France. Perhaps the greatest pleasure John experienced during his second sojourn in Europe was the company of John Quincy and Charles. Together, the three became inveterate sightseers who soaked up the rich French culture and art and viewed the magnificent Parisian architecture with appreciation.

John's brief respite in America and his firsthand observations about the challenges his country faced as the war dragged on had convinced him that without active French intervention, the Americans and British would remain stalemated. By the time of John's second visit to France, he believed even more strongly that French assistance was required to tip the balance to the American side. The very day after his arrival in Paris, he visited Versailles in the company of Franklin. Adams was gratified to report that the French foreign minister had enthusiastically declared that France was ready to support the American cause by providing "Effectual Aid to the United States," including arms for fifteen thousand American soldiers.[17]

John grew optimistic and eagerly awaited his upcoming presentation to the king. Unfortunately, he harbored unrealistic hopes about speedy diplomatic progress. To his consternation, Vergennes steered a policy focused squarely on what he considered France's best interests and proved to be exceedingly cautious about encouraging peace negotiations with England. Realist that he was, Adams was not surprised that Vergennes privileged French aspirations, but he was disappointed that the French minister did not share his belief that full independence and American economic success would provide robust benefits for France. Instead, Vergennes was outraged when Adams requested that the British immediately be informed of John's peace mission. After Adams complained of insufficient support from France, Vergennes became so incensed that he ordered his French emissary in Philadelphia to press for John's recall. For Adams, this was a signal that Vergennes was scheming to keep America weak and dependent, a situation he found intolerable, as it rekindled memories of British control.[18]

Despite his suspicion of Vergennes, however, Adams was appreciative of the strengthened alliance with France and inclined to take a favorable view of the nation overall. John wrote Abigail that France reflected everything "that can inform understanding, or refine the taste," but he also insisted that it contained much that could "corrupt and debauch." All the while Adams was posted in Europe, he continued to ponder the ideal makeup of the "new" American. French mores often clashed with John's deep appreciation of New England virtues. Closer to home, he fretted that his sons might fall prey to French temptations and display behavior that was at odds with the republican simplicity and moral habits he viewed as essential to American success.[19]

As much as he admired aspects of French culture, John was loath to spend too much time absorbing French "fine Arts" because he believed that "the Science of government is my Duty to study, more than all other Sciences: The Art of Legislation and Administration and Negotiation, ought to take Place, indeed to exclude in a manner all other Arts."[20] In other words, pursuit of science and the arts would have to take second place for American diplomats as their attention needed to be focused on putting an end to hostilities with England and stabilizing the weak American government of the confederation period. He also expressed concern that Americans were aping their European counterparts and becoming too fond of opulence. "The Usefull, the mechanic Arts, are those which We have occasion for in a young Country," he cautioned, "as yet simple and not far advanced in Luxury, altho perhaps [already] much too far for her Age and Character."[21]

Abigail concurred. Even from afar, she was never one to neglect what she considered her motherly duty to offer guidance to her offspring. In early January 1780, she advised John Quincy not to squander his prodigious natural talents and unprecedented opportunities. "These are times in which a genius would wish to live," she declared, for "it is not in the still calm of life, or the repose of a pacific station, that great characters are formed."[22] Abigail continued her exhortations throughout her son's stay in Europe. In March she provided more detail about the philosophy that she hoped would guide him. "The only sure and permanent foundation of virtue is religion," she maintained. "Justice, humanity, and benevolence are the duties you owe society in general. To your country the same duties are incumbent upon you, with the additional obligations of sacrificing personal ease, pleasure, wealth, and life itself for its defence and security."[23] Certainly a tall order for a teenaged boy, but a maxim both his parents had taken to heart and prescribed for their children. The Adamses' moral framework had been shaped by New England sensibilities and upbringing.

If John Quincy was the most scholarly of John and Abigail's four children, their son Charles possessed the most charm. His residence in

Europe proved unusually challenging for the sensitive and high-strung boy, and for a good part of his time overseas he was either ill or homesick. Years later, when Charles died at the young age of thirty, apparently from complications due to alcoholism and a life of dissipation, John lamented his tragic loss to Thomas Jefferson. Adams insisted that Charles "was once the delight of my Eyes and a darling of my heart, cut off in the flower of his days, amidst very flattering Prospects by causes which have been the greatest grief of my Life."[24] But that was in the future, and at the time John had ambitious hopes for both his sons.

John's first stay in Europe had lasted a relatively short eighteen months, but he could not have predicted that this time he would remain for eight years. Although John had returned to France to negotiate peace and revive commerce with England, this mission turned out to be somewhat premature, as the war did not go well for the Americans in 1780. The British won an important battle at Charleston, South Carolina, and captured over five thousand American troops. That military loss and disappointing political developments left Adams disheartened, and he feared that the Americans would have to accept a truce, perhaps brokered by Russia and France, without accomplishing his country's fundamental objectives.

Frustrated, Adams bided his time in Paris and did little to endear himself to either Franklin or the powerful Comte de Vergennes. John was irritated by the convoluted French style of diplomacy, and he increasingly viewed Vergennes as an obstacle rather than an asset to achieving some level of rapprochement with England. Certainly, Adams wanted complete political independence from England, but he astutely understood that resuming trade with Great Britain would be essential to future American commercial success. Moreover, he believed that a central goal of French policy was to thrust America into a subservient role instead of accepting the new nation as an ally and equal. He wrote Abigail that Vergennes's objective was "to make me [and America] his dependent."[25] Adams astutely summed up his own frank style and understood how it might clash with European-style diplomacy: "My fixed Principle never to be the Tool of any Man, nor the Partisan of any Nation, would forever exclude me from the Smiles and favours of Courts."[26]

Adams and Vergennes locked horns on a number of occasions, from the pressing question of whether the British should be informed about John's peace mission to proposed devaluations of American paper money. The underlying cause of their disagreements was their two opposing worldviews, much of it concerned with future American trade policy and the level of sovereignty to be accorded to the United States after the war concluded. Unsurprisingly, Vergennes was committed to making America a client state and maintaining a favorable European balance of power for France. In his view, the earlier 1778 Franco-American Alliance afforded France preferential treatment in commerce in exchange for French support.

Adams instead focused on ending the war, ensuring that America would be recognized as an independent nation, and restoring robust trade with England. In short, he was determined to accept nothing less than the peace terms conveyed to him by Congress, although communications across the Atlantic were so excruciatingly slow that he and his fellow American diplomats often had to proceed without official direction. Adams appreciated Vergennes's skill and work ethic, but he often regarded the French minister as obstructive, duplicitous, and indifferent to America's well-being. Vergennes, in turn, viewed Adams as an unreasonably strong-willed, interfering emissary, one unwilling to acknowledge America's subordinate status and much too independent-minded. One of the French minister's main objectives had been to degrade England's power, and therefore Vergennes regarded American interests as secondary at best.[27] It did not make for a successful personal alliance. To the sophisticated Vergennes, who preferred to deal with the more obliging Franklin, Adams appeared to be politically unrealistic and an inexperienced "provincial."[28] Still, despite his distrust of Vergennes, as a pragmatist John tried to make the best of the situation and sidestepped him when possible. He remained outwardly cordial and devoted a good deal of his time in France to penning articles explaining the American cause to the British in order to gain popular support in England.

John also conducted a vast correspondence with friends back home, including his fellow revolutionaries Dr. Benjamin Rush and James Warren. One of Adams's most valued correspondents became John Jay, who in 1780 arrived in Europe as the first American minister to Spain. The two often shared their diplomatic frustrations with one another, as Adams was just as stymied as Jay, who had hoped to secure key economic and political support from Spain. In his wry style, Adams summed up for Jay what he found to be the challenges of working with foreign diplomats. "There is something in the European understanding different from that we have been more used to," he maintained. "Men of the greatest abilities, and the most experience, are with great difficulty brought to see, what appears to us as clear as day." For Adams, it was just another example of the customs that separated Americans from Europeans, who were mired in hidebound traditions that he believed discouraged creativity. He speculated that "it is habit, it is education, prejudice, what you will, but so it is." To John it made perfect sense that it was to the long-term political and economic advantage of the French and Spanish to extend loans to the Americans, but he concluded sardonically, "It is in vain to reason in this manner with an European minister of state. He cannot understand you."[29]

John also regularly sent crucial reports about developments in Europe to Congress. He observed that the rival courts of England, France, Spain, and Holland were perpetually in a state of belligerence, and he feared that America would be drawn into their clashes. In April 1780 he summed up his view of unreliable European support for his nation, insisting that many of the countries on the Continent were only fairweather friends with their own self-serving agendas. In a forthright missive to Congress, Adams urged restraint and maintained that America should treat France and Spain "with gratitude, but with dignity." He went on: "Let us above all things avoid as much as possible entangling ourselves with their wars and politics," thus anticipating a main point of discussion during the future Constitutional Convention debates and Washington's later admonishments in his 1796 Farewell Address.[30]

American neutrality was a theme that would resurface many times in John's political outlook, but he was not an isolationist. He recognized before many of his political contemporaries that America, blessed with rich natural resources, vast tracts of land, and raw agricultural goods, had the potential to become a world leader. He gave serious thought to how to best position his homeland in response to global change as the political power of competing European nations waxed and waned and the world community was drawn closer as transatlantic commerce expanded. He later predicted to Jay that America was "destined beyond a doubt to be the greatest Power on Earth."[31] Adams understood that America could never engage in robust trade without also being involved on some level in international affairs. Certainly, he viewed politics, economics, and war as closely interrelated. Therefore, he advocated sending American diplomats to all major European countries to ensure strong commercial connections and peaceful relations.

Economic considerations, particularly his emphasis on the future of American commerce, drove Adams's foreign diplomacy. The American marketplace offered rich opportunities and could serve as the key to effective foreign policy with European countries, which he believed would compete with one another for American trade. Thus, a desirable balance of power could be maintained, but one that would foster American economic success. Later, after the 1783 Treaty of Paris was signed, Adams would find himself disappointed that few new commercial treaties would be executed during his tenure in Europe.[32]

In the meantime, John's relationship with Vergennes deteriorated to the point that the French minister declared that going forward he would communicate only with the more agreeable Franklin. Franklin, exasperated with John's style, informed Congress that Adams's unconventional diplomacy had been a failure in gaining further French support to the extent that "Mr. Adams has given extreme offense to the court here."[33] Frustrated, John decided that instead of wasting time in Paris, his new unofficial mission would be to develop what he considered crucial financial and moral support for American independence in the Netherlands, a country he hoped would be a better match. He knew that the small country had already supported the American cause by engaging in a brisk trade with America in smuggled armaments.

After Vergennes finally agreed to issue Adams the necessary passport, John immediately took his sons out of their Passy school. He set out with them in late July 1780 on a two-week tour of northern France and parts of the Netherlands, passing through Brussels, Antwerp, Rotterdam, and The Hague. It was a peaceful interlude, and they traveled in comfort by horse-drawn carriage and then for the last leg of the journey by the novel conveyance of canal boat. John had intended to stay in the Netherlands for only a few months, but remained for nearly two years. On his own, and for the most part independent of congressional control or the need to consult with other American ministers, Adams would make significant progress.

In mid-August 1780, the Adams party arrived in the bustling metropolis of Amsterdam and experienced their first view of the giant windmills and countless bridges that connected the tree-lined canals, with multistory fine brick houses that reflected the prosperity of the well-to-do merchant class. John took long walking tours to familiarize himself with all Amsterdam had to offer, and he frequented the smoky bustling coffeehouses to learn more about its inhabitants. The Netherlands at the time was a small, independent republic and the commercial hub and banking capital of Europe. Its seven provinces were commonly referred to simply as Holland, the largest of the sections.

Although Adams arrived in Holland as a private citizen, Congress had long agreed with him that the Dutch could be engaged fruitfully. However, due to the slow mail, it was not until mid-September 1780 that John received Congress's formal commission to engage in economic negotiations in the Netherlands, which had been issued in June. Congress instructed him to act as its agent to raise a loan, as Henry Laurens, originally tasked with the mission, had been imprisoned by the British as an alleged spy. After John learned of his authorization, he instructed Thaxter to close up the rooms the Adamses had occupied in Paris and join him in Amsterdam as his secretary.

Adams first secured lodging for himself and his entourage with a local matron in Amsterdam. Both Adams boys were initially enrolled in the city's Latin School, renowned for its exacting educational standards. Their attendance there was short-lived, however, because the rigid environment at the school, where classes were taught exclusively in Dutch and corporal punishment was common, was an unhappy experience for both boys. The oppressive atmosphere may have even led the normally conscientious Johnny to misbehave. The school policies were also unacceptable to his father, who believed in a benevolent approach to learning and education. Adams was horrified when he heard that students were beaten. He unceremoniously withdrew his boys from the school and for a time filled their days with private lessons and visits to the city's most famous sites.

In December 1780, Adams made the decision to send his sons to Leyden with John Thaxter as their chaperone. By January, the two boys began studying at the University of Leyden, then one of the most respected educational institutions of its kind in the world. Gifted in languages, John Quincy soon acquired a working proficiency in Dutch. Charles, deemed too young to enroll as a student, worked privately with a tutor but was later admitted. John's sons' education was supervised by Dr. Benjamin Waterhouse, a young American medical student from Boston, while John stayed in Amsterdam.

Despite his hectic schedule, Adams kept a close eye on his sons' scholarly progress. At the end of John Quincy's first month at the university, John asked Johnny to inform him not only about the state of his health but also his progress in literature. He particularly encouraged John Quincy's study of Roman and Greek classics, but admonished him not to "forget your mother Tongue" in his zeal for those languages.[34] He also urged him to keep in mind his father's underlying philosophy that the purpose of education was to build the American character: "Ever remember that all the End of study is to make you a good Man and a useful Citizen—This will ever be the Sum total of the Advice of your affectionate Father."[35] Johnny had no trouble keeping up with the varied and demanding classes, some of which were taught in Latin and ranged from the study of medicine to law and philosophy. With his father's approval, the teenager also took time to enjoy popular pursuits such as ice-skating on the frozen Dutch canals.

While his sons studied, John continued his efforts to engage Dutch support. Adams soon learned that without formal recognition of America by the ceremonial monarch of the Netherlands, Prince William of Orange, and the powerful parliament, no loans from Dutch bankers or merchants would be forthcoming. While he waited, he began to build relationships with potential financial backers. John found that he shared many values with the members of Holland's thriving industrious merchant class and that some saw themselves as comrades in the cause of liberty.[36]

The financial loans Adams secured came mostly from prosperous entrepreneurs who ran banking and brokerage enterprises in Amsterdam. Some supported the protean Dutch Patriot republican movement in the Netherlands and admired the more representative government of the new American nation, which made Adams sympathetic to their political cause. The Patriots opposed the Dutch royal family, who had aligned themselves with the British, and the incipient revolutionaries were both pro-American and pro-French, a position Adams appreciated.[37]

Astute Dutch merchants also saw an opportunity to expand the scope of their lucrative businesses and increase their profits by working with the Americans. The increased risks of pursuing higher profits were offset by the generally responsible and timely manner in which the Americans serviced their loans. In other words, floating loans for the American cause made good business sense for Dutch businessmen.[38] Adams made some friends among the Patriots, including Adriaan van der Kemp, a Protestant minister in Leyden, and Jean Luzac, a professor of Greek and history, who was also the editor of the influential newspaper the

Gazette de Leyde. Luzac was especially helpful to Adams in his ongoing public relations campaign by publishing John's pro-American articles. The professor also translated John's bold appeal to the government, the "Memorial to the States General," into Dutch. Van der Kemp was later exiled from the Netherlands for his political views, and Adams helped resettle him in the United States, where they remained close friends.[39]

Yet from the beginning, John harbored ambivalent feelings about the Dutch. He found them at times to be avaricious in business, plodding in their negotiations, and almost wholly focused on the accumulation of wealth. Although he at first wrote Abigail that he was "very much pleased with Holland" and the "Frugality, Industry, Cleanliness" he found there, he soon carped about the stinginess of the hearty burghers and "a general Littleness arising from the incessant Contemplation of Stivers and Droits [units of small change]."[40] He found them less welcoming than the French and maintained that "Hospitality and Sociability are no Characteristicks here."[41] He also feared that they lacked the broader sense of public spirit that in his estimation was required for a stable and virtuous republic. Once again, his experience in a European nation helped influence John's views about American nationhood and individual character. Adams found much to admire in Holland, but he never found Dutch society an acceptable model. Adams appreciated fiscal responsibility, but he believed that the Dutch had taken it to an extreme.

Adams was always a hard worker, diligent and disciplined. In an effort to gain official Dutch support, during the month of October 1780 alone, John wrote twenty-six letters to prominent lawyers in Amsterdam to explain the progress and goals of the American Revolution. He worked tirelessly to convince potential supporters in Amsterdam, Leyden, and The Hague to aid the American cause. He even set himself to learning the language by daily reading the local newspaper with the aid of a Dutch dictionary. Although his initial overtures were rebuffed, and John became discouraged with what he perceived as the convoluted government decision-making process as well as Dutch stubbornness, he set out on a concerted campaign to win over the Dutch and enlarge his diplomatic footprint.

At the same time, throughout his residency in Europe, Adams sensed undercurrents of rivalries and alliances that made diplomacy an uphill battle. Adams often worried that Vergennes and his minister in the Netherlands, the Duc de la Vauguyon, were plotting to use their influence in a manner that would derail American interests there. Indeed, Adams likely settled in Amsterdam rather than in The Hague, the seat of the Dutch government, because Vauguyon resided in the latter. Some historians have taken Adams to task for being too independent, being overly paranoid about Vergennes's motivations, and not taking advantage of potentially helpful French diplomacy.[42] Moreover, after John moved to the Netherlands, the war situation worsened for the American side, which made the Dutch more reluctant to offer financial support.

However, circumstances in Europe were slowly changing on the ground in a way that appeared promising. In December, Great Britain issued what amounted to a declaration of war against Holland and began seizing Dutch ships. The ensuing Anglo-Dutch War lasted from 1780 to 1784. Many burghers resented English interference with their trade, and as a result, they looked forward to developing a profitable relationship with the Americans. John welcomed the conflict, as he felt that if England became embroiled in hostilities with so many other nations, including Russia, France, and Sweden, it would not be able to sustain its efforts across the ocean against America.[43]

In the meantime, Adams remained active, for he adhered to the maxim "loose [waste] no time" as a vital moral "Precept."[44] John was never one to hesitate to bend the rules of diplomatic convention when he thought it necessary. Without obtaining prior permission, on May 2, 1781, he took the unheard-of bold step of directly presenting to the parliament of the United Provinces a "Memorial to the States General." He composed the missive as a ringing appeal for Dutch recognition of America and a commercial treaty with the United States. Adams donned formal dress suitable for the occasion and traveled by coach-

and-four to present the document to the "High Mightinesses" in The Hague. He also published the appeal as a pamphlet in English, Dutch, and French. Although he understood that the outcome was uncertain, he felt compelled to "put the seed in the ground," as he told his sons and secretary.[45] In justifying his actions to the American secretary of foreign affairs Robert Livingston, Adams maintained that the "Memorial" was met with "the most universal and unanimous Approbation" in all the local newspapers, "and no Criticism ever appeared against it."[46]

In April 1781, John had relocated his family and assistants from their initial lodgings in Amsterdam with Madam Schorn to new spacious quarters. For a year, John rented a commodious house on the Kiezersgracht that was within his budget but also elegant enough to entertain diplomats and potential business partners. He acquired a carriage, a coachman, and a fine team of horses so that he could conveniently travel the city to gather support for his commercial plans. It left him little time and energy to communicate with an often lonely and sometimes resentful Abigail, who was managing all the family affairs on her own.

Unbeknown to Adams, his diplomatic status had been reduced when his European appointment was amended. On June 15, 1781, Congress removed Adams as sole peace negotiator with Great Britain. French pressure and a letter from Franklin alerting his American colleagues of Vergennes's dislike of Adams's diplomatic style took their toll. The new diplomatic team joining Adams would include Franklin, Jay, Laurens, and Jefferson. Although Abigail chafed at John's prolonged absence, she was more incensed when she inadvertently learned about Franklin's missive and was convinced that Franklin had conspired to sabotage John's singular role. Instead of his original post, John then became the head of an enlarged five-man delegation to negotiate a peace settlement with England. It was fortunate that Adams did not learn about the reorganization for a year. By then he could document significant progress in the Netherlands.

In July, Adams returned to Paris to discuss peace negotiations with Vergennes, but things did not proceed as either had hoped. John was unhappy that Congress had again agreed that France was to have the final say in peace negotiations, and he rejected all of Vergennes's interim proposals for possible negotiations brokered by third parties. Moreover, Adams insisted that he would not participate in any mediations unless American independence was first recognized. Disgruntled with the lack of progress, he returned to Amsterdam, where he remained until the fall of 1782.

Not for the first time, Adams was frustrated that his diplomatic assignments from Congress were often vague. By early 1782, he was receiving unwelcome advice from the wealthy Robert Livingston, who had never traveled to Europe. Livingston criticized Adams's diplomatic efforts in Holland and France, which irritated John, who had always been sensitive to criticism, especially from someone who he thought lacked experience and perspective. Adams's unpleasant interactions with some of his fellow American ministers in Europe and members of Congress played a pivotal role in his growing unease that members of what he considered the American "oligarchy," like Livingston, were subverting the public good for their own selfish ends.

Whether they had become members of the elite by right of birth and family reputation like Livingston or through exceptional charisma and intellectual prowess, as with Franklin, Adams grew worried that Americans had lost the commitment to the civic virtue that he believed was essential to a viable republic. How to control the threat of a rising American aristocracy, which focused on personal wealth, reputation, and power, and instead position them to work toward attaining liberty for all American citizens became a primary concern as Adams continued to ponder the direction of American nationhood. At the same time, he continued to wrestle with balancing obtaining financial support for his country and moving toward a durable peace settlement with England.[47]

Adams's high level of stress and bouts of serious illness while he lived in the Netherlands may have magnified his bleak view of his fellow Americans and his disdain for the leaders of the French, Dutch, and British governments. John's health suffered in the humid climate, where many of the unsanitary canals became breeding grounds for the spread of germs. He contracted an undisclosed "ague," probably malaria, which circulated in the eighteenth century in both Europe and America. His illness, which he termed a "nervous fever of a dangerous kind," became so severe that he apparently lapsed in and out of consciousness and lay near death. "For five or six days I was lost, and so insensible to the Operations of the Physicians and surgeons, as to have lost my memory of them," he reported dramatically to Abigail.[48]

All Abigail could do was to worry, never knowing the state of her husband's health. Under significant stress and without Abigail at his side, John always seemed more susceptible to sickness, and he was likely more vulnerable to disease because of depressed spirits. As he slowly improved, Adams informed Franklin in France that "I am still very far from being a Man in Health and capable of going through much business."[49] Indeed, he was so weak after his health crisis that he did not return to his active schedule for months.

Yet there was some good news. The American victory at Yorktown in October 1781 had turned the tide of the Revolutionary War and heartened Adams. Critical French naval support had served to break the frustrating military stalemate. The combined American and French forces had prevailed over the British army of Lord Cornwallis, resulting in the surrender of more than seven thousand Redcoats. The humiliating British defeat renewed the prospects of a peace settlement, and with his health improved, John recovered his optimism and redoubled his diplomatic efforts with the Dutch. The American victory at Yorktown and the British surrender served to convince Dutch financiers to back what now appeared to be the winning side. Moreover, 1782 had also brought a change in the British government, which made future American negotiations more promising. The defeat had brought down the North ministry, and his successor, Lord Shelburne, was determined to achieve an honorable exit from the hostilities.

There were also major victories of a different sort in the Netherlands. Everyone knew that the Stadtholder, William V, was merely a figure-

Engraving of John Adams from an original painting
by Gilbert Stuart. The globe symbolizes his diplomatic career. Courtesy Library of Congress.

head and that the real power rested in the States General. Still, Adams
understood that as a royal William possessed influence, and he treated
him accordingly. By now Adams had gained experience with European
royalty, and he approached the Stadtholder with "all the Softness, Cau-
tion and Prudence, possible, so that no ill humours might be stirred."
John was not fond of the Prince of Orange and judged him an obstacle
to the cause of liberty, "as incurable as George the third, his Cousin."[50]

Regardless of John's feelings about Britain's King George, when in April 1782, Prince William of Orange and Princess Wilhelmina formally recognized John as the American minister at their palace in The Hague, he was elated. He wrote Benjamin Rush on April 22 that he believed that America would now have a faithful friend and ally and that the declaration of the "Sovereignty" reflected the "most Signal Epocha, in the History of a Century."[51]

In March 1782, even before he had received official government recognition from the States General, John had purchased an imposing five-story redbrick canal house in The Hague to serve as the headquarters of the American legation, the first American embassy the world had ever known. John and his entourage moved into the fine residence at the Hôtel des Etats-Unis d'Amérique in May, when he proudly raised a flag. In a burst of exultation and optimism, John later pronounced it a triumph over British pride and claimed that "not the Declaration of American Independence—not the Massachusetts Constitution—not the Alliance with France, ever gave me more Satisfaction or more pleasing Prospects for our country than this Event."[52] Although John may have minimized those other seminal events, he was correct that without the Dutch loans that followed the recognition of the American nation, the financially beleaguered United States may have collapsed before the republican experiment even got off the ground.

Adams frequently entertained dignitaries, supportive merchants, and bankers in the embassy as he now moved easily in Dutch diplomatic and court circles. His house featured a spacious drawing room decorated with gilded mirrors and crimson damask curtains, and the large dining room table could seat sixteen guests. Clearly, even without his Abigail at his side, Adams appears to have been capable of overseeing a welcoming and dignified setting for diplomacy. Secure in the belief that Abigail remained a loyal wife on whom he could depend, John was able to carry on his diplomatic business with peace of mind, often minimizing the daily stresses that his wife endured in his absence.

A milestone was marked in March 1782, when the Dutch government formally recognized the United States. It was the second nation in the world after France to do so, and on April 19, the States General acknowledged Adams as the American minister. Now treated as a respected and popular public figure in Holland, Adams basked in his unaccustomed adulation. John was especially gratified when he reaped effusive praise from the Spanish ambassador, whom he considered one of the most respected foreign ministers posted to The Hague. Adams proudly reported to Benjamin Rush that the Spanish envoy had lauded John's effort as "the grandest Step that has ever yet been taken. It is you, who have filled this Nation with enthusiasm for your Cause and turned their Heads. It is a most important, and most decisive measure, and it is due, to you." Adams could not resist telling Rush, "Voila! a flour of diplomatick Rhetoric, enough to turn my Head, whether I have turned those of the Dutchmen or not."[53]

Yet as late as mid-May, John was still not confident of Dutch loans. "I have taken every Measure in my Power to accomplish it, but I have met with so many Difficulties that I almost despair of obtaining any thing," he reported glumly to Robert Livingston. He even compared himself to "a Man in the midst of the Ocean negotiating for his Life among a School of Sharks."[54] John must have been ecstatic later in June when he received the first Dutch loan from a consortium of Amsterdam bankers, a significant five million guilders at 5 percent interest. He proudly, if immodestly, told his friend James Warren that his "Dutch Negotiations" were "one of the most extraordinary, in all diplomatic Records. But it has succeeded to a marvel."[55]

On October 8, 1782, John Adams was finally able to affix his signature to a commercial treaty with the Dutch Republic. It was a pivotal agreement of amity and commerce signed at the State House in The Hague. Indeed, the Dutch loans that Adams negotiated between 1782 and 1788 played a critical role in allowing the American nation to avoid bankruptcy.[56] Even the French emissary in the Netherlands recognized

John's success as a negotiator. When John informed Vauguyon that John Jay had summoned Adams to Paris to work on a formal peace treaty with the English, Vauguyon insisted that it was "absolutely necessary" that John be involved because the "immoveable Firmness that Heaven had given me, would be useful and necessary on this occasion." In a moment of wry self-reflection about his sometimes volatile personality, Adams recorded, "I could not help laughing at this and replying, that I had often occasion however for cooler Blood than had fallen to my Share."[57] Adams may have been flattered, but he likely took Vauguyon's praise with a measure of skepticism, and just the following month he observed sardonically, "Compliments are the Study of this People [the French] and there is no others so ingenious as them."[58]

Against the backdrop of a whirlwind of diplomatic events, a significant change in the Adams family dynamics had occurred earlier in the summer of 1781. At the age of barely fourteen, John Quincy traveled to St. Petersburg to serve as the personal secretary and French interpreter to the newly appointed American minister to Russia, Francis Dana. Dana was dispatched in order to establish ties with the Russian government under the reign of Catherine the Great. Although John had misgivings, he liked and trusted Dana, who hailed from Massachusetts and had served as an able secretary to the American legation in France. Adams missed John Quincy and worried about the potential dangers of his travels, but he realized that it was an unparalleled opportunity for his son, whom he and Abigail had groomed for greatness and public service. John implored his son to write him often and, always seeking to increase his own knowledge, Adams asked him to inform him about the state of education in St. Petersburg.[59] Even John Quincy's sister, Nabby, recognized his potential and wrote, "You, my brother, have become so great a traveler that much is expected from you."[60] Abigail was unaware of the exact details of her eldest son's whereabouts or she would have been left even more anxious about his far-flung travels. John Quincy did not return to The Hague until April 21, 1783, via a convoluted journey through Finland, Denmark, Sweden, and the German provinces, with stops in Copenhagen, Stockholm, and Hamburg.

While diplomatic events were unfolding, the Adamses' middle son, Charles, was sent home in August 1781 on the *South Carolina* due to a combination of homesickness and uncertain health. Charles's return trip to America lasted nearly six months in all, and Abigail remained in a state of heightened anxiety as she received almost no updates about his progress home. Charles was chaperoned on his overseas trek by William Jackson, a former officer in the Continental Army. The boy finally arrived home at the end of January 1781, via another vessel, the *Cicero*, but why the trip was so prolonged remains a mystery to this day.

While she awaited Charles's return, Abigail formed her opinion about what she considered the inferiority of life on the other side of the Atlantic. She worried about the threat posed to moral virtue for young Americans abroad, including her son. Soon after Charles arrived, she told her younger sister Elizabeth that to her immense relief and satisfaction he had returned "to his Native Land, undepraved in his mind and morals, by the fascinating allurements of vice, decked in Foreign garb . . . and perfectly attached to the modest [American] republican Stile of Life."[61]

Abigail kept up her campaign to bring John home as well. Despite her pleas, John remained reluctant to allow Abigail and Nabby to join him in Europe. When Nabby expressed her willingness to travel on her own to assist her father as his housekeeper in the Netherlands, he replied firmly that a voyage during war was far too dangerous and that "I have too much tenderness for you, my dear child, to cross the Atlantic. You know not what it is."[62]

Although John primarily focused on molding the characters of his sons, he also frequently expressed his deep affection and concern for Nabby. Writing from The Hague in 1782, John shared parental wisdom about the pursuit of a virtuous life, which was essential to his vision of the ideal American character, traits he often found missing in Europe. When Nabby requested that John send her what he considered mere fripperies from abroad, he admonished her and declared that jewels and lace were superficial ornaments. He advised her that with her superior intellectual talents and personal attributes, she should set her sights on higher ambitions than fashion. "Knowledge in the head and virtue in the heart, time devoted to study and business, instead of show or plea-sure, are the way to be useful and consequently happy," he counseled.[63] John told Nabby that she should not neglect the arts and cultural ac-complishments, but he believed that women had more important objec-tives to focus upon. "Your country is young, and advancing with more rapid strides than any people ever took before her," he asserted. "She will have occasion for great abilities and virtues to conduct her affairs with wisdom and success."[64]

John's advice to his daughter reveals the common outlook about marriage in their era and casts light on his relationship with Abigail, even when separated by distance. Although the religious and popular views of their time stressed that partners in a good marriage had "sym-metrical" roles, such a view did not imply an egalitarian partnership.[65] Clearly, marriage was different in the eighteenth century, and the so-cially prescribed form of marriage during the era was one in which the wife was automatically the subordinate partner.[66] Abigail would never have contemplated deviating from that norm. Marriage was also considered an unbreakable lifelong commitment, and although many early Americans, like the Adamses, undoubtedly married for love, po-litical, economic, and social considerations played a role in the decision to marry as well.

On the heels of his Dutch success, John was unexpectedly called away from Amsterdam in late September. He received an urgent appeal from John Jay requesting that he help Jay and Franklin negotiate the long-awaited peace treaty with England now that the British were will-ing to accept the reality of American independence. John was pleased that some "Symptoms" of peace were visible on the horizon, but appears to have been in no rush to return to Paris, for his health was still un-certain, and he wanted to finalize his Dutch commercial efforts before departing.[67] Adams was accompanied to France by Thaxter and Charles Storer. Storer was a Harvard graduate who was related to Abigail and who was to serve as an additional secretary to the American negotiators. The three took a ten-day coach trip to France through dank weather, stopping in Antwerp and Chantilly to view a number of examples of renowned European architecture, including the magnificent Chateau de Chantilly, and art such as remarkable works by Rubens and Rembrandt, whom Adams appreciated as masters.

Adams arrived in Paris on October 26, and the next day he took time to make himself presentable for his diplomatic tasks by ordering a custom-made French tailored suit, new shoes, and a fine wig. He also treated himself to a stop to wash away the grime of his journey at a popular bathhouse on the Seine, where he was furnished with hot towels. Again, as an American diplomat he had become a man of privilege, but Adams found himself uncomfortable with its trappings. The high costs of the new purchases irritated him, and John observed disdainfully that French modes of fashion were so influential in Europe that only French tailoring was acceptable for diplomacy. "This is one of the Ways," he huffed, "in which France taxes all Europe, and will tax America."[68] This time Adams made the Hôtel du Roi his headquarters as it provided him with more spacious accommodations than were available at his regular rooms at the Hôtel Valois.

Of the five American peace commissioners, Thomas Jefferson was unable to sail from America in time to participate in the negotiations, and Henry Laurens, who had been captured as a British prisoner of war after crossing the Atlantic, languished in prison. Only Franklin, Adams, and Jay remained to carry on. Laurens was later released from the Tower of London just in time to sign the preliminary treaty. With successful economic negotiations in The Hague concluded, Adams was received warmly in Paris. Even his old nemesis Vergennes was noticeably hospitable, inviting him to dine at his home as an honored guest.

Through Jay's intervention, Adams and Franklin were able to maintain at least an outwardly cordial relationship. The team worked productively together, with the three often dining together while working through the complex issues that lay before them, this despite the fact that John was capable of nursing a grudge, particularly when he felt that his reputation had been maligned. John still resented the critical remarks Franklin had made about his diplomatic skills to Congress. As he put it petulantly to Arthur Lee, "I wish it were possible [to] blot out of the Page of History . . . his insolent Persecutions of you and me and others, and the Motives of them a Sordid Jealousy and insidious Selfishness." But to his credit, John's dedication to his mission overrode personal feelings, and Jay helpfully mediated differences between his fellow commissioners.[69]

If the relationship between Franklin and Adams remained somewhat fraught, Jay and Adams got along especially well. The third American commissioner was a decade Adams's junior, but both men were skilled lawyers. Adams knew Jay from the time the two had served together in the Continental Congress, although during that period the two men did not always see political events from the same perspective. Unlike the Adamses, the Jays were part of a wealthy New York family, and they were unapologetic slave owners. Adams, on the other hand, was proud of the fact that he had never owned another person and was a largely self-made man. Despite John Adams's anti-slavery sentiments, however, the fate of African Americans who had supported the British during the American Revolution was sidestepped in the final peace treaty. The issue was discussed, but it was left unresolved largely in an effort to appease the American southern faction.[70]

In Paris, Adams and Jay discovered that their political outlooks had grown more closely aligned. Jay had arrived in France with his wife, Sarah, and their young children from an unfruitful diplomatic stint in Spain. He clearly played a critical role in the Paris treaty talks. Indeed, Adams later declared that Franklin had been cooperative and helpful, but that Jay was the man most responsible among the three diplomats for the ultimate success of the negotiations with the British, an extremely generous and somewhat uncharacteristic gesture by

Adams, who was never one to downplay his own contributions. He even noted privately in his diary that most of the credit "belongs to Mr. Jay."[71] It was certainly true that much of Jay's earlier drafts for the peace treaty remained in the final iteration.[72] When Jay returned to America in 1784, Adams continued his praise: "Our worthy friend, Mr. Jay, returns to his country like a bee to his hive, with both legs loaded with merit and honor."[73] Still, John noted proudly in his diary that the French had taken to referring to Adams as "Le Washington de la Negotiation."[74]

At the start of the peace talks with the English, how to handle France remained a pivotal issue. Both Adams and Jay agreed that they would not allow the French to dictate settlement terms to a newly independent America. And Franklin, despite his earlier close and amiable connections with Vergennes, understood that the American representatives needed to act in harmony if they were to succeed. Jay and his wife, Sarah, became friendly with Franklin while they lived in Paris, and they both found him congenial and witty. Despite some disagreements over how to handle elements of the treaty negotiations, Jay appreciated the elder statesman far more than Adams did.

Yet their agreement over the relationship with France meant that the American diplomats had to disregard, if not outright violate, the earlier Franco-American Alliance of 1778. In that treaty, the Americans had agreed not to make a separate peace with Great Britain. When Adams was reminded of the caveat, he was irritated and threatened to resign his commission. In the end, the three American diplomats ignored the advice from Congress and proceeded directly to negotiations with the British. As Adams perceptively noted in his diary in November 1782, "There was something in the Minds of the English and French, which impelled them irresistibly to War every Ten or fifteen years." Although not unique in this outlook, Adams especially feared American entanglement in European affairs, and he insisted that "America had been long enough involved in the Wars of Europe. She had been a football between contending Nations from the Beginning, and it was easy to see that France and England both would endeavor to involve Us in their future Wars."[75] Thus, John maintained that the best course was for America to connect with European nations through commerce, not through military or political alliances, an approach that had always informed his diplomatic outlook.

Franklin, who in the past had presented an accommodating persona to both the French and British ministers, allowed Jay and Adams to proceed with the single-minded firmness that reflected America's status as an independent nation. The main British negotiator, Richard Oswald, a Scottish merchant, took a conciliatory view toward the United States, and the minister of war, Lord Shelburne, influenced in part by his progressive support of free trade, dealt generously with the Americans. Unsurprisingly, their actions were criticized by other members of the British ministry, as well as by King George III. In addition to Oswald, the American emissaries also had to contend with the British undersecretary of state, Henry Strachey, who insisted that American Loyalists deserved compensation for property and financial losses, a controversial subject that would surface again in the future, even after the signing of the final treaty. In the short run it was sidestepped by Adams, Jay, and Franklin, who was the most adamant among the three in his insistence that no compensation be granted, arguing that it would unreasonably delay peace.

On November 30, 1782, after five intense weeks of negotiations, the American emissaries signed a preliminary but crucial peace treaty with Great Britain at Oswald's hotel. As Adams put it, "We had been very industrious, having been at it, forenoon, Afternoon and Evening, ever since my arrival."[76] Not only representatives of England, but also envoys from France, Spain, and the Netherlands and potential mediators from Austria and Russia all played a part in the complex discussions to end what had essentially become a world war. Although France was at the time America's most important ally, Vergennes and the elderly Comte de Maurepas, the head minister of King Louis XVI's government, understandably always put French interests first. Both had to take into consideration France's finances, strained to a breaking point in part due to support of the Americans, as well as a vocal political faction that urged peace with England. A rapprochement between America and Great Britain was not always perceived as desirable by French leaders, focused as they were on retaining France's strong position in the balance of power.

November 1782 marked the third anniversary of Abigail's separation from her husband, and she often lamented the prospect of several additional years without her "dearest friend" by her side. Just a few months later, John insisted that "the first Wish of my Heart was to return to my Wife and Children."[77] With the signing of the preliminary peace treaty, Abigail had hoped that John would soon be able to return home, but her desire was premature.

The signing of the preliminary peace treaty between America and England left Vergennes astonished, particularly at the degree of British concessions, but Franklin was able to use his considerable diplomatic talents and relationship with the French minister to smooth over potential discord. In the end, the Americans had secured nearly all their demands from Great Britain. These included the right of navigation on the Mississippi River, the annexation of British territory between the Appalachian Mountains on the East and the Mississippi on the West, which doubled the size of the United States, and finally, the acknowledgment of American fishing rights on the Grand Banks and along the coast of Newfoundland.

A final peace treaty, which included not only the formal recognition of American independence and withdrawal of British forces, but generous territorial rights for America, would be executed in early September 1783. At one point, after the preliminary treaty was concluded, only half in jest, John wrote ruefully to Abigail that "my Children will have nothing, but their Liberty and the Right to catch Fish, in the Banks of

Newfoundland. This is all the Fortune that I have been able to make for myself or them."[78] Adams had played a critical role in the negotiations, but he was again left feeling that Congress had not sufficiently appreciated his efforts. He remained dispirited and without a defined role for the future.

Still Adams moved forward. He recorded that on the evening of January 1, 1783, he visited Versailles, where, to his astonishment, he was greeted with exceptional cordiality by Vergennes, to whom he delivered a copy of the treaty draft. This was the very man who had openly maligned Adams to Congress, but John, in turn, was studiously polite. Despite unaccustomed praise from the French minister, Adams kept his counsel and refused to divulge any details of the negotiations. Adams also took the time to attend a palace ceremony "where the Queen [Marie-Antoinette] shone in great splendor."[79] Later in the month Adams paid his respects to King Louis XVI and the royal family and noted that the queen and king appeared in "high Health and in gay Sprits."[80]

Although on one level John admired Louis XVI and Marie-Antoinette, he continued to look with disdain on their ostentatious court lifestyle. Adams viewed Louis XVI (and later even his former enemy George III) as a man of character, a trait he admired, but he confided in his diary that in France "the Demon of Monarchy haunts all the Scenes of Life. . . . [The people] can esteem but one [the king], and to that one their Homage is Adulation and Idolatry."[81] Moreover, John maintained that Vergennes and the other French ministers had often tried to derail American plans, and he insisted that unlike Franklin and some members of Congress he had always adhered to firmness in negotiations, particularly in regard to fishing rights and western territory. Although John felt that he had often been unfairly derided for obstinacy, he reiterated that he had always acted in the best interests of America as the French, through the machinations of Vergennes, were "endeavoring to make my Countrymen meek and humble and I was laboring to make them proud."[82]

Although John Adams has been criticized for being overly suspicious and even paranoid about the motives and intentions of his European diplomatic counterparts,[83] historian Richard B. Morris has ably demonstrated that Adams had good reason to find their efforts suspect. Both Adams and Jay viewed Vergennes as a manipulator who planned to keep the Americans subservient for the foreseeable future. Vergennes was similarly skeptical of the motives of the American negotiators. To his credit, Adams stubbornly refused to acquiesce to any agreements that violated fundamental American goals, and he vocally protested his objections to Vergennes. His consistent arguments put "a spoke in the wheel" that resulted in a favorable outcome for America and effectively ended plans for proposed mediation by third parties. Moreover, Jay had earlier insisted that no peace talks would occur before Great Britain formally recognized his country as an independent nation, a stance that had strengthened the American position from the start.[84]

Morris concluded that "by their shrewdness, discernment, and tenacity the three Americans in Paris won independence and a continental domain for 13 littoral states." The treaty marked the legitimacy of the new American nation. In the final analysis, Adams, Jay, and Franklin had surmounted the knotty issues surrounding the discussions and had refused to compromise on all essential points, for the American commissioners viewed themselves as "instruments of the new revolutionary society and as such would not settle for less than total victory."[85] Certainly, Adams saw himself that way, a committed warrior on behalf of his native country. He continued to worry about European aggression and French jealousy of the American nation, which he considered to be but a "brittle Vessel." John told his friend James Warren that he considered America "at Peace, but not out of danger. . . . Amidst all the Joys of Peace, and the glorious Prospects before Us, I see in Europe so many Causes of Inquietude."[86] Hardly the sentiments of a man who was later accused of abandoning his republican principles in veneration of monarchy and European life and society.

Living in France had sharpened John's political thought and helped shape his views on the best course for the future of his country. Although he had seen the failings of feudalism and "the Demon of Monarchy" firsthand, he had developed a measure of respect for Louis XVI as he would later in England for George III. John was always fearful of both the potential excesses of democracy and the creation of a powerful elite oligarchy that often thrived in republics. With his customary dry wit, he ridiculed the tendency of Americans to decide "every Thing by a Majority of Votes. We put it to vote whether the Company will sing a Song or tell a Story."[87] Adams would always be the staunchest supporter of the creation of a strong executive branch in the United States to keep elite power in check. As he would famously write Jefferson at the end of 1787 when the Constitution was under debate in America, "You are afraid of the one—I, of the few. We agree perfectly that the many should have a full fair and perfect Representation.—You are Apprehensive of Monarchy: I, of Aristocracy. I would therefore have given more Power to the President and less to the Senate."[88] Still, Adams always appreciated the critical difference between those who governed and those who ruled.

After a series of tension-producing complications, the final treaty with England was finally consummated and ready for signatures in the fall of 1783. Adams, along with Franklin and Jay, signed the long-awaited document on September 3, 1783, with diplomat David Hartley affixing his signature on behalf of King George III. It was executed at Hartley's lodgings at the Hôtel d' York located on the Rue Jacob in the Left Bank of Paris. Later in the day, a separate treaty was signed between Britain and Spain. The treaty between France and Great Britain was executed at Versailles, where Vergennes lavishly entertained the American diplomats at dinner. Although it was unrecognized at the time, the treaty signaled the death knell of the French monarchy, which would crumble amid financial ruin during the French Revolution of 1789.

With so many players and competing interests, the execution of the preliminary treaty and later the final Treaty of Paris in 1783 had been anything but smooth. Not only did it reflect the underlying struggle between America and Great Britain, but it also indicated that American objectives were sometimes at odds with those of its presumptive allies, France and Spain.[89] It is all the more impressive, therefore, that Adams and Jay (for a good portion of the time Franklin had been sidelined with an acute attack of kidney stones) had been able to prevail in most of their demands and achieve significant concessions from the British. This despite the fact that numerous attempts were made by foreign ministers to reject points that were seen by the American diplomats as being in the best interests of their country. As Adams told Oswald, "All the powers of Europe will be continually maneuvering with Us, to work us into their real or imaginary Ballances of Power."[90] Franklin is often given the most credit for the treaty, but in reality it was Adams and Jay who ensured its success.

The signing of the Treaty of Paris was truly a momentous historic occasion, one that came about after nearly a decade of strife and sacrifice, not only for John and Abigail Adams, but also for John's diplomatic partners, as well as their fellow Americans in the former thirteen colonies. The treaty terms were far better than Congress could have hoped. It reflected full recognition of American independence but it also allowed for the incorporation of a significant section of territory, much more in retrospect than appeared justified by modest American military successes.[91]

Despite his often blunt manner and refusal at times to follow traditional diplomatic protocol, Adams had at critical moments turned out to be a tough negotiator. Franklin had grown irritated by what he considered Adams's lack of diplomacy at times. Franklin's ire sparked his famous comment to Robert Livingston in the summer of 1783 that despite the elder statesman's belief that Adams was well-meaning, always honest, and often wise, at the same time John was "in some things, absolutely out of his senses."[92] Yet it was Adams who had ensured commercial agreements that were so essential for the stability and growth of the American economy. At the close of the year, Abigail reported that a friend has asked her whether she would have consented to his mission if she had known that John would have been so long abroad. Abigail recorded (at least for public consumption) that in the light of John's successful peace efforts and his exemplary commitment, she felt "a pleasure in being able to sacrifice my selfish passions to the general good."[93]

Yet even before the finalization of the peace treaty, by the summer of 1783 Abigail clearly wanted John home and refused to accept any excuses. In June she wrote her husband, "You have before this day received a joint commission for fostering a commercial treaty with Britain. I am at a loss to determine whether you will consider yourself so bound by it, as to tarry longer abroad." Although she conceded that America had a pressing need for "able statesmen and wise counsellors," she insisted to John, "I do not wish you to accept an embassy to England, should you be appointed. This little cottage has more heart-felt satisfaction for you than the most brilliant court can afford."[94] John seemed at first to consider Abigail's plea but made no commitments. In August he wrote Nabby that he hoped his superiors would soon allow him to return home, but that if instructed to stay abroad by Congress, he would make a decision once he was informed of the details of a new commission. "One thing is certain," he maintained, "that I will not live long without my family."[95] In the end, John still chose to remain in France with Franklin and Jefferson to foster commercial relations with other foreign powers.

Abigail was far from surprised when John disregarded her desires, for as she wrote him in the fall of 1783, "Your letter, which informs me of your determination to pass another winter abroad, is by no means unexpected. That we must pass it with a vast ocean between us is reflection no means pleasurable, yet this must be the case." By then Abigail realized that she would have to join John in Europe to reunite the family, and she mounted a campaign to convince him to agree. Practically speaking, she could not leave before spring. Moreover, she did not look forward to interacting with British royalty or English aristocrats: "I should have very well liked to have gone to France and resided there a year; but to think of going to England in a public character, and engaging, at my time of life, in scenes attended with dissipation, parade, and nonsense,—I am sure I would make an awkward figure."[96] In the end, despite her apprehension and personal inclination, Abigail would spend eight months in France and nearly three years in England.

The death in September 1783 of Abigail's father, Parson William Smith, removed one more of the obstacles that had prevented her from sailing across the Atlantic. She had been proud of her parents and was especially close to her father. Abigail referred to his passing in an emotional letter to John Quincy, in which she maintained that his grandfather bequeathed him a legacy more valuable than wealth. She told her eldest son, "He left you his blessings and his prayers that you might return to your country and friends, improved in knowledge and matured in virtue; that you might become a useful citizen, a guardian of the laws, liberty, and religion of your country, as your father . . . has already been." She concluded her letter with her wish for him to return to complete his education in America at Harvard, an institution she regarded as the equal of any in Europe.[97]

In another letter written to John Quincy the following month, Abigail again felt compelled to remind him of his proud American heritage: "The history of your country and the late revolution are striking and recent instances of the mighty things achieved by a brave, enlightened, and hardy people determined to be free." Perhaps she was fearful that her son had become too impressed by the courts that he had viewed firsthand in Europe. Abigail admonished him to learn from the example of his wise father to "despise wealth, titles, pomp, and equipage, as mere external advantages, which cannot add to the external excellence of your mind, or compensate for want of integrity and virtue."[98]

In a reversal of his earlier position, John now entreated Abigail to join him, but still she dithered over traveling to Europe. "The State of your health gives me great anxiety, and the delay of your return increases it. . . . The Scenes of anxiety through which you have past, are enough to rack the firmest constitution, and debilitate the strongest faculties," she observed in October 1783.[99] She missed John deeply, but fear of an ocean journey, particularly in the more dangerous winter months, domestic arrangements, and family issues at home, including a potential unsuitable suitor for Nabby, made her a reluctant traveler.

It now appeared almost certain that John would become the American minister to England, an appointment he welcomed, and now more than ever, he wanted his wife by his side. For Abigail's part, she recognized the connection between stressful situations and John's ill health. In the fall of 1783, Adams contracted yet another serious fever, possibly a debilitating case of influenza, which laid him low. John Quincy had returned from his diplomatic secretarial post in St. Petersburg the previous July. Father and son had reunited in The Hague before returning to Paris together in August, the month before John and his fellow commissioners had signed the final peace treaty with Great Britain.

In October, Adams in the company of John Quincy journeyed to England, where they visited London and Oxford. John also sampled the renowned curative powers of the resort spa of Bath in order to recover his health, but he took time out for his first visit to the British capital with his son. The Adamses appeared to have been impressed with London, and for nearly two months they visited its cultural and historic landmarks. During that stay John sat for portraits by the leading American artists of the era, John Singleton Copley and Benjamin West, who then resided in England.

The artists proved a conduit to an introduction to some of the city's elite political figures. At one point during John's visit, West secured an invitation for the Adamses to tour Buckingham Palace in the absence of the royal family. John professed himself delighted with the elegance yet relative simplicity of the royal residence. As he put it, "In every apartment of the whole house, the same taste, the same judgement, the same elegance. I could not but compare it, in my own mind with Versailles, and not at all to the advantage of the latter." He was especially impressed with King George III's robust library, and because of their shared love for books, it even predisposed John to develop a fondness for the monarch, who had served as the most visible symbol of the enemy during the American Revolution. John and his son also toured many famous attractions, such as Windsor Castle, Westminster Abbey, and the well-known Wedgewood porcelain factory, where he delightedly viewed the company's renowned decorated fine china.[100]

By that time, John's friendship with American diplomat John Jay had blossomed. Jay had traveled from France to England in the hope that the famous Bath waters would improve his uncertain health, and at times Jay joined Adams and John Quincy on their tour of London sites. Although the Adamses appeared to have appreciated their foray into British history and culture, Jay was far less impressed. He later wrote his wife, Sarah, who had remained behind in Paris, that "nothing has as yet exceeded my Expectations, and I shall probably return to America fully persuaded that Europe collectively considered is far less estimable than America."[101] It was a sentiment that was echoed by Abigail Adams when she later joined her husband in the Old World.

In late December, John left for Bath, famed for the supposed healthful powers of the mineral waters. However, his recuperative visit was short-lived, as he was entreated to travel to Holland to help ward off yet another American economic crisis. The loans Adams had secured the previous summer were already exhausted. He too was exhausted and had little hope that he would be successful on the new mission: "It was winter, my health was very delicate, a journey and voyage to Holland at that season would very probably put an end to my labours."[102]

Still, as he had done so many times in the past, John marshalled his energy, determined to do his best for his country. As he stoically put it, "Nevertheless no man knows what he can bear till he tries."

He returned to London with John Quincy, and the two set out on their trek from Harwich on January 3, 1784, to cross the tempestuous North Sea. For nearly a week, the pair traveled over dangerous seas and an icy, snow-coated terrain amid "violent agitations by sea and land." The Adamses had their first experience of travel on an iceboat and were forced to embark and disembark numerous times when the ice became too brittle to carry them and they were plunged into frigid waters. At the conclusion of their sea voyage, they took an uncomfortable journey by carriage to The Hague. Somehow, to his surprise, John survived the ordeal, and on March 9 he secured a second major loan in Amsterdam to save American credit. Despite his initial misgivings, John was successful "beyond my most sanguine expectations, and obtained a loan of millions enough to prevent all the bills of congress from being protested for non-payment."[103] John's heroic efforts turned out to be one of the great successes of American diplomacy in Europe.

In Amsterdam, John had also made significant strides in securing a much-desired commercial treaty between the United States and Prussia when he met with that country's foreign minister. From the distant shores of Europe, Adams astutely understood that the American republican experiment stood on the edge of collapse. Squabbling states, financial instability, and a fragile confederation government did not inspire confidence. Even during the revolution, John had recognized that future American success depended on robust trade that would move American foodstuffs, such as wheat, corn, and fish, and other products like whale oil across the Atlantic to foreign markets.

Just a few months later, the Confederation Congress would name John, along with Franklin and Jefferson, as commissioners to negotiate treaties of friendship and commerce with over twenty European and North African nations. John drafted a treaty with Prussia in June 1784, which was finally executed in 1785, after Jefferson had arrived in Europe with additional congressional instructions. That treaty would serve as a model for future negotiations with Portugal, Denmark,

Tuscany, and Morocco. In the spring of 1785, Jefferson replaced the aging Franklin, who longed to return to Philadelphia, as the American minister to France. The camaraderie between Adams and Jefferson would help move diplomacy forward. And 1784 would also mark an important development in John's personal life, as he would finally be joined in Europe by his long-suffering wife and "dearest friend," Abigail, who would experience her own firsthand encounter with the Old World.

THREE

Abigail in France

From the New World to the Old

House and Garden [in Auteuil] with all its decorations, are not so dear to me as my own little Cottage connected with the Society I used there to enjoy, for out of my own family I have no attachments in Europe, nor do I think I ever shall have.

Abigail Adams to Mary Cranch, September 5, 1784

I know not whether I shall be able to content myself to tarry out my two years [in Europe]. My Heart and Soul is more American than ever. We are a *family by ourselves.*

Abigail Adams to Dr. Cotton Tufts,
Auteuil, France, January 3, 1785

[An] amaizing difference . . . subsists between those Countries [in Europe] which have past the Zenith of their glory, saped by Luxury, and undermined by the rage for pleasure and a Young a flourishing a free, and I may add, a virtous Country [America] uncontrouled by a Royal Mandate, unshackled by military police, unfearfull of the thundering anathamas of Ecclesiastic power, where every individual possest of industry and probity, has a sure reward for his Labour, uninfested with thousands of useless virmin, whom Luxery supports upon the Bread of Idleness, a Country where Virtue is still revered; and modesty still Cloaths itself in crimson.

Abigail Adams to John Thaxter,
Auteuil, March 20, 1785

EVEN AFTER YEARS OF YEARNING TO REUNITE WITH HER husband, Abigail was ambivalent about the prospect of joining John in Europe. Fear of the long, potentially dangerous sea voyage and concerns about leaving her two youngest children behind made her absence difficult to imagine. She also worried that she was unprepared to assume the demanding role of the wife of an American diplomat who would be required to move among royalty. "I think if you were abroad in a private Character, and necessitated to continue there; I should not hesitate so much at comeing to you," she mused to John. "But a mere American as I am, unacquainted with the Etiquette of courts, taught to say the thing I mean, and to wear my Heart in my countanance," she fretted she might be an embarrassment to her country.[1]

Yet Abigail was being somewhat disingenuous, as she was one of the most intelligent, politically sophisticated, and well-read women of her era; and she had always been at ease in encounters with a host of American leaders of prominence who lived in or visited Massachusetts. She could be charming, but at the same time Abigail was a formidable woman with a powerful personality. Abigail's tongue-in-cheek reference to her being a "mere American" foreshadowed the manner in which she viewed European society. Throughout her residence in the Old World, Abigail remained proud of her New England roots and the openness and honesty that she believed defined the American character. Almost daily in her correspondence to family and friends at home she would comment on what she considered the undesirable behavior and manners of most Europeans, reinforcing her worldview that society in her native land, particularly in Massachusetts, was superior to that found in France or England.

A lengthy sea voyage was not to be undertaken lightly for a refined woman from New England like Abigail, who had strict notions about propriety and respectable accommodations. Moreover, on many occasions John had deemed such a trip for Abigail and their only daughter, Nabby, too challenging to undertake, and he adamantly dissuaded them from embarking on such a perilous excursion. As late as the spring of 1783, he had cautioned Nabby, "You know little the difficulties of a voyage to Europe, even in time of profound peace. The elements are unstable in peace as in war, and a sea life is never agreeable, not ever without danger."[2]

Yet we do have an example of the wife of another American diplomat who happily accompanied her husband to Europe. In September 1779 John Jay was named minister to Spain in order to seek financial and political support for the new nation. His wife, Sarah Livingston Jay, refused to be separated from her husband, and so she sailed with him in October, but they left their son Peter, a toddler at the time, behind with relatives. Although a voyage for both Abigail and Sarah would have been dangerous at the time, Abigail had more household responsibilities to keep her at home than the younger Mrs. Jay, who was a woman of means.

Moreover, Sarah Jay was traveling *with* her husband, so the voyage was less daunting. Sarah had previously joined Jay in Philadelphia when he served as president of the Continental Congress, so she had already spent time entertaining political figures and foreign emissaries. Similar to Adams's experience in France and England, Jay would find himself stymied in his diplomatic efforts with the Spanish, who refused to accept him as the official American representative. Despite family wealth, Sarah, like Abigail later, would resent the meager salary provided by Congress to American diplomats, which hampered social efforts, essential to building alliances. At one point in his posting in Spain, John Jay wrote, "I never loved or admired America so much as since I left it," a sentiment that would soon be shared by Abigail.[3] If the Jays were unhappy in Spain, they would find themselves more at ease when they moved to France. Sarah hosted a number of popular social receptions there, and Jay and Adams experienced gratification over their successful joint efforts to negotiate the peace treaty in Paris with British representatives.[4] Although Abigail and Sarah Jay did not cross paths in Europe, when the Adamses later moved to New York City when John served as the first vice president of the United States, the two women became friends and even attended political debates in the House of Representatives together.

In the meantime, Abigail remained lonely back in Braintree and increasingly out of touch with her distant husband. Communications between the couple had often been excruciatingly slow, which served to heighten Abigail's anxiety and irritation, especially as the few letters she received were often brief and businesslike. She concluded that their current separation, which had stretched over four years, was untenable. In the final tally, until John left public office in 1800 they lived apart for much of their married lives. It is true that John and Abigail were lifelong soul mates, but their marriage has often been idealized. One wag is said to have observed that the reason their marriage was so successful was that they were forced by political circumstances to spend so much time apart. There may have been a kernel of truth in the jest, for their separation provided Abigail with the opportunity to develop greater self-reliance.

As time passed, Abigail understood that John had become frustrated with his diplomatic mission and that he now longed for her to join him. Perhaps the deciding factor that at last propelled her to set sail was John's heartfelt plea that "if you and your daughter were with me, I could keep up my spirits. . . . I am weary, worn, and disgusted to death."[5] Abigail was terrified by the thought of crossing the ocean, but she gathered her courage. Dr. Waterhouse, who had crossed paths with John often in the Netherlands, advised her that John's health would benefit from her presence. She was likely even more motivated by the prospect of being reunited with her "long long separated best Friend and dear companion."[6]

Abigail confided to John that the proposed journey, undertaken without any male relative escort, was "a situation which I once thought nothing would tempt me to undertake," but she hoped that she would be "benefitted by my voyage as my Health has been very infirm and I have just recoverd from a slow fever."[7] In this, Abigail reflected the contemporary view that sea air was curative for a variety of ills. Another indirect benefit of the voyage for Abigail and John was that it provided the opportunity to put distance between their nineteen-year-old daughter, Nabby, and a potentially unsuitable mate, Royall Tyler.

Tyler had trained as a lawyer and came from a respected family. Abigail liked the personable young man but could not ignore whispers of an illegitimate child and other unsavory rumors about his character. Because Abigail was uncertain about Tyler, she may have felt that a lengthy separation would test the true depth of the couple's commitment. Nabby had been reluctant to part from Tyler, but she accompanied her mother to Europe out of a highly developed sense of duty. She later ended her understanding with Tyler and in 1786 married the dashing secretary to the American legation in England, Colonel William Smith, who turned out to be an unreliable husband.[8]

John's revolutionary comrade Thomas Jefferson had stopped to meet Mrs. Adams while on a visit to Boston just before she and Nabby prepared to set sail. Jefferson, who would head for Paris as a newly appointed emissary to France, had offered to accompany Abigail to Europe in the hope of "the pleasure of attending" her and "lessening some of her difficulties to which she may be exposed," as he put it in a letter to John. However, Abigail had already secured her passage from Boston to London and was unable to change her arrangements at the last minute to join Jefferson, who planned to leave from New York in July.[9] Before departing Braintree, Abigail made sure that all the family's affairs were in good order. She leased out the Adams farm, placed the house rent-free under the supervision of her loyal servant and her father's former slave, Phoebe Abdee and her husband, and left the family's financial concerns in the capable hands of her uncle Dr. Cotton Tufts.

Abigail and Nabby received an emotional send-off from their Braintree neighbors, with many tears shed, then spent two nights in Boston before boarding ship. The two arrived at Rowe's Wharf on a Sunday and sailed on the *Active* from Boston harbor on June 20, 1784. They were accompanied by their two loyal servants, Esther Field and John Briesler. Abigail also brought a cow along to provide milk aboard ship. John and

Abigail's two younger sons, Charles, then fourteen, and Thomas, twelve, had been left behind with Abigail's sister Elizabeth Shaw, who would provide affectionate substitute maternal care. Elizabeth's husband, John, a Calvinist minister, supervised the boys' education as they prepared to eventually enter college at Harvard. Sensitive to the fact that the Shaws lived on a circumscribed budget, Abigail paid for her children's room and board, and once in Europe often sent both her sisters generous gifts as tokens of her affection and appreciation.

The long sea crossing provided an opportunity for Abigail to muse about what she anticipated she would find in Europe and to affirm her faith in the American future. On July 4, the anniversary of American independence, she was moved to offer both a pronouncement and a heartfelt prayer. Before she even set foot in the Old World, she wrote in her diary, "Whilst the Nations of Europe are enveloped in Luxery and dissipation; and a universal venality prevails throughout Britain, may the new empire [America] Gracious Heavens, become the Guardians and protector of Religion and Liberty, of universal Benevolence and Phylanthropy. May those virtues which are banished from the land of our Nativity [England], find a safe Assylum with the inhabitants of this new world."[10] Abigail's antipathy for European society, which she had not yet personally experienced, could not have been clearer. At the same time, she had detailed her hope for her new nation's bright future.

From almost the moment she set foot on board the ship, Abigail was wretchedly ill with seasickness. The *Active* was aptly named. Confined to her small room, in a cabin of about eight square feet and buffeted by the stormy seas, Abigail was prostrate in bed for ten days. In her journal she wrote, "To Those who have never been at Sea or experienced this dispiriting malady tis impossible to discribe it, the Nausia arising from the smell of the Ship, the continual rolling, tossing and tumbling contribute to keep up this Disorder, and when once it seazeis a person it levels Sex and condition." Lack of circulating air must have magnified their queasiness, and the women were forced to keep their cabin doors open at night to provide minimal comfort. Her first terrible days aboard ship left Abigail so weak she was unable to make her own bed or even put on her own shoes. To make matters worse, her cherished cow suffered severe injuries after being tossed about during a fierce gale and had to be put down and thrown overboard.[11]

The dampness of the ship also aggravated Abigail's rheumatism, and she developed a fever. Abigail described her overall misery and her seasickness to her elder sister Mary Cranch as the "most disheartening . . . malady." "We crawled on deck when able," she reported. She decried the particular indignities visited on female voyagers who had to compromise their notions of "decency and decorum" against the backdrop of lack of privacy, primitive sanitary conditions, and malodorous smells arising from the cargo of potash and whale oil. For Abigail, there were standards that needed to be upheld, even in the most challenging of circumstances. Another source of annoyance was the poor fare offered up by the black cook, whom she found to be dirty and lazy and whom she described in what today we would deem racist terms as a man "with no more knowledge of cookery than a savage." Although Abigail staunchly opposed the institution of slavery, she held ambivalent feelings about African Americans. She noted caustically that the men on board seemed to be satisfied if they were fed five times a day, but women like her and Nabby had more refined sensibilities.[12]

Life on ship posed many challenges. Only about a dozen passengers joined the crew, narrowing the possibility of suitable social interactions for Abigail and her daughter, but Abigail enjoyed the company of several people, including an amiable physician named John Clark. Often confined to her cramped airless cabin, one of only two staterooms on the merchantman ship in quarters she shared with Esther Field, Abigail described the vessel as "a partial prison." Still, when the weather was fine and she felt well enough, she spent pleasant time on deck reading, including a heavy tome about political life in Great Britain. The author's description of England further reinforced her view of the superiority of the American nation, including the climate and terrain. Reading the book encouraged her optimistic view that "as our Country becomes more populous, we shall be daily maeking new discoveries and vie in some future day, with the most celebrated European nation."[13] It was a prophetic declaration.

Once Abigail overcame her ailments, she regained her equilibrium and felt more like her usual industrious self. Soon, she proceeded to provide advice to their captain, Nathaniel Byfield Lyde, about improving the sanitary conditions on the ship, and she set out to direct a thorough cleanup of her surroundings. When the weather cooperated, Abigail took the opportunity to observe the pristine beauty of a becalmed ocean, which she described as "stupendous." As time went on, Abigail became more accustomed to sailing and even took great pleasure in sitting on deck, especially at night when it appeared to her that the ocean sparkled as if jewels had been scattered over its dark expanse. As they neared the end of the journey, however, the ship once again encountered severe winds, and Abigail and her party were rocked by dangerous waves and pelted with rain. After a month at sea, the weary party arrived on English terrain on July 20, 1784. "Heaven be praised, I have landed safely upon the British coast," Abigail proclaimed with obvious relief.[14]

Just as Abigail arrived in Europe, John Jay and his wife, Sarah, were returning to America after four years overseas. As was the case with the Adamses, the Jays enjoyed parts of their stay abroad, particularly the cultural and shopping opportunities and congenial social events with fellow Americans living in Europe. But the attractions of their native land always beckoned. Jay once averred that during his residence in Europe he had "met with neither men nor things on this side of the water which abate my predilection, or if you please my prejudices, in favor of those on the other. . . . [My] affections are deeply rooted in America."[15] If the exact words differ, they reflect remarkably well the sentiments that Abigail would share with friends and family back home time and time again.

Although they had landed, Abigail, Nabby, and their two servants were not yet at the end of their journey. To access land, they had to first transfer from the ship to a rickety, bobbing pilot boat swirling in the crashing six-foot-high surf. They disembarked at the coastal town of Deal, propelled on shore by a massive wave, with Abigail, in her soaking wet clothes, hanging on to an obliging gentleman for dear life. Once safely on land, they sought lodgings in a local inn. The next morning, they rose at dawn to travel by post chaise, a closed horse-drawn carriage, which jolted and bumped along the road to London, where highwaymen frequently attempted to rob passengers.

Still, Abigail and Nabby experienced a superior form of carriage travel for the time, as their coach seats were comfortably upholstered and afforded them a pleasant view of the passing landscape through large side and front windows. The four-wheeled vehicle was drawn by four horses, which were exchanged by the coachmen for new animals at every post stage stop. They finally arrived in the busy London metropolis on the evening of July 21, having first dined at another inn in Chatham along the way. Abigail was struck by the elegance she witnessed there. She and her party were served by waiters in powdered wigs, who offered them eight different main course choices in addition to vegetables, in keeping with their elevated status as customers who could afford a post chaise and fine dining.[16] From the beginning of her stay in Europe, Abigail realized that she now enjoyed a level of privilege not available to most of her friends and relatives back home, and she struggled with how to reconcile that newfound privilege, which made her uncomfortable, with her professed beliefs in a more austere existence.

Because John Adams was unsure of the exact date on which Abigail and Nabby were to arrive and due to pressing business in the Netherlands, he could not be on hand to greet them. It was likely that John was anxious of the possible negative influence European society might have on his only daughter, particularly in his absence. Although he certainly admired aspects of life in France and England, he was concerned about the corroding effects that residing there could instill in American females. When he earlier visited Princess Wilhelmina in The Hague, he told her that the "Great Cities as Paris and London were not good Schools for American young Ladies at present."[17] But as soon as he received news of Abigail's safe landing, John wrote her ecstatically that it has "made me the happiest Man upon Earth" and that he would send John Quincy, "a son who is the greatest Traveller, of his Age," to meet them.[18] Therefore, due to the lack of effective communication, Abigail and Nabby had to mark time in London on their own, but with the assistance of two distant male cousins who resided in London, mother and daughter found temporary lodging at Low's Hotel in Covent Garden.

Abigail disliked the hustle and bustle of their surroundings, as Low's was surrounded by a cacophony of noise made by the heavy carriage traffic in the teeming streets. She soon moved her group to the more elegant but less expensive Adelphi Hotel, not far from the Thames River, located in a more secluded area off the Strand. They recovered from the rigors of the journey in an attractive suite of rooms that included a spacious drawing room and a large bedroom. To Abigail's astonishment, as part of their fee, the Adelphi also provided them with a cook, waiter, and chambermaid, another mark of her newly privileged existence.[19] While in London, Abigail had the opportunity to visit a local seamstress, milliner, hairdresser, and shoemaker, all of whom conspired in her opinion to turn her into a "fashionable Lady." It made for a pleasant interlude, and Abigail told her younger sister Elizabeth Shaw that she was "better pleased with this city than I expected."[20]

Nevertheless, as she remarked to a niece, Abigail had mixed feelings about her temporary residence in London. Like many of her fellow supporters of American independence, having experienced the deprivations of the Revolutionary War firsthand, Abigail had long regarded the British as enemies. She admitted to Betsy Cranch, "I believe England should have been the last Country for me to have visited."[21] How to balance her American patriotism with an appreciation of British culture posed a dilemma. Yet Abigail and Nabby passed more than a week enjoying the busy English capital. They attended church on Sunday, shopped (but bought little), and visited famous London sights, such as the beautiful botanical garden at Kew Palace, and venerable cultural institutions like the British Museum. Most impressive was Westminster Abbey, the grand church where England's kings and queens had been crowned and buried since 1066. At other times, they took long, fatiguing walks over the wide and winding cobblestone streets.

One area literally dazzled Abigail. She told her sister Mary that the "most delightful Spot my Eyes ever beheld" was the grotto designed by the English poet Alexander Pope at Twickenham.[22] Pope had decorated the cave-like structure with a variety of sparking geological specimens, including impressive stalagmites and crystals. During her stay in France and England Abigail would often be more charmed by her surroundings than she was willing to admit. At other times, like many Americans, she had to revise her antipathy for all things British. Nevertheless, she always declared America to be superior to all other nations.

During the ten days that they waited to reunite with John and John Quincy, Abigail and Nabby met many of their old American acquaintances, even former Loyalists, who had opposed the revolutionary cause. As Abigail put it, "I have so many visitors, I hardly know how to think myself out of my own country, I see so many Americans about me." Although Abigail had often visited the American urban center of Boston, it paled in comparison to the storied history and culture of London. The grand residence of the British royal family, St. James's Palace, was located just a few blocks from her London hotel. Yet Abigail expressed surprise to her sister that except on formal occasions, British women, especially those she met in London, appeared to dress more plainly and informally in company than people in America and they often set a rather modest table.[23]

During her London stay, Abigail was pleased to have the opportunity to view what is now a famous portrait of John Adams, which had been painted the previous year by expatriate American artist John Singleton Copley. The acclaimed painter had developed a reputation for finely executed pictures of members of the elite in their resplendent finery. Abigail enthusiastically approved of Copley's rendering of her husband, visibly proud that John's elevated status now merited a formal portrait.

On July 30, Abigail was reunited with John Quincy. After so many years of separation, she marveled that her boy had grown into an impressive and cultured, almost unrecognizable young man of seventeen. John apologized to Abigail that he felt it a "cruel mortification" he could not yet join them, but he promised that they would soon be setting out together as a family for France and insisted that it was "the first Time in Europe that I looked forward to a Journey with Pleasure."[24] John arrived in London a week later in early August. If the reunion with John Quincy had been joyful, seeing John again after a nearly five-year separation must have been an overwhelming emotional experience for Abigail. By all accounts, their long marriage of almost sixty years was a loving, enduring partnership, attested to by well over a thousand affectionate letters. From the beginning, it appears that John recognized and appreciated Abigail's keen intelligence, strong character, resilience, and generally cheerful disposition. In the face of frequent separations, their marriage endured because of shared values, deep mutual affection and respect, as well as a match in intellect.

It is apparent that even after their long years apart, John and Abigail had retained their close bond. They quickly resumed their normal family life, and even though each had functioned as a single parent for long periods of time, that does not appear to have posed a challenge. As Abigail summed it up, "We were a very happy family once more."[25] Still, there must have been at least some degree of readjustment and a measure of the shifting of their roles. For years, Abigail had capably acted as a "deputy" in John's absence, shepherding their finances and overseeing the family farm and their children's education during his years away in Philadelphia at the Continental Congress and then during his diplomatic missions across the Atlantic.

Yet even after Abigail joined her husband in Europe, John appears to have been content to leave a good deal of their financial business to his wife. As she told her uncle Cotton Tufts, as a busy diplomat, John exhibited little interest in their day-to-day domestic and economic affairs, generally leaving it to Abigail to "write and think about them and give directions."[26] Still, John asserted his male authority later in London when the couple disagreed about the possible purchase of a mansion back in Braintree. And he firmly rejected Abigail's desire to purchase another property before they later settled on buying the old Borland estate.

Abigail was apparently so proficient at stewarding the Adams finances that Jefferson later acknowledged her financial acumen in a letter to James Madison. Jefferson admired her management of the family's "pecuniary affairs," which he witnessed firsthand in Europe, and noted that Mrs. Adams was one of the "most attentive and honourable economists."[27] Despite grumbling from both the Adamses about the meager salary that John received from Congress, they managed to return to America in a stronger financial state than when they had departed. Although never wealthy, unlike Jefferson and other revolutionary leaders from the southern aristocratic planter class, the Adamses ended up comfortably off in their elder years.

Just a day after John arrived in London, on August 8, Abigail, John, and Nabby departed for France, where John and the other two American commissioners were to commence their deliberations. Once again, commerce would become the core of their diplomatic efforts. Benjamin Franklin, Adams, and Jefferson became part of a small corps of American emissaries who worked to boost the credibility of the United States in Europe. Before they confronted the reality of European power struggles, all three idealistically envisioned a cooperative international spirit in which enlightened nations would engage in free trade. One of their primary goals was to negotiate reciprocal treaties that would bolster the fragile economy of their new nation. They hoped that if European countries, particularly France, would remove tariffs on America's abundant raw materials and agricultural products, it would open up a thriving market in America for French manufactured goods that would benefit both countries.

The Adamses sped to France by a combination of vehicles, including a crowded coach to the Channel, with the servants following in a rented post chaise. At the coastal town of Dover they boarded a channel boat for the overnight crossing to Calais, and after landing they shared yet another horse-drawn coach that transported them on the two-hundred-mile trip to the glittering French capital, from which John had been absent for almost a year. They arrived in Paris on August 13, preceded there by Jefferson and his young daughter Martha. Abigail's first order of business was a visit to a Parisian milliner in order to replace the four caps that she had lost during her travels so she could retain the customary modest covering for her hair. While Abigail and Nabby toured Paris with John Quincy, whose fluency in French made him an ideal guide, Adams began consultations with Franklin and Jefferson. Even though John had described French society to Abigail in his letters, we can imagine the cultural shock she experienced at her first encounter with the grand homes, rich and often unfamiliar food offerings, and royals who exuded privilege and lived in palaces that dwarfed even the most imposing residences of the wealthiest residents of Massachusetts.

Soon the Adams party settled in the Paris suburb of Auteuil, located about four miles from the capital. They rented a formerly luxurious three-story home, which was perched on a hill above the banks of the Seine River, from the Comte de Rouault. Despite its size and grandeur, it was an edifice badly in need of repair. The house was sparsely furnished, and the Adamses were forced to rent additional furniture to make it comfortable. Still, the Auteuil residence was a marked contrast to their humble seven-room saltbox house in Braintree. It took some time for Abigail and Nabby to become resigned to the use of French chamber pots instead of the outhouse privies that they had been accustomed to back home.

Although the house could provide sleeping accommodations for many guests, its expanse of around forty uncarpeted rooms made it hard to heat. Abigail found it irritating to oversee a retinue of temperamental servants, including a personal hairdresser named Pauline (considered *de rigueur* in France) for the two Adams women. She lamented the fact that each of her French servants would perform only specialized duties,

The exterior of the home the Adamses rented in Auteuil, France. Courtesy Massachusetts Historical Society.

making them, in her eyes, inefficient and sometimes even disrespectful. One male servant's time was devoted exclusively to sweeping and waxing the floors, while one of the maidservants focused only on making the beds. Pauline, who also served as Nabby's chambermaid, found favor in Abigail's eyes as she was kind to their American servant Esther when she took ill.

In addition to the challenges she encountered with servants, Abigail complained that it was expensive to run the household on John's modest salary of $9,000, and the Adamses did their best to economize, curtailing as many social occasions as possible. Although she was likely exaggerating, Abigail grumbled to Mary about Congress's stinginess and complained, "We spend no evenings abroad, make no suppers, attend very few public entertainments, or spectacles, as they are called, and avoid every expense that is not held indispensable. Yet I cannot but think it hard, that a gentleman [John] who has devoted so great a part of his life to the service of the public . . . should find it necessary to so cautiously calculate his pence."[28]

John agreed with Abigail's assessment. Meeting fashionable standards was critical to diplomacy, and he told his fellow American diplomat John Jay that it was "impossible to live upon what is now allotted us, without disgracing our Country, and obstructing its' service and Interests."[29] Yet the amount was actually enough to cover all their expenditures, with some to spare, and there were other compensations, including opportunities to play host to foreign ministers and fellow Americans such as Jefferson and Franklin for dinner. Abigail developed great affection for Jefferson, but she treated Franklin with only polite respect, as she believed his criticism of John to Congress had caused her husband to lose his earlier commission to France in 1779.

The Adamses were also pleased with the commodious bedroom suites available for the entire family on the second floor, all of which overlooked the verdant garden that bloomed in season with a rich array of colorful flowers and fragrant orange trees that created an attractive vista. The second floor also provided a reception room where the family gathered to socialize and which served as a meeting area for guests who visited John during the morning. Abigail also enjoyed two small but handsome rooms, decorated with flowered chintz-covered walls, curtains, and furniture. Adjacent to her bedroom, these two additional areas afforded her a comfortable private space in which to sew, read, and write. Abigail loved the melodic notes of the nightingales, whose songs punctuated the quiet countryside evenings when the windows were open.

With obvious pleasure, John reported in his diary on August 17 that "the house, the garden, the situation, near the *Bois de Boulogne*, elevated above the river Seine, and the low grounds, and distant from the putrid streets of Paris, is the best I could wish for."[30] In fact, the view over the parkland was stunning. And life at Auteuil offered a longed-for domestic respite for Abigail and John, who was delighted to have his family, and particularly his wife, by his side, a circumstance that always brought out the best in him and bolstered his health. As John put it with obvious contentment, although distance prevented him from interacting with his American friends back home in person, "I have made a little America of my own family."[31]

It also afforded John Quincy, now a brilliant, accomplished young man on the cusp of adulthood, the opportunity to again experience a normal family life and spend time with his mother and sister, from whom he had long been separated. For Abigail it provided time to read, think, and write reflective letters to family members in America. Although she still rose early and set herself a number of mundane tasks, including darning socks, she had far more leisure than she had experienced in Braintree, where she had even had to tend to her own turkeys and chickens.

Nabby wrote her cousin Elizabeth Cranch that every morning she prepared tea for her mother and brother and hot chocolate for her father. After breakfast, Nabby occupied herself with reading the works of French writers such as the playwright Molière, translating sections of French books into English, and composing letters before joining her mother to have their hair dressed daily by their French maid, as was the Parisian custom. Every day, John took long walks of several miles in the park with his son, and the two often studied together, for John Quincy was preparing to attend college back home in America at Harvard. When he was not tutoring John Quincy, Adams took the opportunity to examine scholarly works on his own, including the writings of Plato. In the evenings, if there were no guests for dinner, the Adamses often read companionably and then played an enjoyable card game of whist together before John retired for the evening shortly after ten o'clock.[32]

For practical reasons, the Adamses needed to reside near Franklin, who was often bedridden at Passy, but the Adamses also hoped that their Auteuil estate would expose them to an invigorating country environment away from congested, dank Paris. Abigail insisted that the repeated attacks of fevers John had endured in Europe obligated them to live outside cities where the air was reputed to be healthier. She found Paris to be filthy, airless, and malodorous and its crooked streets crowded and narrow, but she was pleased with the lovely park near their Auteuil home, the magnificent Bois de Boulogne, the site of many pleasant rambles.

Nabby found that she adjusted quickly to living in France, but she still felt that life there was inferior to what she had been accustomed to in America. Like Abigail, Nabby maintained that society at home had been more congenial and that Americans exhibited a more natural type of sociability than she encountered in France. Despite fashionable elegance and artistic culture, for Nabby, Parisian high society lacked the warm ease of interaction of New England. After less than a month in Auteuil, she admitted to Mercy Warren that "the contrast is by no means so remarkable between America and Europe, as is generally supposed," but "I am happy to assure you, that I give the preference to my own country, and believe I ever shall."[33]

Abigail, despite her embarrassment about speaking little French (although she had studied the language as a young woman and could read and write tolerably well) and having to often rely on John Quincy to be her interpreter, remarked positively on her travels. She told Mrs. Warren that in her opinion "the cleanliness of Britain, joined to the civility and politeness of France, could make a most agreeable assemblage."[34] Abigail told her niece that with the aid of a dictionary she had tasked herself with improving her French reading skills by setting a goal of completing one play a day, including the works of Racine, Molière, and Corneille, and she reported that she was pleased with her progress.[35]

Abigail's letters to her sisters provide an engaging window into her years in Europe, filled with revealing, often amusing details, which reflect not only Abigail's experiences in both the social and political culture but also the contours of contemporary life in France and England. Her stay abroad afforded her time for serious contemplation. Like many Americans in Europe, she often shared details about the latest fashion trends with her female relatives back home, but they were mixed in with astute political observations and comparisons to life in New England. She never tired of contrasting the decadence she observed among the French elite with the simpler, more virtuous lifestyle that she maintained characterized society in America.

The Adams household in Braintree had always been a lively center within their close-knit neighborhood, and Abigail regretted the loss of her formerly busy but comfortable life among longtime friends. She noted to her sister Mary that although Auteuil was located only a few miles from Paris, in the midst of December she found the location isolated. "It is a very agreeable summer situation, but in winter I should prefer Paris, on many accounts; but upon none more than that of society," she declared. "The Americans who are in France, and with whom I have any acquaintance, all reside in Paris; they would frequently fall in and spend an evening with us; but to come four miles, unless by particular invitation, is what they do not think of; so that our evenings, which are very long, are wholly by ourselves. You cannot wonder that we all long for the social friends whom we left in America, whose places are not supplied in Europe."[36]

The Adamses remained a social couple, however, and despite their distance from Paris, they made "it a pretty general rule to entertain company once a week. Upon those occasions, our company consists of fifteen, eighteen, or twenty." Abigail took charge of paying all expenses from her household account and often complained that costs were unreasonably high. Still, they entertained many visitors, since "every American who comes into Paris, no matter from what State, makes his visit, and pays his respects, to the American ministers, all of whom, in return, you must dine. Then there are the foreign ministers, from the different courts, who reside here, and some French gentlemen. In short, there is no end of the expense, which a person in a public character is obliged to be at." She ended with a touch of bitterness, "Yet our countrymen think their ministers are growing rich."[37] However, long part of a political family unit, Abigail understood full well that entertaining guests was an important diplomatic responsibility and that her social skills helped advance her husband's political aims and served as an opportunity for persuasion and alliance building.

Abigail continued to complain about the high prices. She told her uncle Isaac Smith about her purchase of fish and poultry, which she considered inferior to the seafood and turkey, geese, and ducks found in Massachusetts, but conceded that French capons were very tasty. She again remarked on the exorbitant expenses that were required of those who were involved in diplomatic public life, as "attendance upon Courts cannot be done in the small way." Abigail was alternately awed, overwhelmed, and disgusted when she visited the residences of other diplomats stationed in Europe or the estates of the French nobility. She concluded that she had no affection for her required lifestyle and "no ambition for a life of this kind. . . . It is my wish to return to America, where frugality and oconomy are, or ought to be considered as virtues."[38] Reading between the lines reveals both Abigail's pride in her country and her concern that republican principles were perhaps already compromised in her homeland.

Yet despite her complaints, there were some American women residing in France with whom Abigail enjoyed socializing, including Anne Willing Bingham, the attractive, pampered, and highly cultured wife of the wealthy Philadelphia merchant and politician William Bingham. The vastly different world outlooks exhibited by the two women soon became apparent. The Binghams had embarked on a grand tour of Europe in 1783, combining business with pleasure. William and Anne were accompanied abroad by their toddler daughter as well as Anne's aunt and a retinue of servants. Like Abigail, Anne suffered from severe seasickness on the voyage, but in Anne's case it was exacerbated by morning sickness, for she was about two months pregnant at the time. In contrast to Abigail, Anne became an ardent, unreserved admirer of European elite society.

The Binghams began their stay in a rented house in London's fashionable Bloomsbury Square before moving to another fine home in Cavendish Square. In England, William attempted to better relations between Great Britain and America and tried to encourage a business treaty that would benefit him as well as other American merchants. He and Anne moved comfortably in high society and frequently dined with leading politicians in London, including Lord Shelburne, the former British prime minister. They also visited the popular Bath spa, where they took the renowned waters, made purchases in elegant shops, and spent their evenings attending card games and glittering balls. From England, they traveled to the Netherlands. At The Hague, they crossed paths with John Adams, who introduced them to the Princess of Orange, who was charmed by the vivacious Anne. The Binghams arrived in France before the Adamses and rented a suite of rooms at the luxurious Hôtel Muscovy. From the start, Anne became enchanted with the grace and manners of the French.[39]

Before long, the Adamses invited the Binghams to dine at their house in Autcuil, part of a group of twenty guests. Even early on, Anne appeared to Abigail to be far too enthralled with French culture. In September 1784, Abigail shared her impressions of Anne with Mercy Warren, combining appreciation for Mrs. Bingham with subtle criticism. "Mrs. Bingham is a very young Lady, not more than 20, very agreeable, and very handsome," she wrote. But she also opined that the Philadelphia socialite was "rather too much given to the foibles of the Country for the mother of two Children, which she already is." Abigail had little admiration for the excesses she saw displayed at the French court and in the popular salons of the day.[40] Abigail was already constructing her picture of the ideal American, and the French emphasis on opulence and the pursuit of pleasure did not fit into her vision. She fretted about the tendency of some Americans to look to Europe for *la mode* in pursuit of a fashion that emphasized unnecessary fripperies.

By the end of the year, Abigail retained her admiration for Anne's beauty and graceful elegance but became increasingly critical of the younger woman's attachment to her European lifestyle. Abigail wrote her niece that Anne was "a fine figure and a Beautiful person, her manners are easy and affable," but that she was too young to have traveled abroad without a wise guide, as she "gives too much into the follies of this Country."[41] Abigail was inclined to pardon Anne because of her youth and charm, but it is obvious that she regarded Anne as deficient in elements Abigail prized in the American character.

Nabby came to share her mother's impression of Anne. At first, Nabby very much enjoyed socializing with the cultured young woman who was close to her age. She appreciated that Anne was a skilled and amiable conversationalist and an elegant dresser (who shared a dressmaker with Marie-Antoinette), but she thought Anne had become a bit too much of "a Frenchwoman." Perhaps somewhat jealous of Anne's immense popularity, Nabby found that Anne lacked a certain dignity that she claimed was reflected in one's intellect rather than outward appearance.[42] Both Abigail and Nabby were troubled by the fact that Anne was enraptured by Parisian life, to the extent that she told Nabby that she was "so delighted with Paris, that she [Anne] says she shall never go [back] to America with her own consent; she expects to be carried in the Spring." Such sentiments were unfathomable to the two Adams women, who looked upon their European residence as a temporary duty to their country. They regarded Anne's outlook as decidedly unpatriotic, even what today we would term "un-American."[43]

While she lived in France, Abigail did establish some superficial friendships with French women, and she, John, and Nabby even attended some of the famous Parisian salons, overseen by accomplished women such as Madame Houdetot and Franklin's favorite, the flirtatious and aging Madame Helvetius, whom Abigail detested. Abigail often found the salons pretentious, and she was appalled when Helvetius nonchalantly used the hem of her dress to wipe up after her pet dog, who had wet the floor during one of the social gatherings Abigail had attended. Certainly, Abigail was far less enamored of the French-style salons and the high fashion exhibited by the elite than her fellow American Anne Bingham.

The lively and sociable Anne was over twenty years younger than Abigail, and she not only enjoyed the sophisticated, opulent style of

French dress, but basked in the intellectual circles that included so many accomplished elite Parisian women. In a famous letter written to Jefferson after the Binghams returned to Philadelphia, Anne maintained that French women were "more accomplished and understand the Intercourse of society better than in any other Country." Moreover, she told Jefferson admiringly that she believed that French women "interfere in the politics of the Country, and often give a decided Turn to the Fate of Empires," certainly not an influence Jefferson admired. He, in turn, advised Bingham that she and other American women should be "too wise to wrinkle their foreheads with politics," but instead should confine themselves to "soothe and calm the minds of their husbands returning ruffled from political debates."[44] Jefferson's words reflect his admiring opinion of what would later become the popular prescription in the early United States for the ideal republican wife.

When the socially prominent, wealthy Binghams later returned to Philadelphia in 1786, Anne became the leader of Philadelphia upper-class society. Philadelphia became the site of a national political elite group when the United States capital moved there temporarily between 1790 and 1800. The elegant Bingham Mansion House, patterned after an English upper-class London estate, was furnished with the most elegant examples of French and English furniture and other accoutrements. Anne hosted numerous salons there, modeled after those she had attended in Paris, although American salons were more intentionally political than their French counterparts. Many of the prominent political figures of the day, including those who were fervent Federalists, including the Washingtons and Adamses, and Democratic Republicans, such as Thomas Jefferson and James Madison, often mingled at Anne's events. Bingham prided herself on bringing together people with diverse points of view in the conversations and harmonizing differences in the style she had witnessed at the Parisian salons. Abigail and Nabby, however, became less tolerant of her than they had been while they all resided in Europe. The Adams women felt that Anne's Philadelphia home, dress, and manners were far too ostentatious, and they became among her harshest critics.[45]

Unlike Anne, for the most part, Abigail found French women overly demonstrative and ironically rather informal in manner and dress, despite the French emphasis on fashion, and they often did not meet her exacting standards for proper dress in public. Perhaps because of her disdain for French mores, she had only limited interaction with French women. She confessed to Mary, "As to speaking French, I make but little progress in that; but I have acquired much more facility in reading it. My acquaintance with French ladies is very small." However, she did admire some aspects of French manners such as the elegant way some elite French women conducted themselves, especially their poise, confidence, femininity, and ease of intelligent conversation.[46]

One French woman who did find great favor in Abigail's eyes was the Marquise de Lafayette, Adrienne Francoise de Noailles, who spoke English "with tolerable ease." While Sarah Jay resided in France, she had also interacted often with the Marquise, and the two became good friends. The Marquise, who was born to a leading French family and married to the prominent French supporter of the American cause, the Marquis de Lafayette, welcomed Mrs. Adams. Of course, Lafayette's favorable attitude toward her nation made Abigail inclined to view him and his wife in a positive light. According to Abigail, the Marquise greeted her "with the freedom of an old acquaintance, and the rapture peculiar to the ladies of this nation, caught me by the hand and gave me a salute upon each cheek, most heartily rejoiced to see me. You would have supposed I had been some long absent friend, whom she dearly loved." She noted approvingly that Adrienne took her marriage vows seriously, was faithful and loyal to her husband, and attentive to her children, not a practice, according to Abigail, that many "ladies of high rank in Europe" adhered to.[47] For Abigail, family and maternal responsibility were highly regarded values, ones she believed Americans took seriously.

When the Marquise returned Abigail's visit, the French woman arrived quite plainly dressed, which seemed to offend the sensibilities of some of Abigail's American guests, who according to Abigail carried "the extravagance of dress to such a height." Yet, despite Abigail's preference for high standards of formal dress in company, she seemed to be very tolerant of the Marquise. In fact, she preferred the Marquise's choice of clothing to that of her fellow American visitors, whom she found too vulgarly ostentatious in their choice of attire and jewelry. She remarked tolerantly that although "there is not a lady in our country, who would have gone abroad to dine so little [plainly] dressed . . . the lady's rank sets her above the formalities of dress."[48] The next month Abigail summarized her impression of upper-class French women in a surprisingly positive way, noting that "the dress of French ladies, is like their manners, light, airy, and genteel." Even Queen Marie-Antoinette was said to have resented the intricate ceremonial rituals and elaborate etiquette to which she was forced to conform, and dressed with relative simplicity when she was not on display at public occasions.[49]

At the same time Abigail looked down upon female dress that was on occasion too informal, she lamented the extravagant costs made necessary by moving in French society and particularly the high expenses she was forced to meet, which made deep incursions on the Adamses' funds, since American ministers abroad received only modest salaries. Abigail told Mercy Warren disapprovingly, "If you ask me what is the business of life here [in France]? I answer pleasure . . . from the throne to the footstool."[50]

Although the Adamses entertained regularly at Auteuil, John devoted the majority of his time to serious diplomatic undertakings, and Franklin, Jefferson, and Adams worked in harmony together. Despite his crowded schedule, the family made time to take in the Parisian sights. They visited the famed Tuileries Gardens, situated opposite the Seine River, where they strolled along its meandering public walks and admired the marble statuary set among stately shade trees. One fine September afternoon, for the price of one crown, the Adamses and Jefferson—and another ten thousand spectators—witnessed one of the new and much-talked-about egg-shaped hot-air balloons as it rose above the ground at the Tuileries. Although Nabby observed dryly that the French were "more attentive to their amusements than anything else," with a touch of honest self-reflection she admitted that it was unjust to criticize others since her family was there with the same intent.[51]

In August, the Adamses visited Chantilly, the seat of the Conde family, located around twenty-five miles north of Paris. John Quincy later reported to his aunt that the estate was magnificent, perhaps the most "elegant of the kind, in the world." The Chantilly stables housed between 160 and 170 horses and 150 dogs, and the vast grounds included a theater, an armory, and acres of well-tended grounds that featured terraced flower gardens. In addition to the main castle, there were also a number of small, well-appointed buildings with exquisite furnishings.[52]

The level of opulence the Adams family witnessed in France like that at Chantilly was literally a world away from what they had been accustomed to in America. The vast expense of keeping up the luxurious residences and massive grounds, occupied by just one family, reminded Abigail of the chasm between the rich and poor in Europe. The visit moved Abigail to declare to a friend that though there were "many customs in this Country worthy a transplantation to the Soil of America . . . there are others which would lead me to repeat in the words of the Church Service, 'Good Lord Deliver Us.'"[53] Her words demonstrate the conflicting emotions Abigail experienced about class and society during her time abroad. All that Europe had to offer was measured against what she considered the superior American lifestyle.

Balance and moderation were always key aspirations for Abigail and John in their personal lives as well as their views on American governance, and they found that the pendulum had veered too far toward decadence in Europe. They witnessed extreme wealth and dire poverty, excessive luxury instead of the refinement they appreciated. They met powerful members of the elite who oppressed the powerless common people. From the first, Abigail disapproved of much she found in the pleasure-loving French society, especially the excesses of the royal court and its lavish entertainments. Evidence of Parisian immorality, dissipation, and self-indulgence assaulted her at every turn and offended the long-held tenets of her Puritan heritage. Often she struggled with reconciling her New England standards with the radically different culture she encountered in France. For example, she was shocked that most Parisians appeared to be more interested in endless recreation, showing off their latest exquisitely tailored fashions and attending social events instead of church on Sundays. Yet she conceded that one had to sometimes join in their amusements or remain isolated at home. As she noted to Mary Cranch, "Fashion is the Deity everyone worships in this country and from the highest to the lowest you must submit."[54] Before Abigail and Nabby had sailed to Europe, John had already warned them that "the polite life in Europe is such an insipid round of head-dressing and play."[55]

Moreover, the glittering surface often hid deep fissures in French society. Abigail lamented to an aunt back in America that working-class women there labored as hard as the men in the fields, primarily for only the benefit of landowners. They often sowed, plowed, and reaped crops alongside their male counterparts and received only coarse bread and watered-down wine for their toil.[56] She sadly understood that for the peasants, starvation threatened when crops failed or the already crushing taxes were raised unexpectedly. Many other women, forced by circumstances into prostitution or unwelcome marriages, entered into restrictive and unhappy arrangements for economic or social gain only.

Abigail was even more troubled that "thousands of these miserable wretches perish annually with Disease and Poverty; whilst the most sacred of institutions [marriage] is prostituted to unite titles and estates."[57] Abigail was impressed with the level of charitable care offered by nuns at the French orphanages she visited, but it saddened her to learn that the institutions were filled with babies who had been born out of wedlock and given up by their mothers. Abigail's parents had modeled responsibility for the needy, and she viewed taking care of the less fortunate as essential to being a good Christian and a good American.

Although there was much Abigail decried in France, she was gratified that their time in Europe enabled Nabby and John Quincy to renew their relationship, as for many years the siblings had spent little time together. The two studied separately during the morning, but often attended cultural events side by side in the afternoons and evenings. And despite her disdain for incessant Parisian "amusements," Abigail visited the French ballet and attended the theater, as those entertainments had long been banned in Boston. She enjoyed the performances of many of the plays she had read and admired, but complained that the crowds and the activity on stage often left her with a headache, perhaps brought on by a sense of guilt for having participated in what friends and family may have considered frivolous pursuits.[58]

From the beginning of their residence at Auteuil, Abigail and John knew that their stay in France would likely be relatively brief. Once Jefferson arrived, he, Adams, and Franklin attended weekly gatherings hosted by Louis XVI at Versailles and frequently met with Vergennes and other French diplomats. While John conducted business, Abigail took advantage of her time in France. Although her stay at Auteuil was less than a year, she began to appreciate some aspects of French culture, and she developed several robust friendships. She valued the company of Jefferson, whom she viewed as a highly cultured man and delightful conversationalist. On many levels, the Adamses and Jefferson were intellectual equals. Adams and Jefferson had first met in the summer of 1775 when they both served as delegates to the Continental Congress in Philadelphia, and they had often found themselves allies. When John learned of Jefferson's appointment to France, he wrote his fellow Boston patriot James Warren that the news "gives me great pleasure. He is an old Friend with whom I have often had occasion to labour at many a knotty Problem, and in whose Abilities and Steadiness I have always found great Cause to Confide."[59]

Jefferson, his eldest daughter, Martha, and the Adamses frequently dined together in France, and both John and Abigail developed a strong bond with the young, personable Virginian, facilitated in part by Abigail's lively presence and her people skills. Abigail could sometimes be tart and critical, but like Jefferson, who was only a year younger, she was fundamentally optimistic in spirit. Jefferson was charmed by Abigail, who likely fulfilled his domestic ideal as a supportive wife and involved mother, one who stood in stark contrast to many of the Parisian women he regarded as too forward and politically active.

Abigail certainly helped bolster Jefferson after the death of his young wife, Martha. They became fast friends but exhibited different outlooks about financial prudence. Not only did the southern aristocrat spend lavishly on his beloved Monticello, but in Paris and later on a trip to London he proved to be an inveterate shopper who relished fine clothes, magnificent art, stylish furnishings, and the best wines. Despite his idealized vision of the simple life, Jefferson never was able to bring his quest for civilized elegance and extravagant luxuries under control. Although at one time he had been one of the wealthiest planters in Virginia, he died in considerable debt, unlike the Adamses.

Nabby and Abigail befriended Jefferson's daughter in France, and they even attended a profession ceremony for two young novices with Jefferson at Martha's elite Catholic convent school. Jefferson, in turn, became a fond mentor to John Quincy, who often visited the Jefferson residence in Paris. When the Adamses left France for England, Abigail told Mary that "I shall really regret to leave Mr. Jefferson; he is one of the choice ones of the earth."[60] Jefferson reciprocated the sentiment. After the Adams family departed Auteuil, Jefferson wrote to John that "the departure of your family has left me in the dumps."[61] From London, Abigail told Jefferson that, due to the strong friendship and trust that had developed between the two men, she had been loath "to leave behind me the only person with whom my Companion [John] could associate with perfect freedom and unreserve."[62]

Although in some ways Jefferson became a great admirer of French art and culture, like the Adamses, he would look askance at much of the dissipation he witnessed among members of the aristocracy. He particularly detested the monarchy and the intrigue at the French court. According to Brian Steele, most of Jefferson's letters from France, like Abigail's, "emphasized American differences, and superiority, to the Old World, and his anxiety about the potential corrupting effect of European mores on American people and institutions . . . and imagined an essentially classless society."[63]

Neither of the Adamses would have agreed that America was a classless society. Certainly, they knew that American slaves in the South faced a more difficult situation then even the lowest members of European society. They also both understood that a hierarchy existed even in their beloved Braintree, and that America housed the rich as well as the poor, although most Americans were of a "middling" level and poverty was neither as widespread nor as severe as what they encountered in Europe. It was one more aspect of American life that Abigail pointed to with pride. An abundance of land and resources allowed most who were willing to work hard to sustain their families in some measure of comfort and prosperity, an observation Abigail repeatedly asserted.

Although their political outlooks were already diverging, the two American families would retain their close ties even after the Adamses moved to London. Mrs. Adams and Jefferson often purchased clothing and household supplies for one another. At times, Abigail ordered table linens and even bespoke English shirts and men's silk stockings for the Virginia aristocrat, who was fond of fashionable accoutrements and good food. When Jefferson returned to America in 1789 he was said to have shipped over 680 bottles of French wine to Monticello.[64] In turn, from Paris Thomas bought fine French wine for John and sent porcelain statuary, stylish women's shoes, and ladies' gloves in many colorful shades for Abigail and Nabby.

Separated by distance, the two families kept in frequent touch. News in 1785 of the death of Jefferson's youngest daughter, two-year-old Lucy, who had remained in Virginia with relatives, was heartbreaking, and it prompted Jefferson to send for his other remaining daughter, Maria (nicknamed Polly), to join him in France. After she heard of Lucy's demise, Nabby recorded in her journal, "Mr. J. is a man of great sensibility and parental affection. . . . This news has greatly affected him and his daughter."[65] Jefferson had long found Mrs. Adams to be a sympathetic personality, and though by the time of Lucy Jefferson's death the Adamses were stationed in England, she urged Jefferson to reunite the family. When Polly sailed to England from Virginia, Jefferson turned to Abigail to care for his daughter until she could be brought to Paris. Sally Hemings, then a young enslaved teenager on the Jefferson plantation, accompanied Polly on the voyage, and she later attended to both Jefferson's daughters at their Catholic boarding school.

Jefferson had brought Sally's older brother James Hemings with him to France, where he trained to become an accomplished chef and culinary expert. Abigail disapproved of Sally at first sight, but did not outwardly remark on the young woman's status as a slave, merely telling her sister Mary that she found the young girl very immature but good-natured and fond of her young charge. Abigail and John were both opposed to slavery on moral and practical economic grounds, although neither appears to have been willing to risk their friendship with Jefferson or later southern political support for the new nation over a serious debate about slavery. Abigail's reaction to Sally Hemings serves as an example of her conflicted feelings about African Americans, a mixture of enlightened liberalism and prejudice. Abigail professed herself happy to watch over precocious Polly, and almost immediately the two developed an affectionate relationship before Jefferson sent one of his servants to bring his young daughter to Paris.[66] All of Abigail's motherly instincts appear to have been rekindled by Polly's stay, and she soon pronounced her an exceptionally bright and endearing girl who "is a child of the quickest sensibility, and the maturest understanding, that I have ever met for her years."[67]

Later in March 1786, in an effort to encourage American commerce in Europe, Jefferson would visit London, where he renewed his close friendship with the Adamses. In many ways it was an attraction of opposites: Jefferson was a romantic idealist, who was almost pathologically optimistic, but Adams often took a darker view of humanity and what he considered the inevitable frailties of human nature. Yet the two men shared a deep love for their country and an appreciation for learning, culture, and convivial conversation, even if Jefferson was the more sophisticated.

During their time in Europe, it was the practical Abigail rather than John who primarily attended to the household finances, and she proved to be an exacting steward. As the mistress of such a large household in Auteuil, Abigail was occupied most mornings with domestic supervision, but the presence of numerous servants to take care of housework lightened her responsibilities and reduced Abigail's regular physical activity. Moreover, the rutted French local roads discouraged the formerly slender Abigail from taking her regular walks. As a result, she complained in 1784 to her sister Elizabeth Shaw, "I suffer through want of exercise, and grow too fat." She ruefully commented that the many mirrors at their house in Auteuil only served to magnify her girth. Two years later, the problem had grown in proportion, and she informed her older sister Mary Cranch, "'Tis true I enjoy good health but am larger than both my sisters compounded! Mr. Adams keeps pace with me."[68] Abigail still fretted over her husband's health, but John was strong enough to take his daily constitutional in the adjacent park despite the rough roads. As Abigail reported, "Mr. Adams makes it his constant practice to walk several miles every day, without which he would not be able to preserve his health, which at best is but infirm."[69]

John Quincy would soon leave France to attend Harvard College in America, and after he arrived home he was tutored by his uncle the Reverend John Shaw. The young man matriculated in March 1786. Frugal Abigail must have been pleased that her son's tuition was waived in recognition of John's long years of devoted service on behalf of his country. Soon John Quincy's younger brother Charles, the charmer who was less academically inclined, followed the same educational path. John believed that although universal education would never eliminate social classes, an educated public and its leaders were essential ingredients for future American success, and he wanted to ensure that his boys would be prepared to rise to the occasion.

Their time in Europe, where they observed that the masses had few opportunities to obtain even a rudimentary education, made the Adamses even more committed to broader access to learning. Abigail supported the entry of her sons at Harvard because she viewed the venerable institution as a superior training ground for developing moral character compared to what she found abroad, even though the Old World universities were established long before their American counterparts. Early Harvard offered a classic curriculum on the English university model but conformed to the Protestant religious tenets Abigail admired.

She wrote Mary Cranch that she believed that their native country was the proper site "for a young fellow who has any ambition to distinguish himself in knowledge and literature."[70] To a friend she declared, "The more . . . that I see of Europe the more I am attached to the method of Education persued in the state of Massachusetts," where her boys would be exposed to the "purer manners of our own Country."[71] Later, she would affirm with satisfaction to Mary, "I have never once regretted the resolution he [John Quincy] took of quitting Europe, and placing himself upon the theatre of his own country, where, if his life is spared, I presume he will neither be an idle or useless spectator."[72] Her words were prescient: John Quincy was destined to play a pivotal role on the American political stage.

In addition to educational matters, Abigail was afforded a close look at the institution of monarchy. The Adamses experienced numerous opportunities to observe the French court at the glittering Palace of Versailles firsthand and to meet King Louis XVI and Queen Marie-Antoinette. On New Year's Day of 1785, Nabby recorded in her diary with a touch of sarcasm, "Papa went to court. . . . The ladies were much dressed; the king and queen received first the ambassadors, then went to mass for an hour, then dined in public to give all the world the opportunity to see them eat and drink."[73] Virtually every action the royals took was scrutinized, even the most mundane activities. The pageantry of the French court impressed the Adamses and at the same time provoked their disapproval and fueled their disgust with the constant pomp and veneration of the monarchs, who were after all, in their opinion, only human and certainly not divine.

After Marie-Antoinette gave birth to the Dauphin, the French male heir to the throne, in the spring of 1785, the Adams family, along with Jefferson, were invited to the lavish ceremony, which was held at the Notre Dame Cathedral. Louis XVI, decked out in an elaborate bejeweled and embroidered costume, made a dramatic appearance. Everyone of any prominence in Paris joined in the festivities. The crowds were so large, Nabby recorded, that Jefferson speculated that the Parisians thronging the surrounding streets outnumbered the population of Massachusetts or that of any other American state.[74]

That Nabby and her parents thought little of the grandeur of the French court and viewed the institution of the monarchy with mixed emotions was evident after the Dauphin's arrival. Nabby recorded that "as soon as a prince is born, he has a house, servants, carriages, horses, tutors, governors and governesses, and every other attendant to him, while he, poor thing, is insensible to every thing." She concluded in bemusement, "The whole nation are taught to look upon them as their guardians and support. In a government such as this, where all power and authority are vested in the King, it is undoubtedly necessary that he should be respected from the moment he exists, then through his life." Still, Nabby observed realistically that "however wrong it may be," given the need of the French king to retain his power, the shows of splendor were "unavoidable."[75]

Despite Abigail and Nabby's disenchantment with many aspects of French life, by 1785 the Adamses had developed a pleasant routine at Auteuil. Ironically, once Abigail was comfortably settled and had worked out a satisfactory relationship with her French servants, she was forced to contemplate a second European move, one in which she would be required to play an even more central public role, including offering regular formal presentations to the British court. As early as January, she wrote Mary she anticipated that "we will be obligated to give up our house, dismiss our servants, and make a journey to England. This is not yet fully agreed upon; but I suppose the next letter from the Court of England will determine it; and this has been Mr. Adams's destiny ever since he came abroad."[76] It was Abigail's staunch belief that John was central to the American cause and that had allowed her to justify his frequent absences and now provided her with the rationale for their extended European stay.

Precisely eight months to the day after Abigail set sail for Europe, she took stock of her time abroad and observed that "many new and interesting scenes have presented themselves before me. I have seen many of the Beauties, and some of the Deformities, of this old World." Her time in France left her with conflicting views about the progress of civilization. Though she deplored much of the French lifestyle, she came to admire the famous *politesse* and civility that prevailed there. She maintained, however, that her time in Paris left her "more than ever convinced that there is no Summit of virtue, and no Depth of vice which Human Nature is not Capable of rising to, on the one hand, or sinking into on the other." Regretfully, she related that she had reconciled herself to some of the immodest customs she encountered in France, such as the scantily clad young women prancing across the stage at the ballet. At the same time, she appreciated her introduction to the sophisticated musical and artistic culture and marveled at the intricate dances and elaborate costumes she viewed in Paris.[77]

While the Adamses remained in France, John continued his frustrating efforts to make progress with the French foreign minister. With both Franklin and Jefferson sidelined with illness, John met on his own with Vergennes to discuss a possible solution to the ever-present threat of piracy by making a treaty with the Barbary States and Morocco. The shrewd diplomat listened politely, but conveniently concluded that the subject was out of his purview. To John's chagrin, Vergennes asked Adams to write up all the American concerns, and he told John that he would then simply convey the information to the minister of marine.[78] Nothing was resolved, and Adams and Jefferson had to revisit the piracy issue later once John moved to London.

John and Abigail had many enjoyable experiences while they lived in France, and would later be appalled at the terror unleashed by the

French Revolution. Although they believed that the political and social structure of the nation needed transformation, unlike Jefferson, they believed that moderate reform instead of the overthrow of the monarchy could address the issues. The resulting mob rule and chaos would make them highly critical of the nation they had once counted as an ally. In late February 1785, Congress appointed Adams the first United States minister to Great Britain, but it was not until April 26 that John received official notification of his new assignment. Jefferson, soon to be named minister to France, brought Adams the welcome news along with instructions that John was to appear in London by the time of King George's birthday celebration, which was scheduled to take place in early June. Jefferson and Adams were tasked anew with negotiating commercial treaties in Europe, and they hoped that the British invitation that had welcomed an American ambassador at the Court of St. James's served as a positive sign.

In early May, John again met with Vergennes, who congratulated him on his new appointment and told John, "It is a great Thing to be the First Ambassador from your Country to the Country you sprung from."[79] Abigail was less pleased with her husband's new posting. She confided to Mary Cranch, "It would be vastly more to my taste, and much more to my satisfaction to return to my own Country and live in that social Friendship and Simplicity in which I formerly rejoiced. I take no pleasure in a life of ceremony and parade."[80]

Abigail again complained to her uncle Cotton Tufts that in Europe she had found that instead of the warm friendships she had enjoyed at home, social interactions focused on mere amusement and had resigned herself to only socializing at ceremonial occasions. Still, Abigail admitted to her uncle that, given her husband's long experience in Europe and his unwavering commitment to promoting the welfare of his country, John was more likely than a "New Hand" to succeed in England in obtaining an economic treaty.[81]

On May 10, 1785, Nabby recorded the news of her father's upcoming position matter-of-factly in her journal: "Papa went to Versailles today, and took leave of this court; he has been appointed to England. Mr. Jefferson succeeds him here."[82] With mixed emotions, Abigail, John, and Nabby left their house in Auteuil on May 20. John fretted that living in London would be more expensive and politically challenging than in France. Moreover, he was uncertain whether he would "meet a candid or even decent reception in England" or whether he would make any headway moving American objectives forward. "It is not to be expected that I should be cherished and beloved," he observed sardonically, but he took a certain grim comfort in the words of a London gentleman he had met in The Hague, who told him, "I certainly know there is no Man in public Life whome the English fear as much as you."[83] Before he left France, John echoed Abigail's distaste for the pomp of European courts and expressed regret for the time wasted on ceremonial distractions instead of pressing diplomacy. He wrote John Jay that "the Essence of Things is lost in Ceremony, in every Country of Europe. We must submit to what We cannot alter."[84]

John Quincy had already left for Boston earlier in May to continue his studies at Harvard. Although she missed her son, Abigail supported his return to America. She told her uncle Cotton Tufts that she and John strongly believed that their sons needed to acquire the necessary skills to earn a living, which would be served best by returning to his native country. Although she appreciated that her eldest son had first-hand exposure to the splendor of the European courts, she retained the fervent hope that he was "Republican enough to leave these Ideas in their native Soils, and to exhibit an example of prudence and frugality" that his parents revered.[85]

Abigail later expanded on this theme, which emphasized the need for all young American men to be educated in America. The Adamses especially missed their youngest son, Thomas, while they resided in Europe, but Abigail stressed that she and John were convinced that their younger boys were best off at home. It was in America that they would "acquire an inherent Love of Liberty and a thorough acquaintance with the Manners and taste of the Society and country of which

Portrait of John Quincy Adams by John Singleton Copley. Courtesy
National Park Service, Adams National Historic Park.

he is a Member. He will find a purity in the Government and manners,
to which Europe has been long a stranger." For Abigail, that combination of civic virtue and reverence for liberty were values to be prized and
necessary ingredients in the formation of an American character. Only
after a young man had matured in judgment and experience and cultivated those traits should he be allowed to visit other nations so as not
to be corrupted by undesirable foreign influences.[86] Nabby regretted her
brother's departure, as she and John Quincy had become close friends in
France, and both would miss the camaraderie they had developed. Still,

they kept up a robust correspondence for many years, which has provided posterity with intimate insight into John Quincy's development as a future American statesman as well as vivid details about Nabby's and her parents' move from France and their stay in London.

No matter Abigail's misgivings about residing in Europe, their sojourn in France had brought the Adamses a rare tranquil family interlude. Abigail shared her reluctance to leave Auteuil with her sister Elizabeth Shaw. "Delightful and blooming garden, how much I shall regret your loss!" she wrote wistfully. At the same time, the resilient Abigail noted with dutiful resignation that "all things must Yeald to Business." Again, she complained about the expense of moving from one country to another and the fact that since John had arrived in Europe, he had been unable "to live a year at a time in one place." Although Abigail looked forward to residing in a country in which she would not need an "interpreter," she was apprehensive about how she would be welcomed in England as the wife of the first American minister. Some of her tolerance and appreciation for the French stemmed from the fact of their strong political alliance with the United States, but that, of course, was not the case with England. She also expected to be subject to more scrutiny in England than she had been in France. Abigail even regretted that she would have to leave behind the cherished pet bird she had acquired in Paris, but she was consoled that Jefferson would care for it. Fortunately, on the boat to England, a fellow passenger whom she had assisted presented her with a pair of his songbirds, which she enjoyed in London.[87]

Abigail expanded on her feelings about the move in a letter penned to her niece. "I shall have some regret, I assure you, in quitting Auteuil, since I must leave it for London instead of America, that being the destination that Congress has assigned us. . . . In many respects, I think I shall feel myself happier in London; but that will depend much upon our reception there, and the course which politics takes."[88] The family would arrive in London on May 26, as Abigail and John opened a new chapter in their European sojourn. The Adamses would spend more than three years in England. The day after their arrival, John would meet the British foreign secretary, Lord Carmarthen, who received the American minister with a measure of respect. By mid-June, Adams would begin talks with Carmarthen to discuss the future of the American and British economic relationship.

During their days in France, the Adamses were afforded the opportunity to enjoy one another's close company as well as the best of French culture, and they had access to magnificent vistas and historical sites. Still, their stay in France had convinced John and Abigail more than ever of the superiority of their home country and deepened their appreciation for America. Abigail confided to her sister Mary, "Can my dear sister realize that it is near eleven Months since I left her [America]? To me it seems incredible; more like a dream than a reality. Yet it ought to appear the longest ten Months of my life, if I were to measure the time by the variety of objects which have occupied my attention. But, amidst them all my heart returns, like the dove of Noah, and rests only in my native land."[89] As John put it even more succinctly when later asked about his origins by a foreign ambassador, "I have not one drop of blood in my veins but what is American."[90]

FOUR

Abigail and John in London

American Yankees in King George's Court

I must avow to your Majesty, I have no Attachments but to
my own Country.

John Adams to King George III, June 1, 1785

I long, dear madam, to return to my native land: My little
cottage, encompassed with my friends, has more charms for
me than the drawing-room of St. James, where studied civility and disguised coldness cover malignant hearts.

Abigail Adams to Mercy Warren, May 14, 1787

WITH A POPULATION OF CLOSE TO ONE MILLION PEOPLE, London was the largest city in the world when John and Abigail Adams took up residence there in late May 1785. John initially viewed his appointment as America's first minister plenipotentiary to the Court of St. James's in the British capital as the high point of his diplomatic career. Instead, it was his negotiations to obtain multiple Dutch loans at critical junctures during the American Revolution, and in the following years of the early fragile American nation, that would mark his greatest success. After he received official notification of his new role, Adams wrote optimistically to John Jay, who had conveyed the welcome news, "The appointment to the Court of Great Britain demands my most grateful acknowledgements to congress, and the utmost care and diligence in the execution of it."[1] It was a pronouncement that John took to heart, and he proceeded thoughtfully to rebuild the American relationship with Great Britain in a manner he hoped would benefit his home nation.

Still, when John learned afterwards that his appointment to England had been debated at length in Congress by those who accused him of vanity and believed him temperamentally unsuited for the position, his pride was wounded. Elation turned to indignation and disappointment, for he believed that his knowledge about foreign affairs, long years of experience, and sacrifices on behalf of his country were unappreciated by the American public and his political colleagues. Yet after much soul-searching, John's commitment to the public good propelled him forward. His response was to redouble his efforts.

John, Abigail, and Nabby took leave of Auteuil in mid-May, and began a leisurely trip to London by a combination of horse-drawn carriage and a boat across the Channel. At first, they traveled in only short segments by post chaise—when they found one available. Due to the throng of travelers trying to escape the unusually hot weather in France that spring, there was a shortage of suitable vehicles. Moreover, John wished to proceed slowly, as he was "determined not to be in a hurry about nothing from the Beginning to the End of this Adventure." He intended to use their journey to enjoy the company of his family and to mull over the best course of action for his upcoming diplomatic overtures. As he put it succinctly to Jefferson, "It is best to give myself as well as others time to think."[2]

Abigail reported to Mary, "About the 28th of May we reached London, and expected to have gone into our old quiet lodgings of the Adelphi; but we found every hotel full. The sitting of Parliament, the birth-day of the King, and the famous celebration of the music of Handel at Westminster Abbey had drawn together such a concourse of people, that we were glad to get into lodgings at the moderate price of a guinea per day, for two rooms and two chambers at the Bath Hotel in Piccadilly, where we are yet." London was always a city on the move. Even at that modest temporary residence, John and Abigail were surrounded by the hustle and bustle of the great city, and they heard the almost constant clattering of carriage wheels over the cobblestone roads and the cries of roving street vendors hawking their wares. "This being the Court end of the city, it is the resort of a vast concourse of carriages. It is too public and noisy for pleasure, but necessity is without law," she remarked resignedly.[3]

In the Old World, the customs at royal courts had been developed over centuries, and the prescribed protocol was precise. The Adamses understood that European monarchs at the time were the most powerful people in the world. It was no wonder that the displaced American Yankees were understandably anxious about moving among British royalty. Despite the animosity the American patriots had displayed toward the British monarch during the revolution, the gregarious king was a man whom John came to respect. Before the outbreak of the war, reverence and even affection for the reigning British monarch had long been ingrained in the colonial American character.[4] George III and Adams were of a similar age and both were well-read, conscientious leaders who were devoted family men, and they shared a common affinity for farming and a love of books. Adams may not have possessed the usual qualities of dissembling and flattery so common to the customs of diplomatic protocol, but he was fervently committed to the American cause, which provided ample motivation for his endeavors. Moreover, he was tenacious and eminently pragmatic, qualities that stood him in good stead during this deeper foray into European diplomacy.

We are able to vividly reconstruct the initial meeting between King George and Adams through John's eyes. Indeed, his remains the only firsthand account, so it reflects *his* perceptions. Accompanied by Carmarthen, who had provided his personal carriage to transport the new American minister, a dapper and visibly nervous John, attired in a somber but fashionable suit and a newly purchased powdered wig, and wearing an impressive ceremonial sword, made his way through the palace before he was conducted to the anteroom. It was crowded with British ministers, foreign diplomats, bishops, and members of the British aristocracy, all awaiting an audience with the king.

Even a sober New Englander like Adams realized the need to project a persona that reflected the refinement in dress required of those who moved among royalty. He was sensitive to the stares of the members of the British court who surveyed the American minister with skepticism and was gratified that the Dutch and Swedish ambassadors cordially engaged him in conversation and made him feel welcome. John was guided through the monarch's "Levee," or grand reception room, and after being announced as "His Excellency the American Minister," he was finally ushered into the king's private reception chamber, known as His Majesty's "closet."[5]

Once in the presence of the king, John recorded that he made the three required "reverence" bows. As John noted, he was following the age-old prescribed modes of protocol of "Usage established at this and all Northern Courts of Europe." Adams told John Jay that he then presented King George III with his formal appointment documents from Congress, as was customary at an initial meeting between the monarch and a new ambassador, and "addressed myself to his Majesty in the following words: The United States of America have appointed me their minister plenipotentiary to your Majesty." Next, John paid his compliments to the king and told him that he had been authorized to convey the unanimous instruction of Congress "to cultivate the most friendly and liberal Intercourse between your Majesty's Subjects and their Citizens, and of their best Wishes for your Majesty's Health and Happiness, and for that of your Royal Family." It was a conciliatory gesture, which George III seemed to appreciate.[6]

Despite the high costs of the Revolutionary War, the British were still left in a strong economic position, so they retained the upper hand in trade negotiations with the Americans. During his years in London, John would do his utmost to foster an amicable relationship between America and England, as his most pressing goal was to secure a favorable trade agreement. In his presentation to King George, Adams was respectful and dignified; he understood that in the late eighteenth century, the government *was* the king's, regardless of the advice or opinions of His Majesty's ministers, and he was intent on making a good impression and persuading the monarch to support economic treaties.

Adams told the king that he would "esteem myself the happiest of Men, if I can be instrumental in recommending my Country more and more to your Majesty's Royal Benevolence, and of restoring an entire esteem, confidence, and affection . . . between People who, though separated by an ocean, and under different Governments, have the same Language, a similar Religion and kindred Blood."[7] It was a tall order, but John's sincerity met with more success than he had anticipated. He wrote Jay that the British monarch "was indeed much affected, and I confess I was not less so."[8]

Despite the understandable awkwardness and residual injured feelings, John reported that King George told him, "I not only receive with Pleasure, the Assurances of the friendly Dispositions of the United States, but that I am very glad the Choice has fallen upon you to be their Minister." When the monarch asked Adams for details about his feelings toward England's rival, France, John responded without hesitation that his full loyalty was only to America, not to any European powers.[9] The king appeared pleased with the frank response. Adams reported to Jefferson that his presentation was treated by the British monarch "with all the Respect, and the Person with all the Kindness, which could have been expected or reasonably desired, and with much more, I confess, than was in fact expected by me."[10]

Following an exchange of pleasantries, as protocol demanded, the king bowed to signal the end of the interview and Adams took his leave, retreating backwards. John had cleared the first hurdle successfully; he was accepted as the legitimate diplomatic representative of an independent country, even though privately the king, his ministers, and courtiers had little confidence in the survival of the fragile American government. Adams's first audience with the king seemed a personal as well as an American triumph.

Several weeks after John's first meeting with the king, Abigail shared with her sister Mary a description of the encounter and noted that her husband had been required to make "some little address," as Abigail described it with understatement. She told Mary she was not at liberty to quote King George's words verbatim, but noted that His Majesty was cordial to John. John also later met with Queen Charlotte, who told him, "Sir, I thank you for your civility to me and my family, and I am glad to see you in this country." Then she made polite small talk and asked John about his housing arrangements.[11]

Abigail also detailed to her sister the set rules surrounding the Adamses' formal introduction to the British monarchs: "The ceremony of presentation [for John], upon one week to the King, and the next to the Queen, was to take place, after which I was to prepare for mine. It is customary, upon presentation, to receive visits from all the foreign ministers; so that we could not exchange our lodgings for more private ones, as we might and should, had we been only in private character. The foreign ministers and several English lords and earls, have paid their compliments here, and hitherto [all] is civil and polite."[12]

Yet John and Abigail would soon find that courtesy and fine manners did not necessarily translate into action or the desired acknowledgment that they were the equals to the British. Within a month, John grew pessimistic about his ability to negotiate a favorable commercial agreement, as he believed that England was set on a path to hinder American economic success. Indeed, the British Ministry, including Lord Carmarthen and Prime Minister William Pitt, continued to thwart Adams throughout his stay in England. John often felt he had encountered a brick wall when he visited the foreign minister at Whitehall or the prime minister at 10 Downing Street, yet another reason for him to disdain British diplomacy.

Abigail had spent only eight months in France; she would reside in England for nearly three years. Although the war for American independence had been over for almost two years when the Adamses moved to London, unsurprisingly, the English did not always welcome the couple who had played such a pivotal role in the colonial rebellion. Each side accused the other of violating the terms of the 1783 Peace Treaty. Adams placed most of the blame on Great Britain, but he conceded that the American government had not always kept its part of the bargain, and he insisted that his nation needed to be scrupulous about following the "sacred faith" of agreements.[13] Nor did many British leaders believe that America deserved official recognition. Indeed, some regarded the American republic as an experiment destined for collapse and believed, not without reason, that the states were united only in name.

Even at the start, all was far from idyllic. Abigail noted to her sister that almost immediately, "the Tory venom has begun to spit itself forth in the public papers, as I expected, bursting with envy that an American minister should be received here with the same marks of attention, politeness, and civility, which are shown to the other ministers of any other power."[14] In a letter written to Jefferson shortly after she arrived in London, Abigail reported with wry humor that one of the local newspapers had commented condescendingly, "An Ambassador from America! Good heavens what a sound!"[15] Soon after, the London *Times* observed in a perturbed tone, "Can there be a stronger proof of the mutability of human affairs than the arrival of John Adams, Esq. in the capacity of Ambassador from North America. This gentleman, who was formerly proscribed as a *rebel* to this country, now appears invested with all the privileges and rank *annexed* to the representative of a free state; and the title of *Excellency* is now substituted by those very persons who formerly styled him *traitor*."[16]

Abigail was irritated with critical British attitudes and the frequent slights that appeared in the newspapers. Fortunately, Boston newspapers, which often reported on the Adamses, cast a more positive light on their activities abroad. Throughout her days in London, Abigail would often complain of the falsehoods reported regularly in British publications about her husband's diplomacy and the "despicable" efforts of the press to belittle them both. Jefferson professed himself unsurprised at the "squibs" from those whom he sarcastically termed the "polished, mild tempered, truth speaking people" of England.[17] Abigail later declared to Jefferson with more than a kernel of truth, "So great is their pride that they cannot endure to view us as independent, and they fear our growing greatness."[18] It would be another six years before England appointed a minister to the United States.

The Adamses were not alone in their feeling of being looked down upon; the group of fledgling American diplomats all endured similar experiences. When Jefferson later visited London to try to assist John in negotiations with the British, he too met with a good measure of disrespect. Jefferson believed that he had been snubbed by King George, and the interaction served to heighten his already considerable antipathy toward England. Jefferson's feelings were soothed, however, by the warm welcome he received from John and Abigail, who frequently hosted him at their rented town house in the elegant Grosvenor Square, the site of the American ambassador's headquarters in London.

Abigail would eventually meet some congenial acquaintances in England, but at the beginning, she was skeptical about forming any meaningful friendships. In her eyes, the enmity between Americans and the English was still too apparent and raw. Early in her stay, she told her sister Mary that though she was not as physically isolated as she had been in Auteuil, she felt little of the easy sociability she had enjoyed in Braintree. "They tell me I shall get attached to England by and by, but I do not believe it," she declared. "The people must Love my country and its inhabitants better first. They must discover a more amicable temper towards us." Still, Abigail conceded, "Yet there are worthy good individuals here whom I Esteem."[19]

Throughout her residence in Europe, Abigail remained concerned about affairs at home. Contemporary political issues occupied her thoughts, and she closely followed the American newspapers that they received from across the Atlantic. As Nabby reported, during the social calls she and her mother made in London, Abigail proved a lively conversationalist who relished her "dish of politics."[20] The politically astute Abigail continued to serve as her husband's confidante and advisor even after he became the second president of the United States in 1797, and her European sojourn helped prepare her for her role as First Lady. According to writer Judith Sargent Murray, one of the leading American female intellectuals of their era, Abigail was so well-respected by some highly placed men in Boston that they declared that if Adams were to die in office "they should rather see Mrs. Adams in the Presidential chair, than any other character now existing in America."[21] Later, Fisher Ames, a Federalist politician from Massachusetts, declared that Mrs. Adams "is as complete a politician as any Lady in the Old French Court."[22]

Over time, Abigail crossed paths with many Americans who were then living in London, including the famous painters John Trumbull, John Singleton Copley, and Benjamin West, all of whom helped introduce the Adamses to London society. Budding artist Mather Brown, the protégé of the older painters, later completed handsome portraits of John, Abigail, and Nabby at their Grosvenor house, pictures that became treasured family heirlooms, for Abigail proudly regarded Copley and West as *American* artistic geniuses. When Brown executed the family paintings in 1785, Nabby pronounced the likeness of her father the best she had ever seen and her own portrait as "very tasty."[23] Formal portraits became popular among the American founders following independence as a sign of their rising status. Jefferson later commissioned Brown to paint portraits of himself and Adams, completed in 1788. When they later visited London for a second time, Anne Bingham and her daughters sat for a portrait by yet another prominent American artist working in England at the time, the acclaimed Gilbert Stuart.

As Abigail became more accustomed to her surroundings, she gradually found the English to be more welcoming, if not effusive. Certainly, the negative perceptions of the "upstart" Americans by British politicians and the elite class had evolved. Years later, John recalled a conversation in London with a British noble who was astounded at the evident cordial relations between Adams, formerly considered a traitor, and Lord Mansfield. The Londoner, who was a member of Parliament, informed John that during the American Revolution, the same Lord Mansfield had viewed John as a formidable threat to the British Empire and had proclaimed dramatically in the House of Lords, "My Lords, if you do not kill him [Adams], he will kill you."[24]

While John found a more favorable reception from British ministers, he had cause to revise his earlier positive views about George III. Adams

Portrait of John Adams painted in London in 1785 by Mather Brown. Courtesy Boston Athenaeum.

found the king to be "the most accomplished Courtier in his Dominion," and so focused on "the little Things of Life" that he was inattentive to "the great Affairs of Society and Government." Moreover, Adams found the king obstinate. John believed that George III, flattered by the unceasing adulation he received, became so convinced of the correctness of his own ideas that he frequently ignored reasonable counsel, particularly when it came to American economic negotiations.[25]

Despite earlier antagonisms, Abigail soon hosted and received many polite social calls, including some from members of the British aristocracy and gentry. Abigail reserved Tuesday afternoons as her time to be home for visitors. By the end of 1785, prospects seemed to be looking up for the American minister. The Adamses' dinner guests in Grosvenor Square included members of the nobility, and John had met again with King George III at both St. James's Palace and Windsor Castle. At one dinner they hosted, Abigail offered her guests a cooked turtle weighing over a hundred pounds, gifted to them by a ship's captain who had recently returned from the West Indies.[26] On another occasion, Abigail served her American guests an American home-style dinner, which featured salt fish, so popular in New England, as the main course. In some aspects, the Court of St. James's was more to Abigail's liking than Versailles had been because she was relieved to be able to converse in English without an interpreter as well as the fact that the royals were Protestant rather than Catholic.

Beset with a myriad of domestic arrangements, Abigail had little time to write when she first arrived in England. Yet, just after a month, she turned to her neglected correspondence and sent Mary Cranch a detailed account of her first weeks in London as the wife of the new American minister. Even though Abigail had often visited and, for a time, had resided in the bustling port of Boston, it could not compare with the overwhelming size and breadth of London with its huge population. Abigail was often distracted by the incessant movement and commotion of the people who daily swarmed the streets.

At the same time, she was impressed with the variety of cultural offerings and the shopping opportunities she discovered. Tourism was traditionally a patrician affair, and their elevated status abroad allowed the Adamses access to magnificent museums, operas, and theatrical productions that were not yet available in America. The Adams family especially appreciated the beauty of the many fashionable English parks, particularly Ranelagh Gardens, located in Chelsea. A favorite haunt of the ruling classes, it offered not only well-designed walking paths, but also musical entertainments and the opportunity to view classic paintings on display inside one of the ornate buildings. On one level, accessing culture was akin to buying fine porcelain and furniture, a way to add another layer of civilized cosmopolitanism.

From the start, life in London was a whirl of both political and social obligations as well as cultural opportunities. The city was a hub of commerce at the time and a shopper's paradise, offering goods that rivaled and sometimes even surpassed the Paris shops. Despite Abigail's emphasis on frugality and simplicity, their beauty attracted her. Over the span of the next few years, she purchased a number of delicate porcelain pieces to bring back to America and ordered fine clothing for her court appearances. At the same time, she often complained about excess spending on fripperies by her fellow Americans and the high British taxes on virtually all items, including gloves, a fashion necessity.

Abigail's purchase of British luxuries reflected the complex strands of cultural influences that attended the formation of American identity. People from all stations of life, but especially members of the elite, including leading revolutionary figures such as George and Martha Washington, Jefferson, and Franklin, still viewed European goods and art as the epitome of sophistication and refinement, even if that view often clashed with their professed republican ideals. For decades, including the years after independence, the Washingtons continued to furnish their Mount Vernon mansion with exquisite European goods. The Binghams returned to Philadelphia from their European tour in 1786 with fine furniture and decorative objects, including rich carpets, silver serving pieces, delicate French china, and magnificent paintings for their American mansion modeled after an acclaimed London town house. The coaches that carried the Binghams to their ship were packed with trunks full of fashionable gowns, hats, and other finery for Anne; other expensive purchases were shipped separately.[27]

When Jefferson returned to America after his stint in France, he appeared to suffer few qualms about bringing back dozens of crates packed with European goods, including many French and English luxury products. Possession of refined objects was often seen as a reflection of high-level civilization, not just for individuals but for American society as a whole. Ironically, the volume of imports, particularly from Great Britain, increased significantly during the early national period.[28] Jefferson as well as the Adamses were able to rationalize their acquisition of these select objects as tangible symbols of increased levels of gentility and good taste in the new nation as long as the items did not reflect tawdry venality. Although the Adamses were always careful to live within their means, Jefferson was challenged financially, and, as mentioned earlier, he died in significant debt.

Abigail informed her sister that she and Nabby were soon required to appear at Queen Charlotte's circle, an event that she regarded with trepidation: "There is no other presentation in Europe, in which I should feel so much as in this," she maintained. The Adamses were subject to unrelenting scrutiny in London, and she was understandably anxious about meeting the queen due to the fraught American-British relationship.[29] Abigail and Nabby were presented to King George III and Queen Charlotte on June 23, just three weeks after John's first private audience. Given Abigail's long-held sense of propriety and decorum, she understood that fashion was an element of social currency. For the special occasion, she dutifully appeared in an elegantly "simple" hooped gown of lace and lilac ribbon-trimmed white shiny silk lutestring, covered in white crepe as a concession to popular style. It was complemented by a beautiful dress-cap decorated with lace, white plumes, and fashionable pearl jewelry, and she observed the social niceties in a manner commensurate with her new station in life, reflecting refined gentility. Nabby was attractively dressed in a white gown trimmed with lace, but with a petticoat festooned with lovely handcrafted artificial flowers. After the long-drawn-out ritual, Abigail sardonically remarked to a friend, "One pays dear for the smiles of Royalty."[30]

Abigail's first formal presentation was held in a crowded drawing room, so it was not private as John's initial meeting had been with George III. John would be required to attend the king's weekly reception, but Abigail's attendance at the queen's drawing rooms was more flexible. The Adamses and Jefferson understood that in the European courts dress took on great significance as a reflection of rank and social standing. For example, despite his later emphasis on republican simplicity, after he arrived in Paris, Jefferson rushed to purchase fashionable French silk embroidered waistcoats, lace ruffles, and a stylish powdered wig. Unlike Adams, however, Jefferson appeared to take pleasure in conforming to the height of European fashion while abroad.[31]

Nevertheless, all three made a conscious effort to follow the standards of Continental fashion. When John was stationed in London, Abigail and Jefferson often shopped for one another. From Paris, Jefferson sent porcelain figurines for display, delicate china for entertaining, and fancy trims and silk shoes in the most popular colors for Abigail and Nabby. Jefferson, in turn, requested that Abigail order him British tailored shirts and fine table linens. Despite the need to appear *à la mode*, however, Abigail sometimes drew the line. She ridiculed the protruding bustle on dresses that were popular in London and declared that English women often wore ensembles lacking in taste. She advised a niece that American women would be best served if they kept modesty, neatness, and economy at the fore in their fashion decisions.[32] In other words, for Abigail elegant simplicity in dress was the most desirable fit for the American character, even if she did not always follow her own advice.

The frugal Abigail frequently grumbled about the extravagance of the British upper classes—especially the cost of the unaccustomed finery she was obliged to wear in order to attend the queen's weekly "circle"—as well as the need to curtsey to the monarchs. Although Abigail professed her distaste for the luxurious trappings of royalty, she appeared to take secret pleasure in her appearance and the opportunity to glimpse royal life. Still, presaging the republican fashion style she would later adopt when she became First Lady, for her first time at the royal court Abigail had instructed her seamstress "to let my dress be elegant, but plain as I could possibly appear."

Abigail justified her unaccustomed expenses and the need to keep up with the dictates of fashion in England as required by her husband's diplomatic position. She insisted that though some American women might envy her, "in a private station I have not a wish for expensive living. . . . I will most joyfully exchange Europe for America, and my public for a private life." Weary of the formalities and rigid structure of the royal courts and elite circles in both France and England, Abigail shared a sentiment with Jefferson that she would repeat many times while living abroad: "I am really surfeited with Europe, and most heartily long for the rural cottage, the purer and honester manner of my native land, where domestic happiness reigns unrivalled, and virtue and honor go hand in hand."[33]

Abigail understood that the interactions with British royals and members of elite society were not inconsequential occasions. In eighteenth-century England, men as well as women used the social arena for political purposes. In London, court events, private dinner parties, theater excursions, or even walks in the park could be politicized. The visits by Adams family members to court served as an opportunity to build alliances and influence the royals and key politicians to gain support for economic agreements, and even brief interactions could make a difference. Abigail believed that as part of a family unit it was her wifely duty to advance her husband's agenda. Since British women exercised considerable sociopolitical influence, it was in her best interest to develop cordial if superficial relationships with the wives, sisters, and daughters of English leaders who wielded power, including the royal family.[34]

The first time she met the British monarchs, Abigail decided on the spot that George III and Charlotte were rather dull, uninspiring figures and that they were decidedly lacking the superior American virtues despite their golden crowns and finery. Moreover, she looked with disdain upon the drawn-out, intricate rituals that surrounded the London court, where visitors had to pass by lines of guards before they were permitted to enter the palace, and then often had to mark time before the royal couple briefly greeted guests and exchanged social small talk at the queen's carefully orchestrated drawing rooms. For example, for Abigail's first encounter with the British royal couple the Adams family pulled up to the palace in their own fine horse-drawn carriage. After alighting, they were directed to the huge drawing room to join hundreds of select guests positioned in a circle around the perimeter.[35] Nor did Abigail find St. James's Palace as grand as Versailles. Abigail likely favored the French court over that of the English because she had so long regarded Great Britain as the enemy. Still, she admitted to John Quincy that the king appeared good-humored, the ministers and courtiers affable, and that she and John had "no reason to complain of any want of politeness or attention at Court."[36]

Abigail had always been a remarkably self-possessed woman, and despite her professed anxiety, she survived the nerve-wracking, exhausting ordeal, carried off her introduction admirably, and enjoyed parts of her first meeting with the British monarchs. The following morning she wrote Mary, "Congratulate me, my dear sister, it is over. I was too much fatigued to write a line last evening." The next day she described the event to her sister in detail. The drawn-out process had begun at two o'clock in the afternoon, when "we went to the circle, which is the drawing-room of the Queen. We passed through several apartments, lined as usual with spectators upon these occasions."[37]

The presentation rooms were thronged with members of the aristocracy and foreign ministers. When Abigail and Nabby entered the anteroom, they first conversed with the affable Dutch envoy Baron de Lynden, whom Abigail had met previously, as well as with a French nobleman, the British politicians Sir Clement Cotterel Dormer and Carmarthen, and the Swedish and Polish ministers to court. Although Abigail was acquainted with many of the male attendees, "not a single lady did I know until the Countess of Effingham came, who was very civil." Soon several other young women, two of them recent brides, arrived to be presented to the queen. "We were placed in a circle round the drawing-room, which was very full, I believe two hundred persons present," Abigail explained. She even expressed some sympathy for the royals, as she appreciated that the interminable social events must have been exhausting for them: "Only think of the task! The royal family have to go round to every person, and find small talk enough to speak to all of them, though they very prudently speak in a whisper, so that only the person who stands next you can hear what is said."[38]

Abigail explained the ritual protocol followed to the letter by King George and Queen Charlotte: "The King enters the room, and goes round to the right; The Queen and the Princesses to the left. The lord in waiting presents you to the King; and the lady in waiting does the same to her Majesty. The King is a personable man, but my dear sister, he has a certain countenance, which you and I have often remarked; a red face and white eyebrows. The Queen has a similar countenance and the numerous royal family confirm the observation. Persons are not placed according to their rank in the drawing-room, but promiscuously; and when the King comes in he takes persons as they stand."[39]

In a sarcastic tone she continued, "When he came to me, Lord Onslow said, 'Mrs. Adams,' upon which I drew off my right-hand glove, and his Majesty saluted my left cheek; then he asked me if I had taken a walk today. I could have told his Majesty that I had been all the morning preparing to wait upon him; but I replied, 'No, Sire.' 'Why, don't you love walking?' says he. I answered that I was rather indolent in that respect. He then bowed, and passed on." Abigail would often find future meetings with the royal couple at their birthday and anniversary celebrations tedious, as the rituals were repeated *ad nauseam*, and the king and queen asked her virtually the same questions on each occasion.[40]

Abigail was determined not to appear inferior to the royals. She later feistily claimed to her sister Mary, "I know I am looked down upon with sovereign pride, and the Smile of Royalty is bestowed as a mighty Boon." Still, she consciously retained her dignity and pride in being an American: "As such however I cannot receive it," she insisted. "I know it is due to my Country, and I consider myself as complimenting the Power before which I appear, as much as being complimented by being noticed by it."[41] Despite the tedium, Abigail behaved impeccably, always conforming to proper etiquette in the presence of royalty. John agreed with Abigail's sentiments, for he found the social rituals equally meaningless. Soon after the Adamses arrived in London, he wrote Jefferson, "You would die of Ennui here for these Ceremonies are more numerous and continue much longer than at Versailles."[42] John was similarly unimpressed with the lack of serious intellectual focus he claimed to have found in England. A year after he and Abigail had settled in, he complained sardonically to Abigail's uncle that only art and music received popular attention, that the study of history and philosophy had gone by the wayside, and that even "Reading is out of Fashion."[43]

Abigail knew that her sisters eagerly awaited her letters, so she spared no detail about her first court appearance: "It was more than two hours after this before it came to my turn to be presented to the Queen. The circle was so large the company were four hours standing. The Queen was evidently embarrassed when I was presented to her. I had disagreeable feelings too. She, however, said, 'Mrs. Adams, have you got into your house? Pray, how do you like the situation of it?' Whilst the Princess Royal looked compassionate, and asked me if I was not much fatigued; and observed that it was a very full drawing-room. Her sister, who came next, Princess Augusta, after having asked your niece [Nabby] if she was ever in England before, and her answering 'Yes' inquired of me how long ago and supposed it was when she was very young. All this is said with much affability, and the ease and freedom of an old acquaintance."[44]

Abigail continued, "The manner, in which they make their tour round the room, is, first, the Queen, the lady in waiting behind her, holding up her train; next to her, the Princess Royal, after her, Princess Augusta, and their lady in waiting behind them." Abigail seldom found English ladies more attractive than American women, and she found the queen ungainly. She considered the princesses "pretty rather than beautiful, well-shaped, with fair complexions, and a tincture of the King's [ruddy] countenance." The two young women were elaborately "both dressed in black and silver silk," with diamonds decorating their hair, while "the Queen was in purple and silver. She is not well shaped nor handsome," Abigail concluded rather uncharitably, but was wise enough to ask Mary to keep her unflattering opinions confidential. "As to the ladies of the Court, rank and title may compensate for want of personal charms," Abigail wrote, "but they are, in general, very plain, ill-shaped, and ugly; but don't you tell anybody that I say so."[45]

Yet, through their dress, the royal family exuded their privileged status. Back in America, over a decade later and as the wife of the second president of the United States, Abigail often consciously sought to distance her own "court" style from that of her European counterparts. Yet as historian David Waldstreicher has observed, ritual celebrations, initially modeled after English traditions, played a visible role during and after the American Revolution and were often appropriated by revolutionary leaders for their own political purposes. They were later utilized as effective practices in building American nationalism and identity in the early republic.[46] As was the custom for British monarchs, after he was elected the nation's first president, Washington's birthday was similarly marked with a lavish ball. Even Abigail, who scoffed at the birthday celebrations of the British royals, was thrilled when her presidential husband's birthday was later celebrated in New England. And as John predicted, July 4 would "become the most memorable Epocha, in the History of America."[47] Indeed, Independence Day became a central but sometimes contested American national symbol of unity. Beginning in 1776 and to this day, it has been a rite appropriated by groups with competing purposes, often marked by celebratory parades and fireworks.

Once the Adamses met the British royals, John proceeded with his duties as he set out to secure commercial agreements. Abigail remained occupied with finding a suitable house to serve as their official living quarters, but her choices were restricted by John's modest salary in London, which had been reduced to only 2,000 pounds, 500 pounds less than he had received in France. Despite the financial challenges and the high cost of London home rentals, which ran to as much as 200 pounds (not including taxes that added another 50 or 60 pounds), Abigail's "good genius" brought her to an affordable town house in fashionable Grosvenor Square, where they moved in early July.[48] When the Adamses resided there, it was populated with members of London's political and social elite, including the former British prime minister Lord Frederick North and foreign secretary Lord Carmarthen. The Adams rental at number 8, located at the northeast corner of the attractive tree-lined square, came to a surprisingly affordable cost of under 200 pounds. The resourceful Abigail even managed to persuade the landlord to have two rooms painted, which made the house more inviting.[49] Despite her high-profile British neighbors, Abigail claimed to be unimpressed by their social status, and she insisted that she was "too much of a republican to be charmed with titles alone." With her typical wit, she added slyly, "We have not taken *a side with* Lord North but are still *opposite* to him."[50]

Grosvenor Square was one of the pleasantest areas in London and well situated for John's diplomatic duties. In its center stood an enclosed park with gravel walkways designed for strolling, and residents were given a key to enter through one of the gates in the grated fence. The park featured a central garden with geometrically designed flower and plant beds, carefully maintained by workers hired by the owners of the elegant homes surrounding it. At night, some sixty lamps illuminated the perimeter. The stately residence leased by Adams became the first American legation in London. It featured a generous-sized front hall entryway with a staircase, a large basement kitchen, and living quarters for eight servants, including a butler and two footmen. The house also had spacious dining and drawing rooms for entertaining guests, a library, and an attractive suite of four bedrooms on the third floor for family members.[51]

An added bonus for Abigail was her own private study, where she could attend to her voluminous correspondence, read, or just gaze out over the square when she had the leisure. Abigail had always read voraciously, and given her finely tuned intelligence, her penchant for introspection, and her wide correspondence with relatives and friends, the cozy retreat was a much-appreciated boon. It was an opportunity that Abigail had coveted for decades. At the height of the revolution, back in the summer of 1776, she wrote John wistfully, "I always had a fancy for a closet [room] with a window which I could more peculiarly call my own."[52] John admitted that it was a fine house, but he grumbled that Congress's penny pinching guaranteed that the Adamses' limited budget would never allow the American minister to make a proper impression on foreign diplomats and politicians.[53]

Abigail often chafed at the rigidly structured world she encountered in Europe, but whether she approved or not, she was forced to conform to society standards in a manner befitting the wife of the American emissary. A carriage and coachman were a necessity for the Adamses, as they frequently traveled London to attend social affairs. Popular Hyde Park, located near the Adamses' Grosvenor house, included six hundred lush green acres, which had originally served as Henry VIII's hunting grounds. Although Abigail occasionally walked there, more often she rode. Many more servants were necessary in London than in Braintree. Esther Field, the female servant Abigail had brought from America, became elevated to the position of ladies' maid. She was responsible for dressing Abigail's and Nabby's hair, acting as a skilled seamstress, and delivering and picking up all the laundered linens and clothing from a local washerwoman, tasks Abigail would have never contemplated for her maid back in Braintree. Later, Esther married the Adamses' footman, John Briesler, and their baby daughter, conceived out of wedlock to Abigail's shock, was born aboard ship when they returned with John and Abigail to America in 1788.

"As soon as our furniture comes [from France], I will commence housekeeping," wrote frugal Abigail. Expenses weighed on her mind as she told her sister Mary that "living at a hotel is, I think, more expensive than housekeeping, in proportion to what one has for his money." Even once they had settled into Grosvenor Square, finances were tight: "We have never had more than two dishes at a time upon our table, and have not pretended to ask any company, and yet we live at a greater expense than twenty-five guineas per week. The wages of servants, horse-hire, house-rent, and provisions are much dearer here than in France." Abigail was also taxed with hiring additional servants, including a coachman, because "I cannot bear to trouble Mr. Adams with any thing of a domestic kind, who, from morning until evening, has sufficient [diplomatic work] to occupy all his time."[54] Abigail shared her irritation over the lack of efficiency of the eight servants she was forced to employ. Perhaps even more so than in France, she found that her English workers would perform only circumscribed duties that they deemed befitted their positions. The butler, who supervised and served the courses at their formal dinners, appeared competent, but she fumed to her sister, "I cannot but think 3 Americans would do the whole work of the Eight and think they had no hard task."[55]

Meanwhile, over the next months, John Adams exchanged a volley of letters with Jefferson that focused on commerce. The two considered the wisdom of imposing economic tariffs and tried to convince the French and English to remove duties from American goods. At the same time, they worried about potentially dangerous entanglements with European nations. Some American products were plentiful and had the potential for significant economic profit, if only fair reciprocal trade agreements could be executed. Adams was optimistic and claimed that "Time will Shew, both them and the French, that it is better to buy our Oil and Candles and Fins [Fish], and pay for them in Buttons and Ribbons" than resort to onerous tariffs that would have a negative commercial impact on all parties.[56]

Frustrated with the lack of British cooperation, he later wrote John Quincy that it was his hope that Americans would progress in their own development of manufacturing and industry and then find markets, including France, that would serve as substitutes for British trade if the English continued to prove obstructive.[57] Abigail viewed the impasse as driven by the competitive quest for national power. The following year, she caustically summed up the roadblocks the Americans faced in negotiations with Europe's two leading countries: "The French as a Nation do not wish our Prosperity more than the English, only as they have sense enough to See that every indulgence stipulated to us, is a thorn in the Side of the English."[58]

As historian Jonathan R. Dull has observed, it is surprising that American leaders remained so optimistic about the attractiveness of a commercial alliance. Dull maintains that they were decidedly naïve about the importance of American trade to the leading European nations.[59] Adams had butted heads with the French foreign minister on many occasions, but he was aware that Jefferson got along well with Vergennes, so he restrained himself from interfering in the particulars of an economic treaty with France. Yet despite the concerted efforts of Adams and Jefferson, England and France would remain impervious to opening their ports to reciprocal trade agreements. The United States was able to sign liberal trade treaties with Prussia, Sweden, and the Netherlands, but those three small countries offered only a limited potential market for American products.[60] Another minor diplomatic success occurred in early January of the following year, when Adams finalized a modest treaty of friendship and peace with Morocco, and the prospect of a similar treaty with Portugal appeared on the horizon in the spring.

While John worked on negotiations, the Adams family kept busy entertaining regularly. When he formally met with diplomats at home, following the custom of the day, the Adams women were sometimes excluded and often spent those evenings visiting other female acquaintances. Still, both Abigail and Nabby enjoyed many dinners in Grosvenor Square, for London hostesses were expected to serve as both social and political facilitators. Indeed, participating in dinners propelled by "overt or covert purposes" was commonplace among British women whose families were involved in politics.[61]

Abigail and Nabby often resented the superior attitude displayed by some of their British guests, and Abigail complained that her days and nights were dull without the congenial companions she had shared time with in Braintree. Nabby found that the French nobility had been more welcoming than the members of London's elite. At the end of one evening she recorded in her journal, "I find a greater degree of politeness and civility in America, than in the people of this country. And the lower class of people in America are infinitely superior to the lower class of people here."[62] It was just one more demonstration of the advantages of her native country.

Abigail expressed similar sentiments in a letter to her younger sister. After nearly six weeks in London, Abigail was relieved to be residing in a Protestant country where the family could resume their regular church attendance, but she remained convinced of the superiority of American manners and believed that members of the British upper class were even more mindful of their titles than French nobles were. The Adamses often went to Sunday meeting to hear the liberal theologian Dr. Richard Price preach, because he had supported American independence. Although she conceded that "in the cultivation of arts and the improvements of manufactures, they [the English] greatly excel us," in her opinion Americans demonstrated more creativity and ingenuity and enjoyed a wider dispersal of general knowledge than she witnessed among British citizens. "You can scarcely form an idea how much superior our common people, as they are termed, are to those of the same rank in this country," Abigail wrote.[63]

Still, Abigail admitted that she had interacted with some very amiable people—expatriate Americans who resided in England, such as Mrs. Copley and Mrs. West, the wives of the acclaimed artists and one of her favorites, Mrs. Rogers, who was "benevolence itself." But she declared that until the British extended a more "amicable temper" toward her family and learned to appreciate America and its inhabitants, it would be a long time, if ever, before she developed any attachment to England.[64]

Once Abigail received word of John Quincy's safe arrival in Boston, she took the opportunity to provide him with an update about American negotiations. John had been treated with dignity and respect, she wrote, but she was concerned about "the bones of contention between us [England and the United States]" that would prevent the British from accepting the "generous treaty [that] has been tendered them, upon which they are now pondering and brewing." She insisted that the future of American commerce and credit was at risk, for there were still men in the British government who focused on denying American independence and returning the nation to English control. However, she remained optimistic that America would prove its mettle through "industry, frugality, wisdom, and virtue" and succeed at becoming "a great and powerful nation if we will." She ended her missive by exhorting her eldest son to use his talents for his country's welfare and presciently predicted, "One day your country will call for your services, either in the cabinet or the field."[65]

Less than six months after John assumed his ministerial duties, he and Jefferson back in Paris remained stymied by the lack of progress with Great Britain over commercial questions. No matter how diligent the Americans' efforts, the British cabinet stubbornly refused overtures for an equitable trade treaty. In October 1785, Adams wrote Jay in frustration that he could "obtain no Answer from the Ministry to any one demand, Proposal or Inquiry."[66] The situation prompted Abigail to write caustically to Jefferson, "In this country [England] there is great want of many French commodities, Good Sense, Good Nature, Political Wisdom and benevolence."[67] Yet even John understood that the failure of the former colonies to honor parts of the peace treaty afforded the British an excuse to delay negotiations. Moreover, the weak American government under the Articles of Confederation made it challenging to provide one unified foreign policy that encompassed all the states, which caused the British to be wary.

To compensate, John tried to develop a more practical approach to European-American relations. He told Jefferson he hoped that as time passed French trade would become more robust and insisted that Americans needed to devise a method to ship products such as tobacco, oil, and candles directly to France without involving middlemen. Adams had long complained that Europeans were profiting off the backs of American labor. As the thrifty Yankee put it to his Virginia comrade, "As We [Americans] are poor We ought to be Economists: but if we were rich it would not be wise nor honourable to give away our Wealth without Consideration or Judgement."[68]

The previous month, in response to an inquiry from Mary Cranch as to whether the Adamses would remain in England for their allotted three years, Abigail was not optimistic: "Heaven only knows what may be the result of one if any probability appears of accomplishing any thing [in diplomatic negotiations]. Tis likely we may tarry. I am sure that it will be a Labour if not of Love yet of much perplexity and difficulty." Abigail lamented that one stumbling block to progress was the result of the immense debt many American merchants had run up with creditors in England, which angered the British and left the unstable American republic on the edge of bankruptcy. In an overt criticism of her fellow citizens, Abigail fretted over what she considered to be the irresponsibility of many who had not honored their debts. Looking at the bright side, however, she predicted that the British government would end up forcing Americans through necessity to become more frugal and ultimately make the United States a world power.[69]

Similarly, Abigail observed to John Quincy that her countrymen had "obtained a credit that they cannot support. They have shackld and hamperd themselves that they cannot now extricate themselves; merchants [in England] who have given credit, are now Suffering, and that naturally creates ill will, and hard words."[70] At the same time, she and

John both understood that the long eight years of the Revolutionary War had resulted in rampant inflation that had inflamed friction between states as well as among social classes, and the Adamses were sensitive to the challenges that many struggling Americans faced. Friends back in America had informed them of their straitened circumstances, including Abigail's own sister and brother-in-law Mary and Richard Cranch. Abigail's friend Mary Palmer of Pennsylvania told her, "Our taxes come very heavy upon us, Our Money is very Scarce and every one is pressing."[71]

Abigail often echoed John's concerns. He had long preached fiscal responsibility. Pressed repeatedly to seek additional Dutch loans, Adams became increasingly irritated over what he considered a deterioration in American economic integrity. He feared that it not only led to the decline of American moral standards but also fostered European distrust that made his efforts to achieve commercial agreements with Great Britain near impossible. Abigail wrote with bitterness to John Quincy that the English would "never leave us until they drive us into Power, and Greatness that will finally shake this kingdom." Nonetheless, she still predicted a great future for America if its inhabitants stayed the course and adhered to the principles that she believed had guided the American Revolution. "We must struggle hard first, and find many difficulties to encounter," she maintained, "but we may be a Great and a powerfull Nation if we will; industry and frugality, wisdom, and virtue must make us so."[72]

Despite her months in London, Abigail often felt like a social outsider and lamented what she considered the deterioration of the hospitality for which the British had formerly been famous. She maintained that the crowded rooms at ladies' parties made civility and politeness challenging. Most of her days were filled with reciprocating invitations or attending a wide variety of social events. Abigail judged English women as inferior compared to their American sisters and much too informally dressed in company. She viewed her rather cool reception in London as an opportunity to reflect upon the social differences between the two countries, which convinced her even more emphatically of the superiority of her native land. In her eyes, American women, especially New Englanders, were the personification of republicanism and refined manners. She told her sister Mary, "The American ladies are much admired here by the gentlemen, I am told, and in truth I wonder not at it. O, my country, my country! Preserve the little purity and simplicity of manners you yet possess. Believe me, they are jewels of inestimable value; the softness, peculiarly characteristic of our sex, and which is so pleasing to the gentlemen, is wholly laid aside here for the masculine attire and manner."[73]

For the Adamses, the foundation for building an ideal American character was a melding of honesty, civic and personal virtue, coupled with Protestant religious tenets and domestic harmony, values they felt were personified in New England life.[74] Like Jefferson, they venerated and sometimes idealized the centrality of family life in America, but the Adamses also regarded religion as central to their vision for the American future. When he wrote the Massachusetts constitution, John insisted that "the happiness of a people and the good order and preservation of civil government essentially depend upon piety, religion, and morality."[75]

Abigail continued to cross paths with the royal family on a number of occasions, including a visit to St. James's Palace in September 1785, to mark the anniversary of the monarchs' coronations. She deemed it a ridiculous ceremony, and she later attended another special function in the winter of 1786 with her daughter to celebrate Queen Charlotte's birthday, which included an evening ball at St. James's Palace. Abigail and Nabby went elegantly clad in colorful satin, Abigail in lustrous green and her daughter in pink trimmed with crepe and silver fringe. William and Anne Bingham, with whom they dined in Paris, were then visiting England. Anne had implored Abigail to introduce her at court, so she dutifully presented the young woman at the celebration. Mrs. Bingham's beauty and elegance made her a welcome figure in London's high society; and in addition to meeting with Queen Charlotte, Anne and her husband were invited to dine with prominent members of the upper crust like Lord Lansdowne and Lady Lucans. Anne became so popular that London shops sold picture engravings of her, which irritated both Abigail and Nabby. Still, they were proud that she had made such an impression on the British nobility, and Nabby admitted that Anne was a "fine woman."[76]

As we saw when the Adamses resided in France, Abigail and Anne were a study in contrasts, and Abigail's comments to her sister after one of Mrs. Bingham's stays in London help clarify the depth of Abigail's commitment to her homeland. Although Abigail continued to admire Anne's grace and fine manners, she lamented the endless round of European "dissipation and frivolity of amusement which has weaned her [Anne] from her Native Country; and given her a passion and thirst after all the Luxeries of Europe."[77] Anne was so enamored of the European lifestyle that she begged her husband to extend their stay abroad. Abigail repeatedly reiterated her distaste for European excess among the upper classes and increasingly longed to return home.

After the royal anniversary celebration, Abigail wrote Mary that she was exhausted after having been required to attend so many events, but she reported, "The company were very brilliant, and her Majesty was stiff with diamonds." Abigail also observed frankly that she "never expected to become a Court favorite" because she refused to adopt a subservient manner.[78] Although she disapproved, she clearly understood the social hierarchy of the English royal court, with its complex rules and calibrations of rank. More than a decade later, after Abigail became the American First Lady, she would consciously conduct herself in a different manner than the heads of state she had encountered in both Paris and London.

Nabby also reported on Queen Charlotte's birthday celebration and complained that the entryway to the afternoon drawing room had been so crowded she was sure she and her mother would be crushed. She also noted that the king and the Prince of Wales were richly dressed with silver adornments, but the queen appeared in a comparatively plain gown.

The evening ball featured intricate minuets, and the Adams party did not arrive home until well after eleven o'clock, exhausted and relieved to have the opportunity to enjoy companionable cups of tea before retiring for the night.[79]

Another day in early April, the Adamses dined at a magnificent British mansion where Jefferson, who was visiting London, and the Prussian and Venetian foreign ministers were also in attendance. Abigail, John, and Nabby returned home at eight o'clock in order to dress for yet another event. The ball, which included hundreds of guests, was held at the Hôtel de France, the beautiful residence of the French ambassador, located across from St. James's Park. Abigail praised the impressive home, which "agreeably blended the magnificence and splendor of France with the neatness and elegance of England." Because Nabby was feeling under the weather with a cold, the Adamses left "early" at 1:00 a.m., before the fashionably late supper was served.[80]

Abigail shared the details of her exhausting social calendar with another niece and again insisted that the occasions demonstrated the superiority of Americans. She maintained that despite the glitter of the assembly rooms and the diamond jewelry and the rouged faces of European women seen at many of the extravagant London events, none of the splendor matched the simple elegance of American gatherings nor the "blooming health, the sparkling eye, and modest deportment of the dear girls of my native land." She also assured Lucy Cranch that even though the Adams family members were moving in the highest circles, "do not fear that your Aunt will become dissipated or in Love with European manners, but as opportunity offers, I wish to See this European World in all its *forms*, that I can with decency." Still she moralized in disapproving tones that all she had witnessed to date had merely reflected vanity.[81] At the same time, she also lamented that many of the *Americans* living in London had lost their common sense and had fallen into the trap of luxurious living that had reduced some to penury. "Our Countrymen *owe Millions* here, . . . much of this debt . . . for mere gewGaws and triffels," she declared critically to her sister Mary.[82]

Abigail remained especially busy entertaining diplomats from many countries in an effort to aid John's negotiations. The day after the Adamses hosted a dinner for Lord Carmarthen and a group of foreign ministers, fifteen guests in all, she proudly informed Mary that London newspapers had reported the event prominently. Yet Abigail clearly found her role as wife of the American ambassador to be a challenge financially, physically, and emotionally. She complained, "Some years hence it may be a pleasure to reside here in the character of American minister; but with present salary and the present temper of the English, no one need envy the embassy." She was, however, proud that despite what she considered the jaundiced eye of the British press, "they have never insinuated a lisp against the private character of the American minister [John] nor in his public line charged him with either want of abilities, honor, or integrity." She concluded that instead, "the whole venom has been leveled against poor America," and she clearly worried about whether she would be able to "stay the course in England."[83]

As time passed, Abigail became more passionate about the entrenched class divide in Great Britain she had witnessed from her first presentation to King George III and Queen Charlotte. She recalled that she had stood in line for hours for the privilege of a mere hint of a smile from the queen and a salute from the king. That earlier encounter prompted her to reflect on yet another underlying difference between American and British citizens. She insisted that the English elite were occupied with the pursuit of enjoyment and pleasure and that they suffered from depraved manners. Moreover, she was grateful that American society did not exhibit the extreme social divides she witnessed in England. "Neither have we that servility of manners," she declared to her younger sister Elizabeth "which the distinction between nobility and citizens gives to the people of this country. We tremble not, either at the sight or name of majesty."[84] For Abigail, that was one more characteristic that distinguished Americans from Europeans.

Nor did it take long for Abigail to develop an attitude of near despair over the plight of the poor in Europe. To her niece Betsy Cranch she described the disheartening conditions she witnessed almost daily in the teeming streets of London: "Were you to be a witness to the spectacles of wretchedness and misery which these old countries exhibit, crowded with inhabitants, loaded with taxes, you would shudder at the sight. I never set my foot out, without encountering many objects. . . . Covered with disease and starving with hunger they beg." In both England and France, Abigail found that it was unremitting peasant labor that supported the high lifestyles of the nobility and aristocracy, and she lauded America, where workers met with a "liberal reward" and "the condition of our labouring poor is preferable to that of any other country." She concluded her preaching, as she put it, by advising Betsy, "Let it excite us to thankfulness, my dear girl, that our lives have fallen to us in a happier land, a land of liberty and virtue, comparatively speaking."[85]

Abigail observed that members of the English working classes often went hungry and that babies and young children were often abandoned and left homeless. She was correct that, in contrast, small landowning farmers in America made up the vast majority of citizens. The average male in the United States at the time was likely to be at least as or more wealthy than the average Englishman. Moreover, all the American states boasted representative bodies, and propertied white males could vote. Close to 80 percent of men held the franchise in the Adamses' home state of Massachusetts.

As much as Abigail came to appreciate European culture and even take some pleasure in life in England, she remained troubled by the degree of "grandeur and magnificence" that she witnessed in both Paris and London. She described European life as characterized by venality, corruption, gaming, and general debauchery and maintained that society on the Continent was "lost in ceremony and parade."[86] She contrasted the opulent culture enjoyed by the elite with the plight of the poor. "When I reflect upon the thousands who are Starving and the millions who are loaded with taxes to support this pomp and show," she observed to Mary, "I look to my happier Country with an enthusiastick warmth, and pray for the continuance of that equality of Rank and fortune which forms so large a portion of our happiness."[87]

Of course, Abigail knew that there were southern enslaved men and women who experienced a wretched existence and other people in America who lived on the edge of poverty. Following the tradition set by her mother, Elizabeth Smith, Abigail dispensed alms and helped support more than half a dozen impoverished women who lived in her Braintree neighborhood. Her generosity was typical of many people of her class in Massachusetts, and the extreme contrast between the rich and poor she saw in Europe and the high number of indigent people living there were not evident in America. Most Americans at the time owned some land and made their living through agricultural pursuits, and the majority lived in small towns or villages and raised at least enough food to feed their families. In contrast, financial institutions, manufacturing, and mining increasingly drove the English economy. America had its prominent families, but a titled ruling class did not exist. In England, on the other hand, the English aristocracy made up only about 2 percent of the population but owned about 70 percent of the land.

Though diplomacy remained stalled, one of the highlights of the Adamses' time in London was a welcome visit from Thomas Jefferson. Jefferson traveled to England from France and arrived on March 6, 1786, for what turned out to be close to a two-month stay to assist Adams with his negotiations, and he took rooms in Golden Square, the elite neighborhood that was the celebrated residence of diplomats and noblemen. The American diplomats would together make one final effort to execute a successful trade agreement with the British. Although lack of progress was disheartening, and no commercial treaty was forthcoming, Jefferson and Adams hoped to secure at least an agreement with Great Britain that would help protect American seamen as well as ships and cargo and also to sign possible treaties with Portugal and Tripoli. Soon after Adams had arrived in London, Algerian pirates captured two

American ships and forced twenty-one American sailors into slavery. The leaders of the Barbary States of North Africa, which included Algiers, Morocco, Tripoli, and Tunis, were accustomed to receiving bribes in exchange for refraining from pirate attacks on European shipping and expected the same from America now that it had separated from Great Britain.

In response to the brazen seizures, Congress authorized a sum for tribute payment, but in reality the cash-poor American nation left Adams with little available funds. Then an unusual opportunity opened up to negotiate with a Tripolitan emissary, Sidi Haji Abdrahaman, who had approached John surreptitiously. Wearing a traditional turban and sandals, the bearded ambassador had attended the queen's birthday ball and subsequently visited Adams at the Grosvenor house for two hours in mid-February. As a result of that meeting, a few days later John urged Jefferson to join him in London before the opportunity to head off an open American conflict with the Barbary States came to a head and the possibility of scoring a possible diplomatic coup with the Portuguese and Tripolitan ministers slipped through their fingers.[88]

Both Jefferson and Adams met privately with Abdrahaman, and they congenially shared strong coffee and a hookah pipe. They found the minister open to negotiations, but in the end the price the Tripolitan named on behalf of his ruler to ransom American sailors and to sign a peace treaty was outrageous, and the meeting ended in a stalemate. John confided to his brother-in-law Richard Cranch that the $80,000 Congress had allotted was far from sufficient to move forward even though he personally felt it was of critical importance to "make Peace with them" to help ensure the safety of American seamen and commerce.[89] Not until January 1787 would Adams and Jefferson be able to execute an agreement with Morocco, but in the absence of a strong American navy, they were still forced at times to pay extortionate tribute money.

On March 13, Adams had informed Britain's foreign minister, Lord Carmarthen, of Jefferson's imminent arrival and requested a meeting. After he joined Adams in London that spring, Jefferson found himself for the most part ignored by members of the nobility as well as by George III. As a result, the Virginia aristocrat took an almost instant dislike to the monarch, which only increased after he was presented to the king by Adams on March 15. The experience fueled his already negative views of the British. After he returned to Paris, Jefferson wrote bitterly to his friend John Page back in Virginia, "The nation hates us, their ministers hate us, and their king more than all other men."[90] Jefferson came to despise the entire institution of monarchy on principle far more than Adams, who believed that with a properly balanced government, a constitutional republic could thrive even with a king at the helm. Adherence to law and not the whims of individuals was what mattered most to him.[91] Therefore, Adams took a more positive view of George III, for whom he had developed a measure of respect, but he shared Jefferson's disquiet.

The two American emissaries were especially disappointed with their failure to arrive at an agreement to end the piracy on the seas that had long been appeased by European powers. Abigail laid part of the blame for the American diplomatic failures on her countrymen. After hearing another sermon by Richard Price, Abigail renewed her emphasis on public virtue, and she patriotically declared that she believed her fellow Americans "possest of a larger portion of virtue than any other Nation." Yet she cast a critical eye on Congress, which she considered ineffectual. She also worried that the American states lacked the crucial unity that would enable the country to move forward to support a federal government. Abigail believed that such a structure would help regulate commerce and earn America the respect in Europe that would result in successful treaties. Moreover, she deemed the "Tripoline Minister," as she called him, a good man, and lamented the fact that Congress had dithered over effective financial backing and legal issues that might have sealed a deal with the Barbary States and perhaps even secured commercial agreements with the British.[92]

Although Jefferson found the joint diplomatic efforts fruitless, he enjoyed the company of the Adamses as well as the opportunity to shop for fine British luxury goods. Like so many other elite Americans, Jefferson often vocally disdained European excess; nevertheless, for him, French and English accoutrements reflected refinement and sophistication. Science was his passion and lifelong avocation, so one highlight of Jefferson's stay was the purchase of high-quality British scientific instruments, which he treasured and later brought back to America. He also commissioned a portrait of himself by the up-and-coming American artist Mather Brown, who had studied under the renowned Benjamin West, King George's favored artist. Brown had opened his own London studio in 1784, and Jefferson and Adams exchanged copies of the portraits of themselves as a gesture of their mutual esteem, although both original paintings remain lost.[93]

Despite their professional setbacks, Adams and Jefferson took an enjoyable weeklong coach excursion together in April 1786, when they toured twenty magnificent formal English gardens and stately homes outside London. Although a decade later, the two statesmen would be divided by politics, at the time they were still close friends. In the fall of the previous year, Abigail wrote her sister that "in Mr. Jefferson he [John] has a firm and faithful friend with whom he can consult and advise; and, as each of them has no object but the good of his country in view, they have an unlimited confidence in each other."[94] Although Abigail did not appear to begrudge her husband's well-earned vacation, she did tell Mary that it would mark the first time since her arrival in Europe that she had been parted from John. In fact, she reflected wistfully that their time together abroad reflected the longest period they were not separated in all the years of their marriage.[95]

The American pair of ministers began their jaunt in Surrey and shared many of their traveling expenses. Their journey, which totaled about three hundred miles, began on April 4 and ranged from a visit to the site of Shakespeare's modest home to stops at the grand Blenheim Palace and some of the colleges in Oxford.[96] John found many of the blooming gardens that graced the English countryside that spring particularly beautiful. Like Abigail, however, he still regarded the European

Copy of portrait of Thomas Jefferson painted in 1786 in London by Mather Brown.
Courtesy National Portrait Gallery.

landscape as inferior to the more natural settings he had enjoyed back in America. Still, the stately homes and country seats he and Jefferson visited were most impressive, and he observed that, in particular, Stowe, Hagley, and Blenheim were superb. John wrote Abigail that he and Jefferson had seen "Magnificence, Elegance and Taste Enough to incite an inclination to see more."[97]

Yet at the same time, John looked with a jaundiced eye on the opulence he had encountered. "Architecture, Painting, Statuary Poetry are all employed in the Embellishment of these Residences of Greatness and Luxury," he observed. Still, he lamented "the British national debt of 274 millions sterling" that helped produce "all this Magnificence." He frowned upon those excesses and expressed his hope that the emphasis on grandeur would not corrupt the simpler American virtues that the Adamses so valued. "It will be long, I hope before Ridings, Parks, Pleasure Grounds, Gardens and ornamented Farms grow so much in fashion in America," he declared. In his diary, John was unable to resist pointing out what he considered the superior landscape in his native land, where "Nature has done greater Things and furnished nobler Materials there. The Oceans, Islands, Rivers, Mountains, Valleys are all laid out upon a larger Scale."[98]

Distanced from the cares of work, the two American diplomats enjoyed their interlude. On April 20, Jefferson along with the Adamses made one last visit to West London to view two grand local estates owned by prominent members of the British aristocracy. Osterley Park had been the country seat of the late Robert Child, a prominent member of the Child banking dynasty, and Sion House belonged to the Duke of Northumberland. Abigail pronounced the extensively cultivated grounds almost a "Fairy Land," and she told her younger sister Elizabeth that Jefferson and John had been charmed by the beautiful settings they had encountered on their tour. John recorded that the greenhouse at Osterley featured enticing full-blown roses, ripe strawberries, cherries, and plums. Yet his underlying disapproval of the European aristo-

Print of Ranelagh Gardens, including the Rotunda, which was visited by the Adams family while they resided in London. Courtesy Rijksmuseum.

cratic lifestyles was apparent. "The Verdure is charming, the Music of the Birds pleasant," but he noted critically that the British family estates were, on the whole, "mere Ostentations of Vanity." He took the opportunity to remark that most of the elite owners spent little time on their estates but were drawn instead to races, gambling, and other frivolous pursuits in London and that English landowners often raised tenant rents merely to finance their own high living.[99]

For Abigail, the verdant landscapes were perhaps the aspect of British life she most enjoyed. Although she too deplored excess, she found the magnificent ornamented gardens and farms on the grand estates an "Innocent and desirable object" for those who could afford them. They appealed to her aesthetic side, and she declared to her niece Elizabeth Cranch that she found them "Beautiful to the Eye, pleasing to the fancy, and improveing to the Imagination," although she admitted that along with the poet Alexander Pope she agreed that usefulness should be a fundamental moral principle in life. She too was disturbed that some of the estate owners seldom resided for long at their imposing country homes. Despite her appreciation for the gardens, she could not resist adding that she still found that nature was more sublime in America.[100]

Jefferson returned to Paris at the end of April, irritated with the lack of British cooperation. He confided in a letter to James Madison on the eve of his departure from London, "With this nation [England] nothing is done, and it is now decided that they intend to do nothing with us [America]."[101] Although Adams and Jefferson had concluded negotiations for a commercial treaty with Portugal during Jefferson's stay, a formal treaty was never ratified by either country. Nevertheless, Jefferson's trip had not been in vain because he had spent time with the Adams family, and he found their Grosvenor house to be almost a second home.

For all of John Adams's faults of occasional vanity and irritability, Jefferson left full of admiration for his old revolutionary comrade. In fact, he told Madison, "He [Adams] is so amiable . . . you will love him if ever you become acquainted with him."[102] It was a friendship that would be sorely tested in the future as each man developed a radically different vision for the future of the new republic. Jefferson and Adams would part ways in the 1790s during the period of intense partisanship in the United States. Encouraged by their mutual friend Dr. Benjamin Rush, the two men reconciled in old age, but Abigail, who had held Jefferson in such high regard, remained largely estranged from Jefferson for the rest of her life.

Despite numerous dissatisfactions abroad, one development that pleased Abigail was that in London her daughter Nabby would meet Colonel William Stephens Smith, the thirty-year-old son of a New York merchant and a graduate of Princeton University. He and Nabby were married in London on June 12, 1786, at their Grosvenor Square home. Just weeks before his daughter's London wedding, John had left for Amsterdam to try to secure yet another Dutch loan for America, and he returned barely in time for the ceremony. Nabby's parents were pleased with the match to the promising, handsome young man, then secretary to the American legation, whom they considered a genteel man of honor with an unblemished reputation. The previous year Abigail had written approvingly to her uncle Cotton Tufts that Smith seemed a sensible, judicious young man, who reflected the "dignified sentiments of his own Country," and that John was grateful to have him as an aide.[103]

Nabby, with her mother's tacit encouragement, had earlier broken off her unofficial engagement to Royall Tyler back in Massachusetts. Although Nabby likely resented the meddling of her mother and her aunt Mary Cranch, in the end she felt she had made the right decision, as time and distance had already cooled the relationship between her and Tyler. It was a step they later may have regretted. Despite his charm and intelligence, William turned out to be a disreputable man, frequently involved in questionable economic schemes and never settling on a steady profession. However, that was in the future, and at the time of their nuptials, Nabby and William were enamored of one another.

Nabby, who had always been a shy, reticent, and even uncommunicative young woman, appears to have blossomed in London. From the beginning of her residence there, she shared shrewd observations about the people and events she encountered in letters back home to her eldest brother, with whom she had developed a close relationship in Auteuil.[104] When he learned of the impending marriage, once he recovered from his surprise, John Quincy declared that he was looking forward to welcoming William as a brother.[105] Soon after the wedding ceremony, Abigail reported with great satisfaction to her sister that the young couple had been married by an English bishop, who told her that he had never encountered a couple who had exhibited "a better prospect for happiness." Abigail then expressed her heartfelt wish that heaven would grant that his words would be prophetic.[106]

After the wedding took place, Nabby and William moved to their own lodgings on Wimpole Street, not far from Grosvenor Square, but they visited almost daily with John and Abigail, who were delighted to entertain the young couple, and they welcomed William as a son. As custom dictated, the Smiths were required to present themselves at court for a blessing from the king and queen. As the Adamses' only surviving daughter, Nabby had been Abigail's close companion during

Portrait of Nabby Adams in England by Mather Brown. Courtesy National
Park Service, Adams National Historic Park.

John's many absences from home. When she left the family nest, it was
emotionally wrenching for Abigail as well as for John, who seems to
have taken every excuse to visit the newlyweds. Although perhaps in
response to her unhappy experience with Tyler, for which she may have
found her mother at least partially to blame, Nabby became even more
self-contained and taciturn than usual during her early days in France,

but the marriage to Smith appears to have healed whatever breach may have occurred between mother and daughter.

With no end to her sojourn in Europe in sight, in October 1786, Abigail wrote her younger sister to extend her deep appreciation for caring for the Adams sons in her absence. Abigail was pleased that her boys were bound for Harvard. Moreover, she told Elizabeth that she firmly believed they would greatly benefit by being educated, not in Europe, but in their native country, where they might acquire "an Inherent Love of Liberty and a thorough acquaintance with the Manners and taste of the Society and country of which" they were citizens. Again, Abigail took the opportunity to revisit one of her favorite themes—the decline of political and moral standards in Europe. She maintained that an American-educated student would "find a purity in the Government and manners, to which Europe has been long a stranger. He will find that diligence integrity Genius and Spirit, are the true Sources of Superiority, and the certain means of rising in the estimation of his fellow citizen; instead of titled Stars and Garters. Far removed be those pests of Society; those Scourges of a free Government, from our Happier land."[107] Abigail's words reflect her underlying belief in American, particularly New England, superiority and her concern that in their rush to rise as a nation, Americans might fall prey to the same ills she felt had infected European society.

Abigail continued to enjoy many of London's cultural offerings, including the opportunity to attend a number of well-acted plays, especially ones that featured the renowned English actress Sarah Siddons in such roles as Lady Macbeth and Desdemona. Despite her anti-slavery beliefs, Abigail was troubled by the interracial romance between the African Othello and a white woman.[108] Yet she remained an admirer of Siddons, who was the subject of a famous portrait painted by the famed British artist Thomas Gainsborough in the mid-1780s. By that time, Gainsborough had become a favorite of both King George III and Queen Charlotte, so Abigail and John may have viewed some of the artist's works when they visited the royal palace. The king was a passionate collector of art as well as fine china, ornately carved furniture, and elaborate clocks. Abigail, too, appreciated great art, but she especially praised the paintings of the American artist John Trumbull, who had studied in England under Benjamin West. West was known as the "painter of the Revolution," and he had rendered many romanticized works of wartime events, which elicited Abigail's approval and heightened her pride in her nation's recent history.

Abigail continued to expand her mind and educational vistas in London, not only by attending the theater and concerts at Covent Gardens, but also by subscribing to a series of scientific lectures, including talks about experiments dealing with electricity and magnetism, both innovative and much-discussed topics at the time. Abigail exhibited a keen aesthetic appreciation of music and art, but she also knew that museums and musical performances provided her with the imprimatur of civilized culture. One aspect of European society that Abigail particularly admired, and in which she felt American society was lacking, was the educational opportunities offered to women. She was delighted to meet the acclaimed British female historian Catharine Macaulay, and the science lectures provided Abigail with the opportunity to criticize sharply the lack of robust female education at home. She commented wistfully to Lucy Cranch that the exposure to scientific subjects was "like going into a Beautifull Country, which I never saw before, a Country which our American Females are not permitted to visit or inspect."[109]

Abigail also enjoyed many excursions in the English countryside and later a trip to Holland. To escape the hot weather of the summer of 1786, she and John visited Portsmouth, about seventy-five miles from London. On their return trip they stopped in Windsor, the site of a retreat for members of the royal family and the imposing Windsor Castle. The Adamses toured the richly appointed palace and expressed appreciation for its gracious rooms.[110]

There was more touring to come. In early August, Abigail and John traveled together in an unplanned visit to Holland, the site of John's greatest diplomatic success. After much foot dragging by Congress, Adams visited the Netherlands to conclude a final commercial treaty with Prussia. It was the one major European agreement that he and

Jefferson had been able to execute, and the document was signed and ratified by Adams and Baron Friedrich Wilhelm von Thulemeyer, the Prussian minister to The Hague, at the Prussian embassy in Amsterdam on August 8. During their stay, John also hoped to learn firsthand about what progress had been made in the constitutional reforms supported by the Dutch Patriots.

The Adamses embarked on August 4 from Harwich, England, about 120 miles from Helvoet, where they were greeted with a military guard and the ringing of bells in their honor. Although they sailed on a spacious, clean vessel, sea travel was always a physical challenge for Abigail, and she was confined to her bed the entire voyage. Once she recovered from the taxing eighteen-hour trip across a stormy sea that had left her miserably seasick and exhausted, Abigail toured the country with her husband by coach.[111] During their five-week excursion, the Adamses visited Rotterdam, Leyden, Amsterdam, Utrecht, and Delft. Despite some monotony in the landscape and Abigail's bouts of ill health, they enjoyed many delightful outings together. She likened the countryside to a vast meadow and was impressed by the system of canals and dykes, and the neat brick houses with well-kept kitchen gardens. On many occasions, the Adamses dined with some of John's Dutch acquaintances as well as foreign ministers, their wives, and other guests from England, Denmark, and the Netherlands.

Because of John's success in The Hague, the existence of a liberal Patriot revolutionary faction, and the fact that it was a Protestant country, Abigail was inclined to display a favorable opinion of the Dutch, whom she found an admirable people, and attribute lofty goals to their efforts. As she wrote Nabby, "If politeness and attention could render a place agreeable, I have had more reason to be pleased with this country [Holland] than any other I have visited. . . . These people appear to think of the past, the present, and the future. . . . They are establishing wise institutions, and forming the minds and manners of their youth, that they may transmit to posterity those rights and liberties which they are sensible have suffered infringements."[112]

The cleanliness of the towns, the modest dress of the inhabitants, and the friendliness of the common Dutch people aligned with Abigail's exacting standards. She told Mary that she had a high regard for the Dutch, who had supported the American cause through generous loans. She also stressed their common love of liberty, which she felt made the two countries compatible. Obliquely, she referred to the political challenges that still lay ahead for Holland when she remarked, "The Spirit of liberty still appears to be alive in them; but whether they will be able to accomplish their views, without a scene of blood and carnage, is very doubtful."[113] Abigail later lamented to John Quincy that Prussian troops had thrust Holland into a humiliating condition, which threatened the freedom of the Dutch people, and revolutionary political strife was visible in full force in the 1780s. In 1787 Prussia invaded Holland to avenge an alleged insult to the Princess of Orange. Abigail claimed that the Prussians were supported by the British, who in her opinion fomented "the troubles in Holland, and seized the first opportunity in her power, to bully [its rival] France."[114]

When the Adamses returned to London after an even more harrowing passage back through a raging storm, to his disappointment John found that there had been no thawing in the relations with England, and any further progress seemed unlikely. Still, he felt he had done his duty. The longer he remained in Europe, the more he became convinced that the future lay in America. He wrote in his diary, "It is an Observation of one of the profoundest Inquirers into Human Affairs, that a Revolution of Government, successfully conducted and completed, is the strongest Proof that can be given, by a People of their Virtue and good Sense." Adams was of course referring to the American Revolution, and for all their faults, he viewed his fellow Americans as able, principled people in comparison to Europeans.[115]

Abigail's travels only served to sustain her belief in the American promise. In Abigail's eyes, even the American climate and terrain were superior to those of France, England, and Holland. Nothing in the Old World could compare to the natural unspoiled beauty at home. Abigail asserted that "nature shows herself in a style of greater magnificence and sublimity in America, than in any part of Europe I have yet seen; everything is upon a grander scale."[116] Abigail even maintained that European birds did not sing as sweetly as those found in America, "Nor is their [European] fruit half so sweet, nor their flowers half so fragrant, nor their manners half so pure, nor people half so virtuous." Realizing that she had perhaps crossed into hyperbole, Abigail cautioned her sister Elizabeth to "keep this to yourself, or I shall be thought more than half deficient in understanding and taste." Perhaps Abigail's dour mood was sparked by her gloomy surroundings for, as she noted, London in November was shrouded in typical winter smoke, fog, and darkness.[117]

Although Abigail found much to disdain in Europe, she knew that conditions were often challenging in America as well. The fragile economy and shortage of hard currency had adversely affected farmers, who were often in debt, which fueled the antagonisms between creditors and debtors. To some degree, Abigail appreciated their frustrations, for she had contended with similar devastating inflation and shortages when she managed the Adams farm during the war. Still, when Captain Daniel Shays, a former Revolutionary War hero, fomented an agrarian rebellion against authorities in Massachusetts in 1786 to protest high taxes levied by the legislature, tight money, and resulting foreclosures, Abigail looked upon the incident with trepidation and viewed requests for printing paper money critically.

The insurrection, seen by some as a clash between the elite and the common people, was short-lived. Chased down by a militia, Shays's group disbanded after a final fight in Sheffield, Massachusetts, at the end of February 1787, and Shays fled to Vermont. Relatives at home kept John and Abigail abreast of national issues as well as local politics in Massachusetts and painted a dark picture of public unrest. Some of the Adamses' correspondents believed that the rebellion had inspired many citizens to support unregulated popular government.[118]

Letters from Mercy Warren may have prompted Abigail's unease. Mrs. Warren had received an uncommon classical education for a female of her era, and she became a fervent patriot and respected writer, a woman whom John Adams once described as "the most accomplished Lady in America." Although they could not vote or hold office, Abigail and Mercy became knowledgeable about politics and were considered what at the time was termed "female politicians." Both had fervently supported separation from Great Britain, and Mercy's husband, James, had applauded her literary efforts and political involvement. Yet, as part of an older generation, the Warrens remained uncompromising supporters of classical republicanism, which eventually played a role in the rupture of their friendship with the Adamses.[119]

Mercy wrote John often while he was abroad, and at the time, the two shared political outlooks. Starting in the late 1770s, she lamented what she saw as a decline in the American virtue seen during the years leading up to the revolution, something both John and Abigail had decried as well. Mercy particularly criticized the conspicuous increase in luxury consumption and displays of wealth. She also viewed with alarm the disruption of the pre-war class hierarchy, which had made the Warrens respected members of a select group of old American elite families. The Warrens now faced a painful decline in their fortunes and status, and anxiety made them critical of new state governments. Although they were sympathetic to the situation that had provoked Shays's Rebellion, they rejected the insurgents' methods.[120]

Based on the information she had received from America, Abigail shared her fears with Jefferson and told him that she considered the protests a threat to American stability and the men involved "mobish insurgents." Moreover, she laid some of the underlying blame for the tense situation on her countrymen, many of whom she claimed had imported too many expensive goods, mere "trumpery," from England. She believed that instead of paying back European loans, they had unwisely saddled themselves with more debt in their deplorable quest for "Luxery and extravagance in both furniture and dress," and she lamented that "vanity was becoming a more powerfull principle than patriotism."[121] Like John, Abigail feared that some Americans were placing personal aggrandizement and hunger for status over the public good.

John, who had always feared the possibility that democratic excess could lead to chaos, shared Abigail's discomfort over the Shays affair, and he took it as a warning sign that Americans may have lost their ability to live peaceably under the rule of popular government guided by the state constitution he had authored. Moreover, he was concerned about the deterioration of what he considered American fiscal ethics. Adams had long decried the push for issuing paper money over gold and silver as irresponsible. In July 1786 he confided his opinion to Cotton Tufts, who was managing the Adamses' affairs back in Massachusetts. "Our country is grown, or at least has been dishonest," John declared. "She has broke her Faith with Nations, and with her own Citizens. . . . She must become Strictly honest and punctual to all the World before she can recover the Confidence of any body at home or abroad." Realizing he had perhaps been overly critical, he continued, "This Censure is too harsh I suppose, for common Ears, but the Essence of these Sentiments must be adopted throughout America, before we can prosper. Have our People forgotten every Principle of Public and Private Credit?"[122]

Shays's Rebellion worried the Adamses, but Jefferson regarded it more tolerantly. After news of the incident reached him in France, he wrote to Abigail, "I like a little rebellion now and then. It is like a storm in the Atmosphere" that was "valuable on certain occasions."[123] According to historian Brian Steele, Jefferson did not support the uprising out of a sense that rebellion for its own sake was desirable. Rather, the rebellion reflected his belief in the special American character. For Jefferson, their unique identity was what allowed Americans to object when tyranny threatened and the government ignored the collective will. The insurrection was short-lived, and some of the irate farmers' demands were addressed, which Jefferson claimed demonstrated how expeditiously Americans were capable of righting the ship and returning to order and political stability. In other words, Jefferson always maintained that his main goal for American governance was to align the political state with the will of the nation as derived from the people. For Jefferson, Shays reflected an admirable "spirit of resistance," which in the light of his belief that Americans were better informed and independent than their European counterparts, demonstrated that they were admirably vigilant against tyranny. He maintained that the dissension had been relatively orderly and was soon extinguished when it was opposed by the majority of "the people."[124]

Perhaps in response to Jefferson's influence, Abigail moderated her initial views about the uprising. She told Mary Cranch that she was upset that Shays had escaped the authorities and still had the potential to stir up future rebellion, but she also expressed her hope that "every rational & reasonable redress of grievances will be granted" in order to restore stability and community confidence in the government.[125] Two months later, she wrote to her younger sister Elizabeth about her hope that the seditious feelings that Shays had encouraged would soon be quelled and that her home state set on a peaceful course. She also shared her increasing frustration and concern over what she viewed as the lack of stable authority in America. "As to our public affairs, they make me sick," she confided frankly to Elizabeth. "Having weathered the storms of War, I had hoped peace would have been confirmed to us the Blessings we had dearly Earned, but this rather proved the wish of Benevolence, than an investigation into the Character of Humane Nature—an unprincipled mob is the worst of all Tyrannies. Wisdom to our Rulers and unanimity to our patriots, and virtue to all our fellow citizens, will remedy the Present Tumults."[126] For Abigail, public insurrections smacked of frightening anarchy despite her earlier fervent support of the American Revolution.

More momentous in Jefferson's view than Shays's Rebellion was the critical 1787 debate about the future of the American government taking place in Philadelphia, which would result in the new Constitution. He believed that it had the potential to create the most enlightened republic in the world. Indeed, according to Steele, "Jefferson's confidence in the American experiment began with Shays."[127] Historian Pauline Maier has pointed out that Americans had a long history of public insurrections launched in order to address public welfare needs, and that compared to Europe such uprisings in America were almost uniformly bloodless and short-lived. Moreover, many American leaders maintained that occasional disorders such as Shays's were a positive feature in a free government, as they reflected the will of citizens to preserve liberty. True, the insurgents in Massachusetts forced the closing of civil courts, but only until a new legislature could address their pressing needs.[128]

Other Americans whom John and Abigail trusted, such as John Jay, even viewed insurrections like Shays's as bringing injustices to light and prompting necessary reforms. Jay wrote that it was important to attack the underlying causes that had led to the uprising. Moreover, he observed that the participants were relatively restrained compared to mobs in England, and they did not commit "any outrages but such as the accomplishment of their Purpose made necessary."[129] As time passed, Abigail internalized a measure of that outlook and acknowledged that the Shayites had some legitimate grievances. In March, after the revolt had been controlled, she told a relative in language similar to Jefferson's, "Ebullitions of this kind will break out in all free governments, like humours in a Healthy Body."[130]

Later in the year, Abigail's thoughts turned from politics to her own troubling physical ills. Soon after Nabby's wedding, Abigail sickened with one of the vague but serious illnesses that surfaced intermittently during her life. Though she first believed that it was her old nemesis, rheumatism, Abigail's English physician instead diagnosed a stomach complaint. In late December her physician sent her to the famous resort of Bath, where people gathered from throughout Europe to take advantage of the therapeutic mineral waters thought to cure a wide variety of ills.

In the company of a group of American friends, Abigail spent a fortnight there in "amusement and dissipation." She attended a round of balls, parties, concerts, and plays. Although Abigail found some of the entertainments enjoyable, she declared that she had little personal taste for the "fashionable Life."[131] The visit may have provided some beneficial placebo effects, but she was troubled by the lifestyle of the elite visitors, who in her opinion appeared to favor social position and wealth over character, which offended her moral sensibilities.[132]

Within less than a year after their marriage, the Smiths made John and Abigail proud grandparents. In early April 1787 Nabby gave birth to a baby boy, whom his parents named William Steuben Smith. After the birth, the Smiths moved from their lodgings in Wimpole Street into the Grosvenor Square house with Nabby's parents, where they remained until they departed for their new home in New York City near William's family in 1788. Just weeks after the baby's birth, Smith was dispatched on a four-month diplomatic mission to Portugal, so living at Grosvenor Square with her parents provided Nabby with congenial company and a helping hand with her new baby.

In May, while William was away, John set out for Amsterdam on yet another emergency effort to seek additional credit in order to pay off interest on a previous Dutch loan. John successfully negotiated that third loan from Dutch bankers, and as he noted with much satisfaction in a letter to Abigail, "I have accomplished the Business I came upon, and have this Day signed the Contract for a Million of Guilders at five Per Cent." John was apparently as enamored of their grandchild as Abigail, for he instructed her to send his love to Nabby and especially give a "Kiss for my Grand Boy."[133]

During the summer, the Adamses decided to take an extended excursion outside London to escape the summer heat and to benefit Abigail's health. Nabby's husband was not due back in England until September, so in July Abigail and John, along with Nabby, little William, and three servants, set out for a tour of western England. Their trip, which covered about five hundred miles, began at Winchester. Late in the summer, Abigail and the family visited the seaport town of Southampton, renowned as a bathing resort. It was there that Abigail "for the first time in my life . . . tried the [outdoor swimming] experiment." She found the experience delightful and wrote Mary that she wished similar "conveniences" could be introduced on the Massachusetts coast. She described a secluded bathing area designated for ladies, supervised by a local woman. When visitors arrived, the matron led them to a small dressing room, where women could don an "oil-cloth cap, a flannel gown, and socks for the feet" in preparation for bathing.[134]

By the time they returned to London, the Adams party had visited several British towns, including Devonshire, Oxford, and Exeter, where they met with members of Richard Cranch's family. The vast grounds of Blenheim Palace in Woodstock, the seat of the Duke of Marlborough, made a deep impression on Abigail. She told her niece Lucy that the duke's "castle," gifted to the family by the crown in appreciation for exemplary service, was the "Grandest scale of any thing I have ever seen." The Adamses entered the park though an elegant Corinthian portal that opened to a magnificent vista of the palace, the surrounding valley, and a bridge spanning a lake. The artwork at Blenheim, which was the only palace in England that was occupied by non-royals, included a painting of the current duke, duchess, and their children by the famed artist Joshua Reynolds, and the library boasted 24,000 volumes.[135]

When she was younger, Abigail had complained about the virtually nonexistent opportunities for women to travel as widely and unfettered as men did. In Europe, Abigail's world expanded, and she was exposed to other cultures and different political models. In both Paris and London, she encountered life in the very powerful royal courts and moved in the highest aristocratic circles. Abigail had the opportunity to view the monarchical form of government firsthand and to compare it to the nascent American republic; she found the European model decidedly lacking.

The more she traveled outside London into the countryside, the more apparent were the disparities between England and America. In the fall of 1787 Abigail shared her increasingly strong opinions with her sister Mary as she lauded American society. "How little cause of complaint have the inhabitants of the united States," she declared, "when they compare their Situation, not with despotic monarchies, but with this Land of Freedom? The ease which honest industry may acquire property in America the equal distribution of justice, to the poor as well as the rich, and the personal Liberty they enjoy, all call upon them to support their Governments and Laws, to respect their rulers and gratefully acknowledge their Superior Blessings."[136]

In language similar to her remarks to Mary, but more nuanced, Abigail described to her younger sister Elizabeth her view of the key elements in American society, which she felt made it politically and socially superior to France and England. After returning from her excursion in Devonshire, she told Elizabeth that although the area was like a beautiful garden, she could not report the same about the condition of its inhabitants. "One part of the people, the Noble, and the wealthy, fare sumptuously," she reported, but "poverty, hunger and Nakedness is the Lot, and portion of the needy peasantry," whose hard labor cultivated the land.[137] She understood that the class divide was indeed deep. Abigail was a keen social observer who was able to look below the surface of the bucolic English countryside, which featured miles of open fields and farms, and confront the harsh realities that faced the impoverished, who were barely able to eke out an existence.

"When I reflect upon the advantages which the people possess in America," Abigail continued to Elizabeth, "the ease with which property is obtained, the plenty which is so equally distributed, the personal liberty and security of life and property I feel grateful to heaven who marked out my Lot in that Happy Land." Yet, despite praise of her homeland, she shared her unease with her younger sister about the quest for power fueled by ambition and a "restless Spirit" she feared might set America on the same path as England.[138]

Although they would remain in England until the spring of 1788, both John and Abigail were already looking forward to the close of their European journey and their return to America. Both Adamses had become accustomed to living in London, but perhaps felt they had become *too* comfortable. In the meantime, as their stay dragged on, Abigail continued sharing her critical opinions of the Old World in her correspondence with relatives and friends back home, perhaps as much to convince herself as the recipients of her letters of the superior life that beckoned in her homeland.

FIVE

The Final Years Abroad

John and Abigail Return to America

I am not at home in this Country [England].
John Adams to Thomas Jefferson, March 1, 1787

But whatever is to be the fate of our Country, we have deter-
mined to come home and share it with you.
Abigail Adams to Mary Smith Cranch,
February 25, 1787

I think we shall return to our country at a very important
period. . . . May Wisdom govern her [America's] counsels
and justice direct her operations.
Abigail Adams to John Quincy Adams,
March 23, 1788

B Y THE SPRING OF 1786, THE ADAMSES HAD BECOME
increasingly restless living in England, and despite John's concerted efforts, they were resigned to the lack of American diplomatic
progress. To make matters worse, according to Abigail since the joint
commission of American ministers expired in May, nothing could be
finalized until the new key players were put into place. In strict confidence she shared with her sister Mary details of the many impenetrable
obstacles that had confronted John in Europe, and she noted with pal-
pable frustration that "whoever has any thing to do with courts, must
have patience."[1] By that time, the Adamses viewed the main thrust of
British policy to be the economic subjugation of America. Normalized

trade with the British would not occur until the 1796 Jay Treaty under President Washington's administration, and that agreement was controversial as the British were at war with the French, who were angry that the Americans whom they had supported during the revolution would make a deal with their enemy.

It was Abigail's fervent hope that she would be able to return to America the following spring, but that would not occur until 1788. She complained bitterly, "There is no office more undesirable than that of Minister of the United States; under the present embarrassments, there is no reputation to be acquired, and there is much to lose." She placed some of the blame on the weak American government and called for unity: "Negotiations with other powers may be and have been effected; but with England there is not the least probability of a treaty, until the States are united in their measures, and invest Congress with full powers for the regulation of powers."[2] Jefferson later echoed Abigail's sentiments when he sympathized with John's desire to leave England. "I do not wonder at your being tired out by the conduct of the court you are at," he commiserated with Adams. Yet at the same time, he urged him to redouble his efforts in Holland and to build on his previous achievements with the Dutch.[3]

Residing in Europe for so many years had broadened the worldviews of both John and Abigail but at the same time had made them even more American in outlook. As historian Edith Gelles has observed, for Abigail especially, her "already passionate patriotism was inflated by her observations, and conditions in England and France reaffirmed her social consciousness and her politics."[4] During her travels through England Abigail had the opportunity to view with a critical eye the deep fissures between the aristocracy and the working classes in British society. The stark inequality struck Abigail as one more characteristic of British life that distinguished the new American nation from its former mother country. "Thus is the landed property of this country vested in lordships and in the hands of the rich altogether," she lamented. "The peasantry are but slaves to the lord, notwithstanding the

Engraving of Abigail Adams from an original painting by Gilbert Stuart. Courtesy Library of Congress.

mighty boast they make of liberty. Sixpence and seven pence per day is the usual wages given to laborers, who are to feed themselves out of the pittance."[5] Abigail was not exaggerating. The English aristocracy, only about 2 percent of the overall population, held the vast majority of land. Members of the laboring classes received meager wages that made it near impossible to support a family.

Abigail's reflections offer us a firsthand account of the plight of the poor, even in the lush English countryside where one would have thought conditions would have been superior to the squalid, teeming, poverty-stricken neighborhoods of the urban centers. "In traveling through a country [England], fertile as the garden of Eden," she observed, "loaded with a golden harvest, and plenty smiling on every side, one would imagine that the voice of Poverty was rarely heard, and that she was seldom seen, but in the abodes of indolence or vice. But it is far otherwise."[6] Moreover, members of the working class, middling British citizens, and even some of the gentry were loaded down with taxes.

According to Abigail, the interiors of the modest homes of the working class were in a pitiful state: "The money earned by the sweat of the brow must go to feed the pampered lord and fatten the greedy bishop, while the miserable, shattered thatched-roof cottage crumbles to the dust for want of repair. To hundreds and hundreds of these abodes have I been a witness in my late journey. The cheering rays of the sun are totally excluded, unless they find admittance through the decayed roof, equally exposed to cold and the inclement season." She sadly concluded, "A few rags for a bed and a joint-stool comprise the chief of their furniture, whilst their own appearance is more wretched than one can well conceive."[7]

Abigail was clearly shocked at the severe poverty she witnessed in England. She decried the plight of poor farm workers who populated the less settled areas along small villages and hamlets: "During the season of hay and harvest, men, women, and children are to be seen laboring in the fields; but, as this is a very small part of the year, the little they then acquire is soon expended; and how they keep soul and body together the remainder of the year is very hard to tell." In her judgment, "It must be owing to this very unequal distribution of property, that the poor-rate is become such an intolerable burden. The inhabitants are very thinly scattered through the country, though large towns are well peopled. To reside in and near London, and to judge of the country from what one sees here would be forming a very erroneous opinion."[8]

The largest urban centers in America, such as New York, Philadelphia, and Boston, held only a fraction of the populations that crowded the European cities of Paris and London. Abigail found conditions for the working classes in England, whether in the countryside or in its cities, appalling, although London and it surrounding areas had in fact become healthier by the 1780s. The death rate had been significantly reduced due to reforms, including better sanitation and the revision of the poor laws, which had to some degree improved the lot of many of the impoverished.[9] But Abigail was correct in her observation that these modest steps still left much to be desired, and challenges for British workers were much more visible compared to their counterparts in America. Certainly, Boston was far healthier than London. The New England diet, which included generous portions of protein-rich cod and beans, even for the masses, was more nourishing than the food choices available for English laborers, and the overall sound environment in Boston translated into lower child mortality when compared to London.

The British lifestyle only made John and Abigail long to return to their Braintree home and reunite with their neighbors and family members. They especially missed their sons. They had not seen their two younger boys for several years, and now John Quincy and Charles were of an age when they were contemplating their future careers. And while she was abroad, Abigail had lost several close family members to illness and old age, including two beloved elderly aunts, an uncle, and her brother William Smith, who died in middle age of complications due to alcoholism.

The Adams sons were at the time all students at Harvard. John and Abigail were grateful that the Cranches and Shaws had lavished so much love and attention on their offspring, but they knew they had been absent at pivotal times in their lives. Abigail regretted that they would miss the graduation of their Cranch nephews and John Quincy, particularly as he was chosen to give an oration because of his outstanding level of scholarship. Harvard commencements had been celebrated for years at Cambridge with grand festivities, which included feasting, drinking, and uncharacteristic revelry, and the Cranches and Adamses were expected to participate actively. In Abigail's absence, Mary and Richard Cranch hosted about a hundred dinner guests as well as another several hundred who came later to enjoy an array of elaborate desserts to mark the occasion.

Unsurprisingly, and despite some apparent nervousness, John Quincy carried out his presentation with his typical high level of competence. The stress of studying and preparing for his oration had an ill effect on his health, however, and Abigail wrote to admonish him because she believed that his physical complaints stemmed from "too close application" to his studies. She provided her son with directions for home remedies to settle his stomach and calm his nerves, but the commencement ceremonies went forward without a hitch.[10] Indeed, after Cotton Tufts praised John Quincy's talk, Abigail echoed the sentiments of mothers and fathers throughout the ages when she wrote her uncle that "there is no musick sweeter in the Ears of parents, than the well earned praises of their children."[11]

To Charles, who was inclined toward the practice of law, John advised that if he conducted his profession with integrity, he would surely succeed. Only half in jest, John told Charles that he hoped he would experience fewer interruptions from public duties than his father had. John Quincy was also training as a lawyer, and Adams reiterated the need to focus on the virtues of honor, humility, and modesty above all and not to allow himself to compromise his principles or be influenced by the demands of business and commerce.[12] John Quincy hoped to apprentice under two Massachusetts judges, but his father, who longed to renew his close relationship with his eldest son, offered to supervise him after John returned to Braintree as he hoped in 1788.[13] Abigail echoed John's beliefs about integrity and public service, but was more concerned that John Quincy was damaging his health and neglecting the social enjoyments of the world by focusing so single-mindedly on his studies.[14]

In January 1787 John informed the Massachusetts delegates in Congress, "To be explicit I am determined to come home." In early February, he wrote John Jay that he wished to leave Europe the following year and declared morosely, "A life so useless to the public, and so insipid to myself, as mine is in Europe has become a burden to me, as well as to my countrymen."[15] Jay would have empathized with Adams's sentiments, as he shared many of his colleague's views about the deficiencies of European life. Near the end of his diplomatic posting in Spain, Jay wrote a friend, "My eyes and affections are constantly turned towards America, and I think I shall return to it with as much real and cordial satisfaction as ever an exiled Israelite felt on returning to his land of promise."[16] Adams was even more forceful about his desire to return to America when he declared to Cotton Tufts, "I am determined not to remain an Hour in Europe after the Expiration of my Commission to the Court."[17]

Despite his plan to depart England and his pessimism about his diplomatic mission, John was successful in securing yet another Dutch loan when he visited Amsterdam in the late spring of 1787. In a letter to Jefferson, John put the object of his excursion to Holland bluntly. "It was to procure Money, and I had the good fortune to obtain as much as was necessary for the then present Purpose," he declared with satisfaction.[18] Adams had undertaken the mission, in part, to help pay off part of the lingering American debt to France, and since he had moved forward without express orders from Congress, he was worried that the necessary American ratification of the loan would not proceed as speedily as the situation demanded.

Earlier in March, Abigail informed her younger sister that she and John hoped to see their immediate family within a year as "we are *determined* to return to America and share the fate of our Country whether she stand firm like mount Atlass—or make it treason to harbor an Idea that she will fail."[19] John and Abigail remained cautiously optimistic about the American future, and Abigail advised Mary that Americans should take heart and remain confident because their country was blessed with robust natural resources and that "patience perseverence industery will accomplish great things."[20] Still, Abigail had become increasingly impatient with British leaders, and in her usual forthright manner fumed to her uncle Isaac Smith about the futility of John's diplomacy, since "England has wholly forgotten that such a place as America even exists."[21]

Although John had already given notice and submitted his formal resignation to Congress at the beginning of 1787, his request did not receive approval until later in the year, when Congress officially recalled Adams from his diplomatic mission. By March, John had set his sights even more firmly on his return to America. He had Abigail's full support, and she lamented what she viewed as the increasing alienation between America and England. She was determined never to return abroad. She wrote emphatically to John Quincy, "The day is fast approaching when we have determined to quit it [England]. God willing I once Set my foot on American ground not all the embassies to Europe consolidated into one shall tempt me again to quit it."[22] Yet in the meantime Abigail took advantage of her access to fine European goods and continued to make additional purchases for family members. She sent generous gifts of clothing, material for sewing gowns, and even the newest type of oil lamp to her sisters and their children in New England.

As soon as Jefferson heard that the Adamses planned to return to America, he expressed his deep regret. "I learn with real pain the resolution you have taken of quitting Europe. Your presence on this side the Atlantic gave me a confidence that if any difficulties should arise within my department, I should always have one to advise with on whose counsels I could rely. I shall now feel bewidowed," he declared dramatically to John. "I do not wonder at your being tired out by the conduct of the court you are at. But is there not room to do a great deal of good for us in Holland in the department of money? No one can do it as well as yourself. But you have taken your resolution I am sure on mature consideration, and I have nothing to offer you but my regrets."[23]

Adams replied firmly that he had arrived at his decision after deep deliberation. In the light of British implacability, he felt that the honor and dignity of Congress as well as his own honor were at stake. Moreover, a prolonged residence in Holland, where he had experienced the most serious illness of his life, might again prove injurious to his heath. Still, the decision provoked considerable anxiety, as John was uncertain of both his reception once he returned to America and what role, if any, he would play in the new government. Somewhat disingenuously, he declared that his preference would be to retire to his own "turnip yard" for the rest of his life. Regardless of the negative aspects of his time abroad, John assured Jefferson that one of his few regrets about leaving Europe was the interruption of their friendship, "which was one of the most agreeable Events in my Life."[24]

Despite John's professed uncertainty about his political future, his daughter, Nabby, was convinced that her father had an important role to play in America. Rumors were already circulating that Adams would be asked to become vice president in the administration of the popular and internationally recognized George Washington, who was the universal choice for president of the newly minted United States. "It is in his [my father's] Power to do His Country essential Service," Nabby wrote to John Quincy, not long before her parents set off for America. "He has it *I believe* in his Power to do as much perhaps *the most* towards establishing her Character as a respectable Nation—of any Man in America," and she astutely concluded that John would never "be Happy in Private Life."[25]

Part of John's discomfort during his last years in Europe was the result of his evolving political vision. Even though he was frustrated by his diplomatic overtures to British policy makers, John's political ideas had moved steadily from his earlier hopeful vision about American republicanism to an even greater appreciation of Britain's mixed government. It was an outlook that he had first developed as far back as the 1750s. He understood the considerable influence the American Revolution had upon European nations and knew that the American rebellion had set off almost a chain reaction on the other side of the Atlantic toward support for popular sovereignty. He therefore took a keen interest in discussions among his contemporaries in France, Holland, and England regarding constitutional reforms, and was a participant in a broader international political and intellectual debate.

John's time in France and his underlying political outlook influenced him to side with moderate, conservative French reformers, known as the Anglomanes, who were proponents of the English model of government. Adams rejected the arguments of the radical reformers, led by former French controller-general Anne Robert Jacques Turgot and the intellectual aristocrat Marquis Nicolas de Condorcet, whom he considered naïve about the realities of human nature. John adhered to a more classical brand of republicanism and took a moderate stance on the ideals of the Enlightenment. He believed that the social and political equality espoused by the disciples of the Radical Enlightenment was an unrealistic goal, no matter how attractive the notion. For Adams, people were *not created equal*, but they all deserved to be *treated equally* by their government in justice and opportunity.[26]

Indeed, Adams insisted that the power of an elite oligarchy, whether based on wealth, intelligence, family distinction, or even attractiveness, would persist even in a modern, more democratic republic like America. It was a fundamental source of his growing distance from leading Americans like Jefferson, who believed that the influence of elites would dissipate after monarchies dissolved and were replaced by a meritocracy. Adams dismissed as mere utopian fantasy the notion that by throwing off British rule and corrupt European influence a pure American character would emerge that would lead to an enlightened society and virtuous self-government.

Of course, Adams hoped that men of real merit would emerge as political leaders, but he believed that the unchecked veneration of celebrity would make that a rare occurrence. Throughout his adult life, Adams remained a practical political scientist and moral psychologist, preoccupied with the fear of oligarchic power and the threat it posed to American liberty. Contrary to what his critics charged, John was never an advocate for monarchy or an aristocracy, and indeed, his moral vision, influenced to a significant degree by Scottish Enlightenment philosophers, was offended by the notion of unequal treatment and the curtailment of freedom.[27]

A complex combination of factors, including John's lack of diplomatic success in England and the potential upheaval in America threatened by Shays's Rebellion in his home state of Massachusetts, likely influenced

Adams to turn his attention back to the unfolding political events across the Atlantic and the upcoming national Constitutional Convention in Philadelphia. He also worried about the very apparent weaknesses of the American government under the Articles of Confederation, as well as the successive failed revolutions in Holland and the growing instability of the French regime. Abigail gave the most weight to Shays's Rebellion and claimed in a letter to John Quincy, "The seditions in Massachusetts induced your Papa to give to the World a book," which he had first intended to share only with friends.[28]

Relatives back in America had voiced their concerns about what appeared to be increasing unrest, resistance to taxation, and feeble state governments, which had alarmed Abigail and John. In the fall of 1786, for example, Mary Cranch, whose husband, Richard, had not been paid for several years for carrying out his public government duties, wrote Abigail that "the excess of Liberty which the constitution [of Massachusetts] gave the People has ruind'd them."[29] Just the following month, Cotton Tufts chimed in with his fears about the instability of the weak confederation government and political life in Massachusetts, where a dangerous "rebellious spirit" had been kindled in some of the western counties.[30] Despite the fraught situation, Abigail remained optimistic that "common sense and plain reason" would be exhibited by a majority of Americans and that through wise firmness order and harmony would be restored.[31] When the situation finally appeared under control, Abigail reiterated that she hoped that clear measures would be taken to avoid "every tendency to future Rebellion," and she advocated that all legitimate and reasonable grievances be addressed to restore public confidence in local government.[32]

John's proposed solution to America's ills came in the form of a blueprint for sound future government, which he revealed in his multivolume book of political philosophy, *A Defence of the Constitutions of Government of the United States of America*, authored in the late 1780s. To achieve his goal of a well-ordered society, he supported a balanced government that required a separation of powers among what he perceived to be the monarchic, aristocratic, and democratic segments of the state. The first hint of the project came in a letter from Abigail to her uncle Cotton Tufts. She confided that John was so deeply occupied in writing a publication about government, which she compared to Plato's work on the subject, that he had little time for correspondence, so she was stepping into the breach.[33] Tufts would later oversee the distribution of copies of the book to family friends, and he sent a supply to a book vendor in Boston. To John Quincy, Abigail wrote, "Your Father is much engaged in a work that may prove of no Small utility to our Country." She summed up the thesis succinctly as "an investigation into the different Forms of Government, both ancient and modern, Monarchical, Aristocratical Democratical and Republican, pointing out that their happiness or misery in proportion to their different balances."[34]

Concern for the stability of American government was very much on the minds of many in the wake of Shays's Rebellion, and both John and Abigail had taken the news of the uprising in America seriously. Some of their correspondents echoed John Jay's concern about the turbulence and reported that fear of anarchy had led many Americans to question the capability of republicanism to maintain order and security.[35] Abigail had given much deep thought to the fraught situation during the rebellion in her home state and was proud of John's efforts to provide sound advice to his countrymen. When Abigail again journeyed to Bath for a visit in December 1786, she told John that she understood his decision to remain behind in London to devote himself to the important subject of "building up Republicks, and establishing Governments."[36]

The following month Abigail wrote her older sister that she was still much concerned about the uprising in Massachusetts, but she was also hopeful that it would influence citizens throughout the country to redouble their efforts to pass wise laws and strengthen their federal as well as local governments. To that end, she again praised John's book project as an aid to help Americans understand "the dangerous consequences of unbalanced power." On an optimistic note, she concluded that if Americans followed a virtuous path, "we have the means of being the freest and the happiest people upon the Globe."[37]

In January 1787, John paid for the publication of the first volume of his seminal *Defence*, followed by the second volume in September and a third in 1788. A coda, a series of essays titled *Discourses on Davila*, was published between April 1790 and April 1791 in the *Gazette of the United States*, a Federalist newspaper. Ostensibly, John's book, which he regarded as a work of empirical political science, was written in response to Turgot's advocacy of a single assembly government in France, a plan he feared might be adopted in America and which he believed would lead only to tyranny as well as the rise of an oligarchy. As far back as the American Revolution, Adams had decried the notion of a single-house legislature. It is important to note, however, that Adams's *Defence* began as a series of letters to his son-in-law, William Stephens Smith, in an effort to educate the younger generation and pass along the accumulated wisdom of the ages for what John considered the best practices for creating the most effective form of government. For Adams, a balanced republic was the ideal model.

Adams believed that studying history and building on tradition rather than destroying it was the key to the improvement of society. In other words, the *Defence* was intended to be a practical handbook for constructing the unfolding American republican experiment based on Adams's examination of past republics. He also hoped to convince leaders in France, Holland, and Ireland that a unicameral legislature was a prescription for failure and a path that would encourage civil war.[38] As time went on, Adams and Franklin, who supported Pennsylvania's unmixed constitution and the French philosophes' push for a single-body government in France, disagreed on the subject. To some degree, both Franklin and Jefferson may have fallen under the influence of the Radical Enlightenment. This disagreement was one factor in their fraught relationship.[39] John also likely believed that the *Defence* could serve as an effective vehicle to thrust him back into an active political conversation with his fellow Americans from whom he had been separated physically for nearly a decade. Adams was one of the deepest political thinkers of his era, judged by one scholar as "America's finest eighteenth-century student of the political sciences."[40]

The ponderous work, written in haste and at times disorganized, was timely, as copies of the first volume had been rushed to America, and its arrival overlapped with secret debates at the constitutional gathering. It was a distillation of many of Adams's long-held views, but his time in Europe had reinforced his thinking and strengthened his belief in a balanced government that included a very strong executive. John's brother-in-law Richard Cranch assured him that the *Defence* was "eagerly read by Gentlemen of all the learned Professions here. It came to America at a very critical Moment just before the Meeting of the grand Convention at Philadelphia. . . . Many . . . gave it as their Opinion that you have supported your System of the Balance in a most masterly manner."[41]

Copies of the book were printed in New York and Philadelphia, and although in retrospect it appears that the publication may have had only minimal influence on the unfolding structure of the American government, it did receive initial praise and was widely read. The *Defence* boasted several well-known supporters in America, including the ardent patriot Dr. Benjamin Rush and former secretary of war Henry Knox, as well as the president of Harvard Joseph Willard. Influenced, in part, by the writings of French moderate reformer Jean Louis de Lolme, who authored *The Constitution of England*, John was probably *the* most vocal American advocate of his time for a mixed government, although many of his contemporaries shared a similar outlook. He maintained that robust checks and balances between three distinct divisions of government, the executive, legislative, and judicial branches, were necessary to keep human ambition and passions under control and ensure liberty for even the common man, not only the influential elite. Adams had long admired what he viewed as that desirable balance in the English government, which he felt displayed a proper division of power between the executive (in the case of Britain, a monarch), the democratic element of common citizens (the House of Commons), and the aristocracy (the House of Lords).

With little practical diplomatic work open to him, John took the time to read even more widely during his last years in England. His political thought was based on a broad amalgam of classical, Enlightenment, and Christian sources, which included the works of Plato, Aristotle, Cicero, Machiavelli, Montesquieu, Jean-Jacques Rousseau, John Locke, Thomas Hobbes, and James Harrington, among other great thinkers over the span of history. Adams envisioned a new era, but one that drew heavily upon age-old European republican traditions.

Beyond a simple debate over the question of whether a unicameral or bicameral government was the best form of government, Adams and his contemporaries approached the discussion from two diverging forms of reasoning and methodology. Adams employed an inductive mode incorporating the scientific methods of Newton and Bacon, while his opponents, including Condorcet, favored a deductive method. French radical reformers viewed Adams's reasoning and his argument as a threat to their political ideals and worked to discredit his book. It was a clash between two opposing belief systems for constructing the best form of government, and the political and intellectual dissonance played a part in the deterioration of the relationship between Adams and Jefferson, who soon allied himself with the more radical French *philosophes*.[42]

Adams incorporated elements of progressive Enlightenment thought in his worldview, but unlike Jefferson, he generally viewed the *philosophes* and their disciples as mistaken in regard to the fundamentals of human nature. He remained skeptical of their view of a continuous improvement of human behavior over the centuries. He and Jefferson differed sharply on the latter's assumption that human nature could be uplifted over time and that social conflict would eventually disappear as an enlightened society progressed. While he believed in the efficacy of widespread education and access to cultural opportunities, Adams never adhered to the outlook of many liberals, Jefferson prominent among them, that exposure to the "civilized" arts and higher learning would serve as a great equalizer of men from all rungs of society.[43]

In this vein, Adams later dismissed the English political theorist Mary Wollstonecraft's book on the French Revolution as naïve and unrealistic. She believed that despite all the terrors of the French upheaval, it reflected a positive and overarching civilizing process. Like other radical reformers of her time, she felt that inequality was the result of the backward and repressive authoritarian forms of government that existed in Europe, especially France. According to this view, the *ancien régime*, with its corrupt hierarchy, was what had led to radicalism; but over time the French moral character would automatically improve, an argument that Adams saw as foolish utopianism. Moreover, he maintained that it was simply ingrained in human nature to admire the rich and influential, which only increased their power. Eliminating formal orders of rank and estate would only be temporary, and these would then reappear in different forms.[44] In other words, powerful social and economic elites would always remain even if aristocratic titles were eradicated.

In his *magnum opus*, John outlined his fundamentally conservative views about human nature and politics and presented his ideal vision of three distinct, separate branches of government based upon his study of past republics in human history. Classical political thought theorized three "pure" forms of government: monarchy (rule by "one" leader), aristocracy (rule by an elite group composed of the "few"), and democracy (rule by the "many"). In his opinion, earlier republics had collapsed because they were improperly constructed and failed to take the realities of human nature into proper consideration. Adams put particular emphasis on a strong executive (the one), who could help preserve widespread liberty and stability by counteracting the dangers of an aristocracy (the few). The latter he feared would descend into an undesirable oligarchy composed of elite members who would wield too much influence and put their own selfish interests above the public good. Even James Madison and Alexander Hamilton, later his political adversaries, agreed with Adams that mere public-spiritedness would not override self-interest.

Adams believed that a powerful executive could effectively offset the pitfalls of a simple democracy, rule by "the many," as he put it. In fact, he proposed that American senators should form some sort of elected aristocracy and that their influence could then safely be limited and confined through the creation of an honorific branch of government. In other words, the "one" would be essential to keep both "the few" and "the many" in check. Adams believed that power would ideally be shared between the three pure divisions of government proposed through classical political thought.[45]

John's concern about the need to control the darker aspects of human nature was not new. As early as 1777, he had written Abigail that "this Passion for Superiority" was ingrained in all humans, including men and women, young and old, the rich and poor, and black as well as white people.[46] In John's prophetic but unpopular view, the balanced government proposed under the United States Constitution could serve to mitigate but never entirely erase the inherent natural social divisions and inequalities in American society, including in the economic realm, where inequality was inevitable. For Adams, the primary purpose of government was to regulate and control those ever-present factors in life to ensure wider access to God-given liberty and opportunity for *all* its citizens, not just one segment of the population.[47]

In Adams's view, the grand American experiment in self-government, if carefully executed, would serve as a model for other nations, for he maintained that "the balance of powers in society is the best guardian of the laws that protect liberty."[48] He believed that America could demonstrate the soundest, albeit imperfect, approach to creating a viable and stable republic. Adams pointed out in the *Defence* that "education, as well as religion, aristocracy, as well as democracy and monarchy, all singly, are totally inadequate to restraining the passions of men of preserving a steady government, and protecting the lives, liberties, and properties of the people."[49]

John regarded his view of human nature as *realistic* rather than pessimistic. He believed that the only way to prevent the abuse of power was to install robust safeguards to counteract the relentless and inevitable forces of self-interest. Indeed, historian Joseph J. Ellis maintained that Adams, despite his blind spots and some significant errors in his thinking, was "the supreme political realist of the revolutionary generation."[50] As his underlying theme, John famously maintained in the *Defence* that "power must be opposed to power, and interest to interest."[51]

Adams had already made a similar point to Jefferson earlier in 1787 after he observed the contemporary situation in Europe. He insisted that neither philosophy, religion, wisdom, nor even self-interest would ever hold sway over nations or factions. "Nothing but Force and Power and Strength," he maintained, "can restrain them." In addition, Adams worried that the republican cause that he and Jefferson had labored for might be "thrown away in the next generation" if Americans abandoned the standards of virtue that had reigned before and during the early days of the War for Independence. He fretted that "Riches Grandeur and Power will have the same effect upon American as it has on European minds."[52] In other words, the virtuous ideals of the revolutionary era might not survive intact as the American nation grew and developed into a large republican enterprise. Unlike Jefferson, Adams did not subscribe to a theory of American exceptionalism and instead believed that all humans operated from the perspective of self-interest and were ruled by their emotions and passions.

Adams was especially concerned about the threat of "aristocrats"—by which he meant anyone with superior talents, from those who possessed wealth, exceptional intellect, beauty, physical power, to the well-born with elevated family connections—who through the admiration they engendered could hold undue influence regarding political or social power. At the same time, he was concerned about giving too much power to the common people, since he viewed unrestrained democracy as a fertile breeding ground for chaos. In some ways, John was influenced by the thinking of the conservative British philosopher and political theorist Edmund Burke, who believed in the necessity of connecting personal virtue with public manners and the importance of religion and the upholding of tradition in bringing stability and morality to society. Adams and Burke diverged, however, in matters that reflected the contrasting social orders in their respective nations.[53]

In John's eyes, social inequalities would always endure, as would jockeying by competing interests to achieve distinction. But all three seats of power in a properly constructed republic, kept in balance by skillful leaders, would help ensure a stable, free government. It was Adams's firm belief that any government that rested all its power in one institution only (a unicameral legislature), even if it was made up of representatives of its people, would result in tyranny and civil disorder. It has been suggested that Adams served as an exemplar in his day of "conservative republicanism," one who staunchly believed in the connection between ordered liberty, justice, and the rule of law but who, at the same time, was committed to the principles of natural rights and equal access to opportunity.[54]

Adams appreciated the considerable advantages America had to offer in its abundance of land and natural resources, but he neither viewed Americans as exceptional nor believed as Jefferson did that their "unique history and environment produced a unique [American] character capable of unique political practices."[55] In his own country, at the close of the revolution, Adams had already witnessed personal greed and the quest for wealth and power begin to erode the republican ideals that he cherished and that he believed had been so widespread among his countrymen at the beginning of the struggle. He even worried prophetically about the rise of a financial aristocracy composed of bankers and investors that would wield disproportionate influence. To counteract this, he cautioned, "Orders of men, watching and balancing each other are the only security."[56] Certainly, Adams's concern still resonates with us today.

At the end of the *Defence*, John concluded with a resounding emphasis on virtue as the underpinning of good government, but noted that it did not come about "naturally" among Americans, as Jefferson suggested. Brian Steele argues that Jefferson described American nationhood as the natural "embodiment of popular aspirations." For Jefferson, American values clashed with "unnatural" European hierarchical structures, which he believed degraded the lives of its citizens and prevented Old World nations from having the ability to create the type of enlightened society he believed had developed in America.[57] Adams disagreed and instead asserted that "Happiness, whether in despotisms or democracy, whether in slavery or liberty, can never be found without virtue. The best republics will be virtuous, and have been so; but we may hazard a conjecture, that the virtues have been the effect of the well ordered constitution, rather than the cause."[58] These were strong pronouncements, and Adams himself realized that his *Defence* was too frank and controversial to be readily accepted by many of his fellow Americans, who were likely uncomfortable with some of the views he had long espoused. In the spring of 1787 he told Jefferson that the *Defence* "is an hazardous enterprise, and will be an unpopular work in America for a long time."[59]

In other words, Adams did not support the more common liberal view that emerged in the early nineteenth century among American leaders like Jefferson. Instead, he felt that public-spiritedness would be the result of a well-defined and carefully designed constitution rather than the other way around. John had absorbed some of the fundamental elements of the Whig creed, particularly its emphasis on the connection between duty, prudence, and an orderly government. It was an outlook that defended the rights associated with property, religious toleration, and due process of law. However, he also believed in the value of cultivating an "aristocracy" of virtuous leaders who could be molded to work on behalf of the public interest.

As Joseph J. Ellis suggested, the key elements that Adams believed should define the new American republic were balance, control, and public responsibility, not the ideals of freedom, equality, democracy, and individualism that characterized much of contemporary liberal American thought.[60] John would later point to the French Revolution as an example of what level of chaos, terror, and ultimate disorder and despotism could be unleashed when the desired balance was disrupted by a quest for the unrestrained rule of "the people." He maintained until the end of his life that his viewpoint had been vindicated by historical events. In 1790 Adams wrote ruefully to his cousin Samuel Adams as he viewed the ongoing French Revolution, "Everything will be pulled down, [but] what will be built up?"[61] John venerated the study of history as a guide for the present and most of all respected prudence and moderation.

With her keen understanding of political theory, Abigail had read the early draft of the *Defence* and provided constructive criticism. Like John, Abigail believed that both law and religion were fundamental to the success of a nation. In the spring of 1786 she wrote her niece Lucy Cranch that "human nature is much the same in all Countries, but it is the Government the Laws and Religion, which forms the Character of a Nation." Abigail's words reveal that she and John were often of one mind. She also agreed with John that republican virtues were being eroded in America and that the main threat to their country was an increasingly influential aristocracy of wealth, which threatened to turn the republican experiment into an oligarchy. She noted to Lucy that "where ever Luxuery abounds, there you will find corruption and degeneracy of manners," and she feared that Americans would be no exception if they did not restrain their growing excess.[62]

This was not a new notion for Abigail either. Back in July 1780, when John was overseas on his earlier diplomatic mission and the war was not going well for the Americans, Abigail wrote hopefully that the situation would improve as "America [will] give Proof of her Virtue when distressed." However, at the same time, she warned that public standards were already on the decline. Abigail shared with John her opinion about the capabilities of several politicians running for office in Massachusetts that summer. She believed that the more capable candidate, whom she had campaigned for and supported, would lose to his more popular, charismatic opponent, the well-known John Hancock. Abigail detested Hancock, whom she viewed as a charlatan and a man lacking in integrity. But she correctly predicted that he would be voted into office by citizens who were influenced by the power he had amassed through his wealth and position. Abigail looked askance at those misguided men who voted for Hancock. She described such voters as "Lovers of the tinkeling cymbal,"[63] or what we would today regard as fans of charismatic individuals with a talent for self-promotion and publicity.

Although Abigail supported the publication of the *Defence*, she understood that John's ideas might prove controversial, particularly his unflinching support for a powerful executive, whom some might view as possessing almost royal authority. She wrote John Quincy, "I tell him they will think in America that he is for sitting up for a King." Still, she told her son that his father insisted that he was only suggesting that state governors be given the same authority as a British monarch in order to maintain the desirable balance of power among the government branches.[64] Abigail's prediction turned out to be correct. John would later be taken to task, especially by Jeffersonians, who incorrectly believed that his intention was to institute monarchy in the fledgling American government and thereby repudiate the guiding principles of the American Revolution. Moreover, many Americans did not venerate the British constitution in the same way Adams did. After the *Defence* had "met with great Applause" and gone through several editions in America, Tufts reported caustically that some of John's detractors insisted that Adams had planned for one of the British princes to "take the Throne in America."[65]

Perhaps the most wounding criticisms of John's political outlook in the *Defence* came from his respected female friend Mercy Warren, and the Virginia politician and Jefferson's protégé John Taylor. In her lengthy, three-volume *History of the Rise, Progress, and Termination of the American Revolution, Interspersed with Biographical, Political and Moral Observations*, published in 1807, Warren asserted that under the influence of John's residence in Europe he had developed an admiration for monarchy due to his life "near the splendor of courts and courtiers." Moreover, she charged that he had undergone "a lapse from former republican principles."[66]

Hurt and incensed, John challenged what he viewed as Mrs. Warren's unfounded accusation in a series of harsh letters and criticized her lack of skill as a historian. Adams had always yearned for distinction, and he believed that Mercy had not sufficiently appreciated his many contributions to the American cause. Yet she stood her ground, insisting in a letter to him that "the pure principles of republicanism were contaminated in your breast."[67] The breach between the Adamses and the Warrens had already appeared before the publication of Mercy's book, when James Warren had dropped out of politics at Mercy's insistence. It was an action that the Adamses had regarded as a lapse in public responsibility. The two families also disagreed vehemently about the Constitution, with the Warrens standing firm as "old Republicans," who opposed a federated republic because they feared it would decrease individual liberty and states' rights and strengthen the national government at the people's expense.[68] Both the Adamses would view a strong federal government as a path to secure America's future and thus would support the Constitution.

In a lengthy tome published two decades after the appearance of the *Defence*, John Taylor also took Adams to task, this time for proposing an outmoded political model for government, one that Taylor insisted was an irrelevant anachronism in the new America, a free nation where, he claimed, social equality ruled. Taylor maintained that the new nation had come about as a logical result of the American Revolution, the principles of which Adams had abandoned. Unsurprisingly, Adams bristled at what he deemed an inaccurate distortion of his *Defence*, one that was based on a political view that was divorced from reality and naïve at best.[69]

However, Warren's and Taylor's searing criticisms were still in the future. At the time John was at work on the *Defence*, despite her reservations, Abigail clearly believed that her husband's monograph had the potential to provide wise and much-needed guidance for the American political experiment. She noted to her sister Mary that change or alterations in governments such as the one that was occurring in America required examination by "skillful artists," counting John among that select group. It was her hope that "the Defence of the American Constitutions is a work which may, perhaps contribute to this end, and I most sincerely wish it may do the good intended."[70] As her husband's most loyal booster, she never tired of bringing up how much he had sacrificed on behalf of his country. Once again, she praised John's diplomatic efforts in Europe. She maintained to her uncle Cotton Tufts, "I believe that History will scarcely find an instance of a person who have held the distinguishd offices that he has been employd in for ten years past, borrowed and transmitted such sums of money as he has, & received so little advantage from it."[71]

Although Abigail was proud of John's erudition, she also feared that his dedication to his writing project, which involved isolating himself in his Grosvenor Square study and working long into the night by candlelight, would ruin his health. She felt that her husband had already sacrificed more than should be expected from one individual on behalf of his country, but John was adamant that he would finish his book. She told Elizabeth proudly that John's *Defence* had initially met with a favorable reception locally, and even a number of Scottish citizens, who had often been critical of the American cause, had said "Handsome things of it" in their reviews.[72] Yet by June, when John was away in Amsterdam, she reported that the British *Monthly Review* had "made open war upon the Defence . . . [and] torn it all to pieces." She and John even suspected incorrectly that one of his political adversaries, the former American diplomat Silas Deane, whom he had replaced in France, had written the critical review.[73]

Abigail later fretted to her sister that she feared that her husband's well-being and future would be affected by the publication. She confided, "I tell him he will ruin himself in Publishing his Books, he says they are for the Benefit of his Country, and he allways expected to be ruined in her service. . . . He has Served the publick Years enough to have been at his ease the remainder of his Life, if half the assiduity had been employd in his private affairs."[74] Abigail could not resist again pointing out that in her opinion John had been paid poorly for his government services and his devotion to his country had resulted in the neglect of the Adams family's own finances.

Despite Abigail's assertions to the contrary, from the beginning the book found many critics, particularly among a group of radical French revolutionaries. It may have also served as the first significant crack in the formerly warm relationship between Adams and Jefferson. Jefferson, with whom John had shared an early copy, first praised the work, telling John that he hoped to arrange for a French translation. In a letter to Adams, Jefferson declared that the *Defence* "will do great good in America. Its learning and its good sense will I hope make an institute for our politicians, old as well as young."[75] However, Jefferson, the eternal optimist, would soon join John's detractors, who mistakenly considered Adams a political reactionary. They claimed that he supported a political elite aristocracy, ignored the will of "the people," and had abandoned his revolutionary principles. John recognized that his *Defence* might mistakenly lead some to think he had rejected his commitment to the American cause. Years later, Adams told Jefferson that from the first moment, "I knew I should give offence to many, if not all, of my best friends in America."[76]

As historian Joyce Appleby demonstrated, initially Jefferson had likely only read the *Defence* on a cursory level. As political unrest in France simmered in 1787, a group of Jefferson's French friends, led by the philosophe the Marquis de Condorcet, worked to suppress Adams's book. Its conservative political ideas posed a threat to their call for radical reform, particularly in regard to the eradication of special privileges of the Church and aristocracy and to their hope of establishing a liberal constitutional monarchy. Condorcet and his followers were opposed to Adams's promotion of mixed government and the program offered by more moderate reformers, who looked to England's form of government as a model. The more radical faction called for the French translation of Adams's book to be suppressed, a move of which Jefferson was likely aware. Appleby maintained that before Jefferson read the *Defence* in depth he had believed that he and Adams shared a fundamental political outlook, but that as time went on it became clear the two men were traveling on divergent philosophical paths.[77]

Recent scholars have maintained that Jefferson's political thought evolved significantly while he resided in France. Therefore, Jefferson and his French intellectual circle found the *Defence* out of sync with their brand of more radical Enlightenment progressive ideals. Adams and Jefferson came to reflect two competing visions about the correct methodology and systems with which to approach the study of politics and how best to frame the Constitution. Their disagreements mirrored the wider cultural, political, and ideological divides that would shape the worldview of thought leaders on both sides of the late eighteenth-century Atlantic.[78] As Adams put it with his usual wry wit thirty years after his publication of the *Defence*, his tract was "misunderstood, misrepresented, and abused, more than any other [book], except the Bible."[79]

The mixed reaction to John's work made the Adamses even more eager to return home. Abigail continued to bristle at any overt criticisms of her husband and aspersions directed at his political motivations. In early November 1787 she reiterated to Tufts that her husband's desire was to "retire to Braintree as a private man." She fumed that John would never compromise his principles for popularity, even if it meant that "he should forfeit by it the highest offices [the presidency or vice presidency] of the united states." She maintained that John would never become a tool of any country or political party as was alleged by his enemies. Abigail concluded despondently that if his "fourteen years unremitted attention to the Service of his Country" had not made that clear to his fellow citizens, there was nothing that could be done to convince Americans otherwise.[80]

Like her husband, after nearly two years' residence in England Abigail became increasingly critical of London society and despaired about the future of Europe. She told Mercy Warren that she had made only "some few acquaintances [in England] whom I esteem, and shall leave with regret; but the customs and manners of a metropolis are unfriendly to that social intercourse which I have ever been accustomed to [at home]." Members of the nobility and gentry she had encountered in London appeared to be focused primarily on the pursuit of wealth and pleasure. She was even more bitter about leaders of the British government and declared that "all virtue is exposed to sale, as to principle, where is it to be found, either in the present administration or its opposition?" She pointed to the heir apparent to the throne as a prime example of the low standards of morality that now permeated the royal court. Prince George Augustus Frederick, the eldest son of George III and Charlotte, pursued a luxurious and dissipated life, later becoming George IV upon the death of his father.[81]

Still, there were moments of great happiness while Abigail resided in Europe. One of the highlights of her stay in London had been the birth of her first grandchild, the son born to Nabby and William Smith that spring in 1787. Abigail doted on the "fine" boy and wrote proudly of his development to her sisters back home. Yet her delight in becoming a grandparent could not dispel her underlying feeling of isolation in London and her growing antipathy toward the royal court and upper-class society. She confided to Mercy Warren that she longed to return to her humble Braintree home and to be released from her obligation to visit St. James's Palace, where she was received with only cool civility.[82]

In the late spring, John was forced to interrupt his work on the *Defence*. He made an emergency trip to the Netherlands to negotiate yet another American loan to help pay off a high-interest debt. In the interim, Abigail and Nabby entertained several local acquaintances, but Abigail felt adrift without her husband. John was successful in securing the funds, yet while he was in Amsterdam, he witnessed violent riots that spelled the demise of the liberal Patriot party, and the dissension fueled Adams's concern about the prospect of a peaceful Europe.

Abigail too was fearful that soon England and France would be at odds over the dangerous situation in Holland or that some other smoldering European tension would ignite and America might find itself unwillingly drawn into the conflict. Jefferson had informed Abigail that the government of France was already crumbling and that Louis XVI and Marie-Antoinette were increasingly unpopular. Abigail wrote John Quincy, "In the general flame, which threatens Europe, I hope and pray our own country may have wisdom sufficient to keep herself out of the fire."[83] Abigail would later view with horror the terror unleashed by the French Revolution and lament the execution of the young queen, whom she believed was maligned unfairly in the press even after her death.[84]

That March, Abigail was again in Bath for her health, but her appetite for news of developments in America continued. She wrote John, who had remained behind in London, and informed him excitedly that a letter had arrived from her son-in-law, William Smith. Abigail told John that Smith's missive had conveyed the welcome information that "seven States [including their own state of Massachusetts] had accepted the Constitution," which had been under debate. She reported that William had been informed that they "may consider the constitution as accepted, and beginning to operate at the commencement of another year." The Adams correspondence demonstrates that the constitutional debates were of great importance to Americans who were living overseas. With high hopes for the future of the United States, Abigail observed to John, "I think we shall return to our country at a very important period. . . . May Wisdom govern her [America's] counsels and justice direct her operations."[85]

In a letter to John Jay written in the previous year, John had questioned whether his public service would be most effective in Europe or in America, but he too was anxious to return home, where he believed he could do more good. He had witnessed chaos and diplomatic machinations abroad that he felt were inherent in European politics, and he feared that America could soon be caught in the crosshairs of the winds of war as England and France vied for dominance.[86] Even before the Constitution was formally adopted, Adams wrote Jay that "the United States of America, therefore, has never more Reason to be upon their Guard: to compleat their Constitution of Government: to unite as one Man to meet with Courage and Constancy, the severe Tryal, which in all probability they will be called to undergo in a few years."[87]

His time in Europe convinced Adams that the former colonies, united only in a "league of friendship" by the Articles of Confederation, represented a shadow of a national government. Now the states needed to coalesce quickly into a single sovereign nation. In the fierce debate between the Federalists and the Antifederalists, who believed that the proposed Constitution would undermine both individual and states' rights and overturn the ideals of the American Revolution, John and Abigail came down firmly on the side of the Federalists. Only a strong central government, with the power to levy taxes and support an army, would be an effective factor in securing American interests abroad. Just a few years earlier John had expressed his hope that the deterioration of civilization that he believed had infested Europe due to creeping luxury and vice could be halted by the example of a sound American govern-ment.[88] The Adamses remained optimistic about America's future if its institutions were set on the right path.

"The Public Mind cannot be occupied about a nobler object than the proposed Plan of Government," John insisted. He wrote Jay approvingly, "It appears to be admirably calculated to cement all America in Affec-tion and Interest in one great Nation." Adams came to believe that only unity between the states would enable the United States to achieve re-spect abroad and take its rightful place in the world. Adams appreciated that accommodation and compromise in the Constitution would still be necessary and that not all of his personal preferences would necessarily be met. But the proposed document, with all its faults, contained the essential principles he considered necessary to establish "Order, Liberty, and Safety." He concluded, "I confess I hope to hear of its adoption by all states."[89] In January 1788, John informed Tufts that he was "for ac-cepting the present Plan as it is and trying the Experiment, at a future Time Amendments may be made."[90] In fact, the preamble regarding protection for American citizens against unreasonable searches and sei-zures that Adams had included in the 1779 Massachusetts Constitution later formed the basis for Madison's Fourth Amendment to the national Constitution.

Long focused on the centrality of commerce, Adams appreciated that the Constitution provided the ability for the federal government to negotiate trade agreements on behalf of *all* the states. He insisted that Americans *must* form a unified strong government in order for the nation to reach its economic potential. John correctly predicted that America would soon be courted by all the powers in Europe, including England and France, and he counseled that the wisest path would be to remain studiously neutral and forge no military alliances.[91]

For the most part, the Constitution reflected John's underlying vision of a balanced tripartite government, with the appropriate checks and balances, although he still believed that the executive should possess absolute veto power. Still, with its guidelines for building a *national* government, it represented the best opportunity to address American weaknesses as the country rapidly matured. Adams understood that building unity was not an easy task. Many years later he maintained that the colonies had developed along such different lines, from their disparate state constitutions to a variety of religious affiliations, national origins, and "customs, manners, and habits . . . [that] to unite them in the same principles in theory and the same system of action, was certainly a very difficult enterprise."[92] John and Abigail viewed New England society and governance as a model for the rest of the nation, but they knew that competing local cultures would require the development of a national culture and identity that would be able to transcend state borders.[93]

How to create a *united* nation would preoccupy American leaders for decades, but now Adams was focused on the creation of a proper form of government. Like many of his contemporaries, he believed that, properly designed, the Constitution could thwart the exercise of tyrannical power within any one branch and preserve the balance of competing interests, but the devil was in the details. Adams believed that it held the promise of restoring the high level of civic and moral virtue that he believed had prevailed in the 1770s, when the American nation was in its infancy. With his focus on the guarantee of individual liberty, however, John almost immediately saw the need for an accompanying

Bill of Rights. At the same time, Adams told John Jay that he was eager to see the American states unified into one "great nation."[94] When the Constitution was formally signed on September 17, 1787, it served as the critical step that transformed the thirteen autonomous American states into a single united nation.

As the Adamses were poised to leave Europe in early February, Jefferson expressed his regret at Abigail's imminent departure and wished her a pleasant, safe voyage. He begged her not to forget that "you have one here [Jefferson] who is with the most sincere esteem & attachment . . . your most obedient and humble servant," reflecting the close friendship they had developed in Europe. Abigail assured Jefferson that she would continue to write to him from America, and she thanked him for the many kindnesses he had extended to her family.[95] In another missive, Abigail reiterated her strong desire to return to Braintree, and only half in jest she asserted, "Retiring to our own little Farm feeding my poultry & and improveing my Garden has more charms for my fancy, than residing at the Court of Saint James's where I seldom meet with Characters So innofensive as my hens & chickings."[96]

Before they departed, the Adamses took leave of the English court, and they said their goodbyes to other foreign ministers and their wives. Granted a final audience with the British monarch, John made a formal farewell call on George III on February 20. The two men parted amicably, but with only a vague promise on the king's part in which he stated that if America honored the peace treaty between the two countries, the British would do the same. In late February Adams traveled to The Hague, braving another round of treacherous winter seas, to bid a formal farewell to the Stadtholder and the States General. By the time he left Amsterdam in March, he had also managed to secure one more loan for the United States with the assistance of Jefferson, who had joined him in Holland, and the two American emissaries lodged at the same hotel. That loan helped repay the nation's debt and stabilize the finances of the new, fragile American government for the next two years while its leaders worked to strengthen the economy.

The Adamses, along with their two American servants, left London by coach for Portsmouth on March 30, 1788, and then traveled to the Isle of Wight to board ship. They first took rooms in the Fountain Hotel in Portsmouth and toured the local sites while they waited for the ship's departure. Before a week was out, Abigail had exhausted the books and sewing tasks she had brought with her to pass the time.[97] After numerous weather-related delays, John and Abigail finally left for America, weeks after they had expected to depart. They sailed from Portsmouth Harbor on April 20, 1788, on the merchant ship *Lucretia*, captained by John Callahan of Boston. Once they departed England, their voyage was anything but smooth, as their arrival home was delayed until June by strong squalls. On the other days, the seas were becalmed with insufficient winds. Fortunately, Abigail suffered less seasickness on the return voyage, but she spent many draining days and sleepless nights, including when her servant Esther Briesler delivered a tiny, fragile baby girl, who according to Abigail miraculously survived.[98] Abigail found this return voyage far easier than the trip that had brought her to Europe. Perhaps having John at her side and knowing what to expect about ship travel had made her less anxious about sailing, and her joy over returning home may have banished her ills.

As they set sail, both John and Abigail looked forward to a peaceful resumption of their domestic life in Massachusetts and to experience once again what they perceived as the distinct advantages of their own country. Their daughter, Nabby, her husband, and their young son had already departed for their new home in New York City. Abigail hoped to be reunited with them soon in the United States, for she had grown happily accustomed to having the Smith family by her side.

John and Abigail also carried with them a wealth of memories and life-changing experiences. Although their European residence had provided them with untold cultural experiences and the opportunity to benefit their homeland, John and Abigail were eager to return to the New World. They had struggled abroad with engaging fully in an unfamiliar world of unprecedented privilege at the royal courts while at the same time their New England roots and moral compass pointed them toward a far more modest lifestyle. Their official duties had worn them down, and both longed for a respite from public life.

They were not yet aware how soon they would be called upon to play a prominent role in the young nation's development, although John undoubtedly hoped to reactivate his political career after his return. In many ways, Abigail's European experiences had prepared her for her own endeavors on behalf of her beloved country and served as an apprenticeship for her role as the future second First Lady of the United States, where she would help establish her own "republican court."[99] When she left England in 1788, she was a mature woman of forty-three, while John, now in his early fifties, had entered solid middle age.

When John and Abigail arrived in Boston Harbor on June 17, 1788, nearly two and a half long months after departing from London, to Abigail's gratification, John was greeted as an American hero by several thousand citizens. They were both feted at a public reception, and the *Massachusetts Centinel* reported that "the bells in the several churches rang during the remainder of the day—and every one testified that approbation of the eminent services his Excellency had rendered his country, in a manner becoming freemen, federalists, and men alive to the sensations of gratitude."[100] John's pride must have been elevated by his welcome, and his political star appeared visibly fixed on the horizon. In less than a year, in March 1789, Adams would be elected the first vice president of the United States and he would continue to make politics the centerpiece of his life. Abigail, who had become part of a political family from the earliest days of her marriage and was a formidable political presence in her own right, continued as his main sounding board and source of unconditional support.

Their residence in Europe had left both John and Abigail with a new veneer of sophistication and culture. Although they had both viewed the opulence and grandeur of the French and English courts with disdain, they learned to appreciate some of the finer things in life. They had visited grand museums and historical sites and attended numerous edifying lectures, outstanding operas, and dramatic performances. Despite many concerns about the pitfalls of luxury, when they returned to America, John and Abigail brought with them fine furnishings, including delicate English china and wallpaper, and impressive decorative French and solid Dutch furniture for their new country gentleman's home in Braintree. The new estate would provide them with a residence more fitting for a family of their elevated social status.

John was particularly fond of a superbly crafted desk he had acquired in Paris, on which he composed many of his lively letters and the *Defence*. He also sent home crates of books that he had collected during his European sojourn. Their purchases demonstrate that objects have social and political as well as material value, and the Adamses' new possessions reflected their rising elite social status. The Borland estate did not compare to the grander houses they had occupied in Auteuil or London, and it required a good deal of repair and remodeling. Abigail had made recommendations from afar, including dictating the choice of colors of paint and wallpaper patterns; she even chose the types of her favorite flowers to be cultivated on the grounds. Over time, however, Stonyfield, or Peacefield as it was nicknamed, became a comfortable, spacious home with a lovely garden, and a significant step up from their old farm homestead.[101]

During their time in Paris and London, both John and Abigail Adams had stood face to face with the heads of Europe, observed European society firsthand, and had the opportunity and leisure to converse about political and broader philosophical topics with some of the best minds of the era. However, neither ever felt fully integrated or at home in European society, even in England, despite the obvious and still robust cultural ties between American and British citizens. To her friend Mercy Warren she had once written, "I do not feel myself at all captivated with the manners or politics of Europe. I think our own country much the happiest spot upon the globe, much as it needs reforming and amending. I should think it still happier, if the inclination was more wanting than the ability, to vie with the Luxeries and extravagance of Europe."[102]

All that the Adamses had encountered in the Old World polished their political and cultural sensibilities, but left them more convinced than ever of the underlying moral, political, and social superiority of the American nation. John feared, however, that without a balanced government to harness the competing elements in the social order, Americans would abandon the virtue that he viewed as essential to the success of republican governments. He worried that his countrymen would fall prey to the same pitfalls as those of the European elites, who he claimed were focused almost exclusively on luxury and pleasure. American leaders would have to be on guard if the grand republican experiment of the United States was indeed to succeed and thrive.

It is interesting to note that John's good friend John Jay had expressed similar sentiments when he returned earlier to America in 1783. He told his fellow New Yorkers that the day he had landed in New York Harbor was one of the happiest days of his life. Moreover, he maintained, "If our views be national, our union preserved, our faith kept, . . . knowledge diffused and our federal government rendered efficient, we cannot fail to become a great and happy people."[103] If Abigail and John had been at the New York City ceremony at which Jay, along with General George Washington and Governor George Clinton, had been honored, they would undoubtedly have chimed in with an enthusiastic and resounding "Amen." The founding fathers, John Adams prominent among them, had secured American independence and then framed a new government. Now as the Adamses returned to America, it fell upon them and their contemporaries to erect a structure that that would ensure the viability and prosperity of the republic and successfully build a new nation.

When Adams was later inaugurated as the nation's second president in 1797, he avowed that the Constitution, which he had first set eyes upon in draft form while still in Europe, provided the framework for the very "system of government as I had ever most esteemed." He wrote eloquently, "Returning to the bosom of my country after a painful separation from it for ten years, I had the honor to be elected to a station under the new order of things, and I have repeatedly laid myself under the most serious obligations to support the Constitution." He concluded, "The operation of it has equaled the most sanguine expectations of its friends, and from an habitual attention to it, satisfaction in its administration, and delight in its effects upon the peace, order, prosperity, and happiness of the nation I have acquired an habitual attachment to it and veneration for it. . . . What other form of government, indeed, can so well deserve our esteem and love?"[104]

Conclusion

John and Abigail in a New America

If I was not attached to America by a Naturel regard, as my native Country, when I compare the conditions of its inhabitants, with that of Europeans, I am bound to it by every feeling of philanthropy, and pray that the Blessings of civil and Religious Liberty, knowledge and virtue may increase and shine upon us, in proportion as they are clouded and obstructed in the rest of the Globe, and that we may possess wisdom enough to estimate aright our peculiar felicity.

Abigail Adams to Lucy Quincy Tufts,
September 3, 1785

I shall quit Europe with more pleasure than I came to it, uncontaminated I hope with its Manners and vices. I have learnt to know the World, and its value. I have seen high Life, I have Witnessed the Luxery and pomp of State, the Power of riches and the influence of titles. . . . Notwithstanding this, I feel that I can return to my little cottage and be happier than here, and if we have not wealth, we have what is better, Integrity.

Abigail Adams to Mary Smith Cranch,
February 25, 1787

Huzza for the new world and farewell to the old one.

John Adams to Thomas Jefferson, December 6, 1787

THE EUROPEAN JOURNEYS OF JOHN AND ABIGAIL ADAMS expanded their life experiences, honed their analytical skills, and allowed them a breadth of perspective they could not have experienced in America. They came face to face with some of the most powerful people in the world and witnessed firsthand national traditions that had been developed over centuries. Yet their time in the Old World only served to enhance their American loyalties as they were transformed from highly intelligent and articulate provincials to sophisticated world travelers. In Europe, they were exposed to an intellectual and cultural environment far richer than they could have imagined. In some ways, their sojourn in Europe played a pivotal role in shaping their notions about American identity and nationhood and provided them with a real-life frame of comparison. The Adamses returned to their homeland with a set of attitudes toward American society that had been reinforced, strengthened, and even evolved from those they had held when they set out.

John's long-held republican political ideology became more entrenched by his residence in Europe, and by the time they left England, Abigail agreed with her husband's worldview in all of its important aspects. True, they found that the Old World provided cultural opportunities not yet found in the United States. For years to come, the "importation" of British culture would still play a part in shaping the identity of the new nation, and Abigail and John respected tradition as a guide for improving society. At the same time, the Adamses believed that European sophistication came at a high price. In their eyes, the European lifestyle, were it to be imported to their fledgling nation, could threaten the health of the new republic through an assault on American virtue, religion, community cohesion, and the moral rectitude they held dear. They and their fellow Americans would have to grapple with how to reorder their society and country as they severed ties with the British Empire, and the new American nation took its place on the international stage.

John and Abigail were strongly influenced by their New England Pilgrim roots. The region's first English settlers, who had arrived on the

Mayflower in 1620, included fervent Calvinists seeking the freedom to practice their religion as they wished, as well as those who came for economic opportunity and the chance to better their lives. Their famous covenant, the Mayflower Compact, declared that they were dedicated to forming a "Civil Body Politic, for *our* better ordering and preservation." Thus, the Adamses had inherited a New England emphasis on faith, mutual cooperation and progress, and, in its limited way, inclusivity.[1] They valued liberty for all but respected prudence and moderation in both personal conduct and governance. For example, they supported the reform of the French monarchy, not its destruction. The challenges to those principles that they saw developing in America could be overcome only by a strong, ordered national government, which had the power to restrain unregulated growth as well as the inherent self-interested passions embedded in human nature. Most worrisome was the threat of the power of an oligarchy, which the Adamses felt was not sufficiently appreciated by some of their fellow Americans. For John and Abigail, the very future of the American republic was at stake.

Although John believed that the British "monarchial republic" was an admirable one, his residence in France and England never led him to esteem either imperial authority or the aristocratic lifestyle. This opinion was shared by Abigail. John abhorred hereditary privilege, and he had long been apprehensive of aristocratic power. He remained so during his entire stay in Europe, where he interacted almost daily with members of the elite, including the highest levels of royalty. As we have seen, the Adamses were uncomfortable with excessive privilege, never admired the behavior of the upper crust, and had no desire to import the trappings of aristocracy into their native land. The problem was that John had *already* seen the challenge unfolding in America through what he perceived as a decline in public ethical standards and too much emphasis on personal aggrandizement over the common good. In fact, from his European vantage point, he became even more convinced that members of what he regarded as the American oligarchy, which included members of Congress and state politicians, as well as a new breed of wealthy men engaged in aggressive and sometimes unscrupulous commerce, needed to be curbed. Some were people like Robert Livingston, with whom he had corresponded; others he had learned about while he lived in Europe. Still, Adams believed that even this rising group of influential American "aristocrats" could make a valuable contribution to the republic, but only if their talents could be harnessed and channeled for the public good.[2]

John Adams always remained a liberal in his unwavering appreciation for public freedom and the rule of law. As early as 1776, he asserted that a true republic was "an empire of laws and not of men," but his former enthusiastic confidence in the good judgment of "the people" had already begun to waver.[3] Public virtue alone, although desirable and important, could not guarantee liberty, but adherence to law and order filtered through a balanced, mixed constitutional government could provide the required stability necessary to guarantee liberty. He adamantly rejected radical reform inspired by Enlightenment ideals about unlimited social progress; he considered such notions to be based on an unrealistic assessment of the potential for change in human nature. For John as well as Abigail, the world order rested on immutable, God-given, natural laws that meant there would always exist an aristocracy of one kind or another as well as a hierarchical pecking order.[4]

An aristocracy, whether it was composed of wealthy, propertied individuals or families, the intellectually gifted, the most attractive, or the supremely talented, was a given. But an aristocracy needed to be controlled by government to make sure it would benefit society. Widespread education was a helpful bulwark against the corrosion of liberty, but it was not enough to ensure stability in the republic. John believed that the broader distribution of property and voting rights among American male citizens was desirable, but he remained opposed to unfettered democracy, and his central goal consistently remained to secure *ordered* liberty. Adams always looked to his own New England region as an exemplar and successful model for building the American character, and he pointed to the town meetings, training days, local schools, and churches as the "four Causes of the Grouth and Defence of N. England. The Virtues and Talents of the People are there Formed."[5]

In other words, the ingredients that he believed were vital to the protection of liberty, such as public-spiritedness, honesty, self-reliance, and trust, were best developed in traditional institutions supported by a strictly defined governmental structure. He sought to restrain and balance both the "Few" (the aristocracy) and the "Many" (the people) by advocating for an executive with robust authority, the "One." In this, he parted ways with many of his contemporary American political leaders after independence from England was achieved, and he diverged as well from their emphasis on the development of a broad democracy. He likely would be pleased that the power of the president has increased over time. Perhaps historian Richard Alan Ryerson put it best when he observed that Adams "was always an ardent republican but never a democratic republican."[6]

As in the case of other Americans before them, such as Benjamin Franklin and the well-known artist Charles Willson Peale, traveling abroad helped John and Abigail Adams define for themselves what it meant to be American in the age of the American Revolution and what constituted "Americanness." The American character was shaped by a complex combination of factors, including geography, nearly limitless natural resources, settlement in initially unexplored areas, the country's distance from the Old World, an exploding population, and the physical breadth of space in America. In fact, John believed that geography was a major factor that set the United States apart from other nations. In overthrowing the European hierarchical model that placed royalty at the top, the nobility in the middle, and common people on the bottom, American founders were intent on pursuing a new vision that eliminated rigid formal ranks and widened access to opportunity for people who were willing to work hard to prosper. As Abraham Lincoln later famously observed in an 1856 speech, perhaps too optimistically, in the United States "every man can make himself." Jefferson believed that Americans had indeed made themselves anew and that a "fortuitous confluence of circumstances and experiences" had merged to create a "new" type of people who had developed a shared exemplary character. He imagined that Americans drew on the wellspring of a "natural aristocracy of talent and virtue" to make a success of the new American experiment of self-government.[7]

John Adams saw things differently. From his perch in Europe in the 1780s, he fretted that an unbridled quest for luxury and power instead of an emphasis on civic and personal virtue, industriousness, and frugality would soon, if it had not already, cross the Atlantic and hold sway in his own country. Indeed, he and Abigail were already convinced that American political and moral life had gone into a decline from its zenith at the beginning of the revolutionary era of the 1770s. Within months after her arrival in France, Abigail's uncle Cotton Tufts, whose opinion she greatly respected, informed her that he was "sorry to find that foreign Customs and Manners are so rapidly gaining Ground amongst us."[8]

At the beginning of 1787, from London's Grosvenor Square, John reminded his Massachusetts friend James Warren that even before the Revolutionary War, some Americans had "run eagerly after foreign manners and Fashions."[9] Reports from trusted friends back in America like Warren, John Jay, and Abigail's sisters served to confirm their anxiety. Even James's wife, Mercy Otis Warren, had lamented that many of her fellow Bostonians were "running mad for their [British] commodities."[10] Abigail repeatedly urged her children to cultivate virtuous habits rather than chasing after luxuries. Concern with maintaining stability and order in American society and improving the quality of the American character had long been a fundamental focus for John Adams, and his stay in Europe provided salutary lessons that only increased his commitment to those values he had long considered essential.[11] Indeed, these values were what distinguished America from the broader world.

Some have regarded John and Abigail's frequent complaints about European society as evidence of negative, querulous personalities. Yet Abigail was known for her sunny disposition and resilience, and although John could be crusty, he was fundamentally optimistic about the long-term future of America. It is more accurate to say that their criticisms of European manners and mores were the mechanism they employed to develop and shape their view of an ideal American political and social landscape. They believed that the key values people needed to succeed in life included industriousness, self-discipline, and thrift. John and Abigail upheld habits that they were convinced led to valuable contributions to one's community and the wider nation, and that encouraged people to become good citizens and virtuous people.

Poised to return home, both Abigail and John gave deep consideration to the formation of an American character and a national identity that was best suited to ensure the future of the innovative political experiment taking place in the United States. Theirs was one of many competing ideas about American identity at the time. John and Abigail's ideal vision was a lifestyle that they had modeled and worked to inculcate in their own children while they resided in Europe. They were proponents of refining moral sentiment. In their letters and conversations, they often reflected on how they believed people *ought* to act and frequently felt compelled to teach not only their children but also their fellow Americans what they considered to be the primary duties of life.

When the four members of the Adams family lived together in Auteuil, mornings had been devoted to study, reading, and contemplation; afternoons were punctuated with walks in the nearby park, where John and his son discussed history and legal, philosophical, and moral issues. Certainly, Abigail and Nabby, and even John and John Quincy, admired and purchased fashionable French and English adornments, but they consciously exercised restraint. When John wrote to a friend that he had made a "little America" of his own in Auteuil, on one level his sentiment reflected an oasis his family had created in the midst of the excessive opulence, moral decadence, and political corruption that they felt surrounded them in France.

The European lifestyle appeared to the Adamses as far removed from the simpler, orderly New England community they recalled with appreciation and frank nostalgia. In their minds, their hometowns of Braintree and Weymouth, where they had spent their youth, exemplified the virtues of civic responsibility, moral rectitude, and the upholding of Protestant religious values. For both John and Abigail, the widespread dissemination of knowledge and inculcation of public virtue were the keys to crafting a stable, enduring republic. American leaders needed to display an unwavering commitment to liberty and justice and possess good character, practical wisdom, and courage to ensure a flourishing society.

It is true that during and after their stay in Europe the Adamses cared about their appearance and the cultivation of good taste and brought symbols of their cultural refinement back with them to America. Despite their revolutionary impulses and their commitment to forging a new national identity, separating themselves from British customs was a complex, fraught task. John and Abigail were frugal by nature and nurture. Like other American revolutionaries, they found there was a fine line between extravagant luxury and a level of materialism that reflected refinement. They returned to the United States with fine china, handsome furniture, paintings, and other decorative objects for their new home, but the house was far more modest than the grand estates they had visited in England. Abigail always maintained her desire to create a level of simple elegance that was befitting an American diplomat and political figure and his close family members.

After John was elected vice president of the United States in 1789 and he and Abigail moved to the temporary capital of New York, they occupied a stately rented mansion in Richmond Hill on the outskirts of the city. At Abigail's first meeting with the nation's inaugural First Lady, she reported to her elder sister that Martha Washington "is plain in her dress, but that plainness is the best of every article. . . . Her manners are modest and unassuming, dignified and feminine, not the Tincture of ha'ture about her."[12] For Abigail, Mrs. Washington personified the ideal of the republican wife, restrained but elegant, and she believed that the American First Lady served as a marked and positive contrast to the royal heads of state that the Adamses had encountered in Europe.

Stonyfield (the old Borland Mansion), the property where the Adamses lived after their return from Europe. Courtesy National Park Service, Adams National Historic Park.

John Adams concurred, and he believed that the only way for the United States to move forward was to learn from the history of the failed republics of the past as well as the flawed European nations of the present. In particular, Adams was long motivated by his firm and expansive belief that a strong executive was necessary to a republic in order to offset inevitable displays of aristocratic power. For John, lack of balance in government constituted a serious threat to the survival of *all* republican nations, whether they were democratic, aristocratic, or monarchial. However, it was during his residency in Europe that his deep-seated fear of an American aristocracy was magnified. His concern was fueled, in part, by his degree of estrangement from the American Congress, made up largely of men he regarded as either uneducated incompetents or haughty and misguided aristocrats who alternately overlooked him or berated him.[13]

In England between 1787 and 1788, Adams penned his most important political tome, *A Defence of the Constitutions of Government of the
United States of America*, which laid out a blueprint for the workings of
an ideal republic. Although many have called Adams a political conservative, it would be more accurate to characterize him as a pragmatic
moderate, one who developed his political views after careful, sober consideration.[14] Influenced by his decade-long residence in Europe coupled
with his Yankee roots, John became increasingly concerned about the
development of a powerful oligarchy in the United States. He noted
his fear of the "many" to Thomas Jefferson, but Jefferson famously declared his greater concern about too powerful an executive, the "one." In
Adams's broad definition of aristocracy, in America that group would
include all men of power, whether their influence was derived from
wealth, keen intelligence, exceptional talents, or superior education.
Such men, he feared, were and would be motivated by unbridled ambition and greed instead of an overriding dedication to the public good.[15]

Historian Richard Alan Ryerson postulates that John's frustrations
and setbacks as a diplomat in Europe made him even more concerned
than he had been about the threat of an elite aristocracy. His anxiety
over inappropriate influence by men of wealth within the American
republic is a view that seems especially relevant today during a period
of heightened political upheaval and uncertainty. Adams not only experienced firsthand the foibles of his fellow American diplomats, including Benjamin Franklin and Silas Deane during his European stint, but
he also had occasion to observe other examples of "aristocratic power"
in his homeland of America. This became apparent in his demeaning
exchanges with Robert Livingston, appointed by Congress to serve as
secretary of foreign affairs. John believed that American oligarchs like
Livingston would use their advantages to exert influence for personal
gain.[16] John viewed inequality as a basic facet of human nature embedded in all societies, but paradoxically, throughout his lifetime he also remained skeptical about popular rule, and may be seen to have espoused
an elitist view of government. Certainly, he believed that without the

moral underpinning of religion coupled with wise governance, the always fragile social order would soon unravel into chaos, an occurrence Adams later insisted had transpired during the French Revolution.

As historian Gordon S. Wood has observed, Adams never fully subscribed to the belief that all men were created equal, the famous dictum voiced in the Declaration of Independence by Jefferson. Adams viewed social conflict as inevitable as individuals competed for position.[17] Neither was Abigail an egalitarian. Moreover, John worried that the existence of powerful legislative branches and frequent elections fostered instability, which, in turn, provided dangerous opportunities for influence by aggressive elites, not to mention meddling by European nations. At the end of 1787 Adams told Jefferson, "Elections to offices which are great objects of Ambition, I look at with terror." Like Jefferson, John was apprehensive of "foreign Interference, Intrigue, and Influence," which he viewed as the inevitable by-product of short terms in office.[18] Today Adams's warnings seem particularly prescient in the light of concerns about Russian meddling in the American electoral process.

Although John had found much to appreciate in Europe, he also bemoaned the fact that America would need to be dependent on European commercial and political ties at least in the short run. He and Abigail extolled the natural riches found in America, which they believed would transform their fledgling nation into an international power. Their experience of European influence spurred their conviction that America would need to follow its own path to take its rightful place in the world. In 1780 John maintained to Cotton Tufts, "Indeed America will never derive any good from Europe of any Kind. Ours is the richest and most independent Country under Heaven, and [yet] We are continually looking up to Europe for Help!"[19] Observing the seemingly endless disagreements and wars between European nations, Adams left feeling more convinced than ever of the potential superiority of the American form of republic. He urged his nation to steer a neutral role in the future, avoiding entanglements in politics on the other side of the Atlantic. John's strong views on the subject, although not unique, preceded Washington's admonitions and the Monroe Doctrine by decades. His main fear seems to have been that Americans might be drawn into overseas conflicts that would distract them from economic progress.

Public virtue became a patriotic imperative for members of the Adams family. Yet despite his apprehension of American involvement in European affairs, at the same time John knew that it would be essential to integrate his country into the transatlantic world to ensure the incipient nation's future. Like his political counterparts around the world, Adams well understood that Americans as well as Europeans would have to figure out how to readjust to global change.

From London in the spring of 1786, Abigail shared her prescription for proper behavior and what she insisted made America superior in all aspects to the nations she had visited in Europe. She wrote to her sister Elizabeth, "The longer I live in the world, and the more I see of mankind, the more deeply I am impressed with the importance and necessity of good principals and virtuous examples being placed before youth."[20] Throughout their lifetimes, both John and Abigail Adams consistently placed public interest above their own, despite strong personal and family aspirations that sometimes pitted ambition against public service. Perhaps it was that outlook, melded with religious and patriotic commitment, that prompted Abigail's declaration about the American potential to her niece. She insisted that "there is no country where there is a fuller exercise of those virtues than ours at present exhibits, which is in a great measure owing to the equal distribution of property, the small number of inhabitants in proportion to its territory, the equal distribution of justice and exercised with impartiality, and to a religion which teaches peace and good will to man; to knowledge and learning being so easily acquired and so universally distributed; and to that sense of our moral obligation which generally inclines our countrymen to do to others as they would that others do to them."[21]

Abigail made the case to Lucy Cranch that America was superior because "it is the government, the laws, and religion, which form the character of a nation." *How* American institutions were formed, developed, and governed remained essential. In her judgment, the excessive luxury she had seen among the elite in Europe had resulted in what she termed "corruption and degeneracy of manners,"[22] a view that had already been germinating in her mind when she embarked across the Atlantic. Though neither John nor Abigail was a strict Calvinist, the philosophy of both was shaped to a significant degree by their New England religious and social heritage.

Their stay in Europe brought into sharp relief all that John and Abigail did *not* want to see become of their fellow Americans. As sociologist James Davison Hunter has pointed out, "Identity is formed not only by our affirmations but by our negations."[23] Both Adamses were critical of excess in all its forms. From emphasis on luxury and opulence to the unrelenting quest for elevated position, personal aggrandizement, and gain fueled by selfish ambition, they deplored what they considered the assault on personal and national standards of morality they had encountered in both France and England. The Adamses steadfastly supported a political structure that focused on simplicity, political stability, individual liberty, and inspirational authority and upheld what they viewed as the distinctive and desirable American values of republican virtue and public service.

From Europe, they had already seen cracks emerging in America, as in Shays's Rebellion. Abigail blamed the unrest at home on the "luxery and extravagance both in furniture and dress [that] had pervaded all orders of our Countrymen and women." She told Thomas Jefferson that it "was hastning fast to Sap their independence" by involving every class of citizen, and that Americans were accumulating debts that they were unable to discharge. For Abigail, vanity was becoming a more powerful motivator than patriotism.[24]

Although the Adamses could be critical of their fellow Americans, they believed that providing necessary governmental restraints would both foster public virtue in their country's citizenry and ensure American success. On the most elemental level, John and Abigail identified themselves fully as Americans, and they exhibited a profound sense of patriotism, nationalism, and duty toward their homeland. Indeed, their own aspirations, ambitions, and dreams for the future of their offspring were inextricably bound up with the fate of their country.

Despite their concerns, Abigail and John retained a good measure of optimism. Writing from London to her sister, Abigail lauded the American nation for having taken the lead in religious toleration and expressed her hope that if Americans proved themselves "equally Liberal in all other respects" and cultivated peace and good will, they would continue to serve "as an example to the world."[25] When James Warren sent negative reports to the Adamses about his fellow Americans at the beginning of 1787, John averred that although he was "Sensible that our Country men have never merited the Character of very exalted Virtue," he remained "very much averse to believe that they are grown much worse." The threat of "general Degeneracy" influenced him to redouble his efforts to ameliorate the situation by offering guidance through his *Defence*. Adams knew full well that his prescriptive advice would likely be unwelcome. Yet, as a principled man of unshakable integrity, he insisted that he felt propelled to risk the displeasure of the "People" if he was to effect any "good in the long run."[26]

As Abigail put it as she contemplated leaving Europe, "I want to return Home, and bring them [her daughter Nabby and family], we should all be happier in America. There we should find sentiments and opinions more agreeable to us, society and Friends which the European World knows not of. It is all lost in ceremony and Parade, venality and corruption, in Gameing and debauchery, amongst those who stile themselves polite People, the fashionable World. . . . Let Learning personal Merit and virtue create the only distinction."[27]

Certainly, commitment to the public good had always been central to Abigail and John's vision for America's future, and few had sacrificed so much on behalf of their nation. As early as the fateful year 1776, John had written patriot Mercy Warren that "Public Virtue is the only Foundation of Republics. . . . Every Man must seriously set himself to root out his Passions, Prejudices and Attachments, and to get the better of his private interest. The only reputable Principle and Doctrine must be that all Things must give way to the public."[28] That fundamental outlook had been a guiding principle for John and Abigail Adams from the beginning of their married life, and it only became stronger during their stay in Europe.

Abigail and particularly John had always struggled with their personal quest for recognition of their roles in history. In Abigail's case, her ambition was primarily on behalf of her husband and later for her son John Quincy. Yet they both regarded the longing for reputation as a moral weakness and believed that a strong civic consciousness was a basic ingredient for American success. They firmly adhered to the precept that it was imperative to live a life embedded in community involvement and responsibility, which would be essential to creating a common national purpose. For the Adams family, love of country trumped personal considerations.

In her diary entry for July 4, 1784, written aboard ship on her maiden voyage to Europe, Abigail had celebrated the "anniversary of our Glorious Independence." She had yet to set foot on British or French soil, but she had already developed preconceived notions about European customs. "Whilst the Nations of Europe are enveloped in Luxery and dissipation; and a universal venality prevails throughout Britain, may the new empire [America], Gracious Heaven, become the Guardian and protector of Religion and Liberty, of universal Benevolence and Phylanthropy," she prayed. She concluded with a blessing: "May those virtues which are banished from the land of our Nativity [England], find a safe Assylum with the inhabitants of this new world."[29]

In the fall of 1787, less than six months before she and John departed Europe, Abigail again voiced her concerns about the ability of Americans to resist the siren calls of luxury and personal ambition. After praising the advantages that America had to offer, she told her younger sister Elizabeth Shaw that she disapproved of what she saw in contemporary Americans, "that restless Spirit, and that baneful pride Ambition, and thirst for power which will finally make us as wretched as our [British]

Neighbors."[30] Of course, people often exhibit contradictory impulses. Abigail and John's criticisms were dispensed, however, almost like that of a fond parent chastising his or her offspring. In fact, they were remarkably similar to the exhortations that the Adamses had directed toward their own children over the years about civic and family responsibility and moral rectitude.

Although Abigail remained optimistic about the future of the United States when she left Europe, her husband took a more ambivalent view. Their differing outlooks reflected their underlying personalities as well as their individual experiences in the Old World. During his years in Europe, John grew increasingly skeptical of the ability of any people to govern and be governed wisely without strict guidelines. It was not simply that he became more conservative in his political outlook as he grew older, but that his mistrust of human behavior grew stronger due to his years in Europe, as did his disillusionment about the American commitment to public virtue. For John, the American character would have to be formed (perhaps even reformed) through the molding of an outside force. And that force would come in the form of a properly framed Constitution that would serve as a guide to ensure continued liberty.

For John, the very moral foundation and order of American society were at stake. He refused to compromise his principles, even when it set him against the popular political tide. As he once told James Warren defiantly, "Popularity was never my mistress, nor was I ever, or shall I ever be a popular man."[31] After he returned to America, Adams would be criticized for displaying monarchial tendencies when he continued to advocate for a head of government that at times appeared to be similar to the British model.[32] Yet Adams's worries about the potential of wealth and celebrity to wield undue influence in American society and in the realms of elections are concerns that strike a chord today.

In a diary entry composed on her return voyage to America, Abigail summed up her sentiments in her usual articulate manner: "Indeed I have seen enough of the world, small as [it] has been, and shall be content to learn what is further to be known from the page of History. I do not think the four years I have past abroad the pleasantest part of my Life. Tis Domestick happiness and Rural felicity in the Bosom of my Native Land, that has charms for me. Yet I do not regret that I made this excursion since it has only more attached me to America."[33] Similarly, while still in England, John shared his prescription for happiness with his son John Quincy: "I have no other Idea of an happy Life: Than Health and Competence, with a clear Conscience and among People who esteem and love you." Despite nearly a decade in Europe, where he had interacted with monarchs and nobles and moved among the highest rungs of society, Adams retained his loyalty to his country, and he looked forward to the companionship of his family and close friends. He concluded firmly, "Home is Home."[34]

As their words reveal, despite mixed feelings and qualms about the future of their nation, at the close of their European journey John and Abigail Adams remained principled, fervent, committed Americans who loved their native land. To borrow a felicitous phrase about John and John Quincy, and apply it instead to John and Abigail, "They studied the world without abandoning the moral geography of America."[35] Perhaps Abigail put it best when early into her European residence she wrote wistfully from France to her elder sister, "What a sad misfortune it is to have the Body in one place and the Soul in another."[36]

Upon their return to America, the Adamses would face multiple personal and political challenges, and there were many journeys still to come, but they remained centrally involved in the growth and development of the United States and devoted to their country's well-being. Their hearts were always firmly rooted in their homeland, and in the end, their European sojourn helped them define what it meant to be an American. Over two centuries after John and Abigail docked at Boston Harbor to return home, we still grapple today with the question of what it means to be an American.

ACKNOWLEDGMENTS

THE OPPORTUNITY TO EXPRESS MY APPRECIATION TO THE many people who provided encouragement, constructive criticism, and lively discussion along the way remains one of the highlights of completing a new book. At the top of the list are the many family members, friends, and colleagues who have served as unwavering "boosters" and sounding boards. My gratitude to Clara Platter, my editor at New York University Press, for championing *A View from Abroad* from the beginning of the proposal stage to the final manuscript, and to her capable editorial assistant, Veronica Knutson, for her invaluable assistance in many technical matters. I would also like to thank my production editor, Alexia Traganas, for her helpful guidance, and Rosalie Morales Kearns for her meticulous copyediting. At the University of Denver, Provost Emeritus Gregg Kvistad, Provost Corrine Lengsfeld, Dean of the University Libraries Michael Levine Clark, Associate Dean Jack Maness, and my faculty colleagues have for years exhibited unwavering support for all of my scholarly research projects.

I am also grateful to those unsung heroes of historical research, the editors of the essential papers and correspondence of America's founders and the archivists across the country who so graciously assist historians in locating primary sources, the essential lifeblood of historical inquiry. Thanks to the anonymous reviewers whose suggestions and criticism helped refine and expand the scope of this book. I am especially grateful to two colleagues and longtime friends, Dr. Frederick Greenspahn, Professor Emeritus at Florida Atlantic University, and Dr. Adam Rovner, Associate Professor at the University of Denver. They spent many hours carefully reviewing each chapter and offered invaluable insights, helpful edits, and practical suggestions to improve the manuscript. I am deeply appreciative of their generous support.

I have continued to be blessed with a wonderful family and a loyal and supportive group of friends who enhance my life on a daily basis. I am especially grateful to my husband, Lewis, and our children and grandchildren for their unwavering love and encouragement and their continued interest in all of my endeavors, scholarly and otherwise.

NOTES

INTRODUCTION

1 Butterfield, *Diary and Autobiography of John Adams*, February 15, 1778, 2:271. Henceforth cited as *Diary and Autobiography of John Adams*.

2 *Diary and Autobiography of John Adams*, June 25, 1774, 2:97.

3 Yokota, *Unbecoming British*, 10.

4 See, for example, some of the more well-known recent works, including Ellis, *First Family*; Gelles, *Abigail and John*; Holton, *Abigail Adams*; and McCullough, *John Adams*.

5 In a letter written to his friend James Warren at the beginning of 1787, Adams pointed out that even well before the American Revolution he had observed that many Americans had eagerly "run after foreign manners and Fashions." John Adams to James Warren, January 9, 1787, *Founders Online*.

6 John Adams to Abigail Adams, April 14, 1776, *Founders Online*.

7 Historian Richard Alan Ryerson, who edited many volumes of the Adams papers, has ably demonstrated this point. For an extremely detailed, insightful, and careful reading of the development and evolution of John Adams's political thought, see Ryerson, *John Adams's Republic*.

8 John Adams, *A Defence of the Constitutions of Government of the United States of America*, in Charles Francis Adams, *The Works of John Adams*, 4:401.

9 Isenberg and Burstein, *The Problem of Democracy*, xii, xiv.

10 Rosenfeld, "'Europe,' Women, and the American Political Imaginary."

11 Abigail Adams to John Adams, May 18, 1778, *Adams Family Papers: An Electronic Archive*.

12 Abigail Adams to John Adams, October 19, 1783, *Adams Family Papers: An Electronic Archive*.

13 Zagarri, *A Woman's Dilemma*, 108–10.

14 Abigail Adams to John Adams, July 16, 1780, in Abigail Adams, *The Letters of Mrs. Adams*, 117.

15 *Diary and Autobiography of John Adams*, 4:4.

16 Gilje, "Commerce and Conquest," 735–45.

17 Ellis, *Passionate Sage*, 12, 13.

18 Wood, *Friends Divided*, 7.

19 For more details about Jefferson's eclectic interests, especially his appreciation for the fine arts, see Wood, *Friends Divided*, 10–12.

20 See McConville, *The King's Three Faces*, 2, 7, 313–14.

21 Yokota, *Unbecoming British*, 10.

22 Saxton, *The Widow Washington*, 103.

23 Ellis, *First Family*, 12.

24 Abigail Adams to John Quincy Adams, March 20, 1780, in Butterfield et al., *Adams Family Correspondence*, 3:313. The *Adams Family Correspondence* is a multiyear, multivolume work, with multiple volume editors, published by Harvard University Press starting in 1963. Henceforth I'll cite it by its title alone, rather than listing the specific volume editors.

25 John Adams to Abigail Adams, May 12, 1780, *Adams Family Correspondence*, 3:333.

26 For a discussion of the building blocks that led to Adams's world outlook in regard to human nature, see Hester, "Puritanism and the Rights of Man."

27 John Adams to Abigail Adams, post May 12, 1780, *Adams Family Correspondence*, 3:342.

28 For a useful case study of the pivotal role of New England, see Kermes, *Creating an American Identity*.

29 Abigail Adams to Mary Cranch, September 15, 1787, in Abigail Adams, *The Letters of Mrs. Adams*, 332.

30 Abigail Adams to Mary Cranch, December 30, 1799, in Mitchell, *New Letters of Mrs. Adams*, 224–25.

31 John Adams to Nabby Adams, July 17, 1784, in De Windt, *Journal and Correspondence of Miss Adams*, 3–4.

32 See Warren, *History of the Rise, Progress, and Termination of the American Revolution*, 3:394–95.

33 John Adams to the Comte de Sarsfield, February 3, 1786, *Founders Online*.

34 Ryerson, *John Adams's Republic*, 3–10.

35 See Mayville, *John Adams and the Fear of an American Oligarchy*, especially the introduction, for a deep examination of Adams's concern about the unchecked power of an American aristocracy composed in part of elite merchants and financiers.

36 Steele, *Thomas Jefferson and American Nationhood*, 10.

37 See Stahr, *John Jay*, xi–xii.

38 William Bingham to John Jay, July 1, 1780, in Johnston, *Correspondence and Public Papers of John Jay*, 364.

39 Steele, *Thomas Jefferson and American Nationhood*, 10, 103.

40 Wood, *Friends Divided*, 207. Several times Wood also accuses Adams of providing his countrymen with a "terrifying picture of themselves" and "a dark and forbidding and un-American picture," 214, 216, 42, 430.

41 Gelles, *Portia*, 173.

CHAPTER I. JOHN ADAMS

1 John Adams to Abigail Adams, July 28, 1777, in Hogan and Taylor, *My Dearest Friend*, 190.

2 John Adams to Mercy Warren, April 16, 1776, in Ford, *Warren-Adams Letters*, 1:223.

3 John Adams, "Travels, and Negotiations," *Diary and Autobiography of John Adams*, 4:5.

4 For a discussion of Abigail's business enterprise, see Holton, *Abigail Adams*, 105–8, 213.

5 *Diary and Autobiography of John Adams*, April 3, 1778, 4:38–39.

6 Abigail Adams to John Adams, December 15, 1783, *Adams Family Papers: An Electronic Archive*.

7 *Diary and Autobiography of John Adams*, February 13–16, 1778, 2:269–71.

8 *Diary and Autobiography of John Adams*, February 16, 1778, 2:272–73.

9 Gelles, *Portia*, xvii.

10 Abigail Adams to John Adams, March 8, 1778, in Abigail Adams, *The Letters of Mrs. Adams*, 93.

11 *Diary and Autobiography of John Adams*, February 18, 1778, 2:274.

12 *Diary and Autobiography of John Adams*, February 21–23, 1778, 2:275–76.

13 Abigail Adams to Mary Cranch, September 12, 1786, *Adams Family Correspondence*, 7:339.

14 *Diary and Autobiography of John Adams*, March 29, 1778, 2:290.

15 *Diary and Autobiography of John Adams*, February 27, 1778, 2:278.

16 *Diary and Autobiography of John Adams*, March 3, 1778, 2:280–81.

17 "Boston Marine Society History," www.bostonmarinesociety.org.

18 *Diary and Autobiography of John Adams*, March 7, 1778, 2:283, and March 19, 1778, 2:287.

19 *Diary and Autobiography of John Adams*, April 8, 1788, 2:296.

20 Dull, *A Diplomatic History of the American Revolution*, 95.

21 Dull, *A Diplomatic History of the American Revolution*, 53.

22 *Diary and Autobiography of John Adams*, April 15, 1778, 4:59.

23 See Hutson, *John Adams and the Diplomacy of the American Revolution*, 12–32.

24 Lopez, *Mon Cher Papa*, viii, 4.

25 Lopez, *My Life with Benjamin Franklin*, 174.

26 Wood, *The Americanization of Benjamin Franklin*, 12–13.

27 *Diary and Autobiography of John Adams*, June 23, 1779, 2:391.

28 *Diary and Autobiography of John Adams*, April 9, 1778, 2:296–97, and April 10, 1778, 2:298.

29 *Diary and Autobiography of John Adams*, April 12, 1778, 2:299.

30 Abigail Adams to John Adams, December 27, 1778, *Adams Family Papers: An Electronic Archive*.

31 Abigail Adams to John Adams, April 10, 1778, *Adams Family Papers: An Electronic Archive.*

32 John Adams to Abigail Adams, December 3, 1778, *Adams Family Papers: An Electronic Archive.*

33 For more details about Franklin's interactions with the women of Paris, see Lopez, *Mon Cher Papa.*

34 See Ellis, *Passionate Sage*, 90–91.

35 Hutson, *John Adams and the Diplomacy of the American Revolution*, 1.

36 Dull, *A Diplomatic History of the American Revolution*, 59–60.

37 Fiero, *The Humanistic Tradition*, Book 4, 62–71. For a lively account of the life of Louis XIV, see Wilkinson, *Louis XIV.*

38 *Diary and Autobiography of John Adams*, April 11, 1778, 2:299.

39 *Diary and Autobiography of John Adams*, May 6, 1778, 2:309

40 *Diary and Autobiography of John Adams*, May 6, 1778, 4:91.

41 Abigail Adams to Mary Smith Cranch, September 5, 1784, *Adams Family Correspondence*, 5:443.

42 *Diary and Autobiography of John Adams*, May 8, 1778, 2:310.

43 *Diary and Autobiography of John Adams*, May 8, 1778, 4:92–93.

44 *Diary and Autobiography of John Adams*, June 7, 1778, 4:131.

45 *Diary and Autobiography of John Adams*, May 5, 1778, 2:308.

46 *Diary and Autobiography of John Adams*, June 2, 1778, 4:121.

47 *Diary and Autobiography of John Adams*, June 7, 1778, 2:316.

48 *Diary and Autobiography of John Adams*, July 4, 1778, 4:143–44.

49 *Diary and Autobiography of John Adams*, November 26, 1778, 2:323.

50 Abigail Adams to John Adams, June 30, 1778, in Abigail Adams, *The Letters of Mrs. Adams*, 97–99.

51 John Adams to Abigail Adams, April 12, 1778, *Adams Family Papers: An Electronic Archive.*

52 John Adams to Mercy Warren, April 16, 1776, in Ford, *Warren-Adams Letters*, 1:222–23.

53 John Adams to Abigail Adams, April 12, 1778, *Adams Family Papers: An Electronic Archive.*

54 *Diary and Autobiography of John Adams*, February 9, 1779, 2:347.

55 *Diary and Autobiography of John Adams*, May 24, 1773, 2:82.

56 *Diary and Autobiography of John Adams*, May 27, 1778, 4:119.

57 *Diary and Autobiography of John Adams*, April 21, 1778, 2:304.

58 *Diary and Autobiography of John Adams*, May 2, 1778, 4:87–88.

59 For a detailed analysis of Adams's evolving views on French diplomacy, see Ferling, "John Adams, Diplomat," 231–37. Nearly three decades before Ferling's article, historian William B. Evans had reached a similar conclusion about the rift between Adams and Franklin: "The evidence leaves little doubt that it was the difference of opinion over the extent to which the United States should depend

upon France which provided the basis for Adams' antagonism and which also produced the unusual revelations of Franklin's anger." Evans, "John Adams' Opinion of Benjamin Franklin," 238.

60 *Diary and Autobiography of John Adams*, July 2, 1779, 2:397.
61 *Diary and Autobiography of John Adams*, May 27, 1778, 4:118.
62 John Adams to Mr. Gerry, a Member of Congress, July 9, 1778, *Diary and Autobiography of John Adams*, 4:149–52.
63 Elizabeth Smith Shaw to Abigail Adams, March 18, 1786, *Adams Family Correspondence*, 7:94.
64 Abigail Adams to John Quincy Adams, June 10, 1778, *Adams Family Correspondence*, 3:37.
65 John Adams to John Quincy Adams, May 18, 1781, *Founders Online*.
66 John Adams to Abigail Adams, December 2, 1778, *Adams Family Correspondence*, 3:125.
67 *Diary and Autobiography of John Adams*, March 3, 1779, 2:354.
68 *Diary and Autobiography of John Adams*, February 12, 1779, 2:353.
69 *Diary and Autobiography of John Adams*, April 22, 1779, 2:361.
70 Taylor et al., *Papers of John Adams*, 6:424. This is another multivolume work with multiple volume editors, published by Harvard University Press. Henceforth I'll cite it by its title alone, rather than listing the specific volume editors.
71 John Adams to Abigail Adams, February 13, 1779, *Adams Family Correspondence*, 3:169.
72 John Adams to Abigail Adams, February 28, 1779, *Adams Family Correspondence*, 3:182–82.
73 *Diary and Autobiography of John Adams*, June 20, 1779, 2:385–86.
74 *Diary and Autobiography of John Adams*, June 21, 1779, 2:389.
75 Abigail Adams to John Thaxter, September 2, 1778, *Adams Family Correspondence*, 3:84–86.

CHAPTER 2. SECOND JOURNEY TO EUROPE

1 For a detailed description of the interior of the house, see Gelles, *Abigail and John*, 21–22.
2 John Adams to the President of Congress, November 4, 1779, *Diary and Autobiography of John Adams*, 4:177.
3 Abigail Adams to John Adams, November 17, 1779, *Adams Family Papers: An Electronic Archive*.
4 Abigail Adams to John Adams, December 25, 1780, *Adams Family Papers: An Electronic Archive*.
5 Gelles, *Portia*, 2.
6 De Windt, *Journal and Correspondence of Miss Adams*, vii.
7 *Diary and Autobiography of John Adams*, November 13, 1779, 2:400.
8 *Diary and Autobiography of John Adams*, December 5, 1779, 2:403.

9   *Diary and Autobiography of John Adams,* December 9, 1779, 2:405.

10 *Diary and Autobiography of John Adams,* December 14, 1779, and December 15, 1779, 2:407, 409.

11 John Adams to Nabby Adams, December 12, 1779, in De Windt, *Journal and Correspondence of Miss Adams,* 12.

12 *Diary and Autobiography of John Adams,* December 27, 1779, 2:415–16.

13 *Diary and Autobiography of John Adams,* December 28, 1779, and January 8, 1780, 2:417, 425.

14 For a detailed study of Adams's anti-Catholic views, see Foster, "'Bienvenido, Mister Adams!'"

15 *Diary and Autobiography of John Adams,* January 11, 1780, 2:426–27.

16 Hutson, *John Adams and the Diplomacy of the French Revolution,* 55–59. Indeed, Hutson is often very critical of Adams and often minimizes Adams's diplomatic contributions in Europe. Many of his arguments have been refuted by recent scholars.

17 John Adams to Congress, February 15, 1780, *Diary and Autobiography of John Adams,* 4:241.

18 *Diary and Autobiography of John Adams,* August 28, 1780, 2:446.

19 John Adams to Abigail Adams, April–May 1780, *Adams Family Papers: An Electronic Archive.*

20 John Adams to Abigail Adams, post May 12, 1789, *Adams Family Papers: An Electronic Archive.*

21 John Adams to Abigail Adams, post May 12, 1780, *Adams Family Papers: An Electronic Archive.*

22 Abigail Adams to John Quincy Adams, January 12, 1780, in Abigail Adams, *The Letters of Mrs. Adams,* 111.

23 Abigail Adams to John Quincy Adams, March 20, 1780, in Abigail Adams, *The Letters of Mrs. Adams,* 113–14.

24 John Adams to Thomas Jefferson, March 24, 1801, in Cappon, *The Adams-Jefferson Letters,* 264.

25 John Adams to Abigail Adams, December 18, 1780, *Adams Family Papers: An Electronic Archive.*

26 *Diary and Autobiography of John Adams,* November 18, 1782, 3:60.

27 For a detailed review and analysis of the diplomatic breakdown between Vergennes and Adams, see Bauer, "With Friends Like These," particularly 664–70.

28 McCullough, *John Adams,* 233.

29 John Adams to John Jay, May 13, 1780, in Johnston, *The Correspondence and Public Papers of John Jay,* 1:330–31.

30 Charles Francis Adams, *The Works of John Adams,* 7:138.

31 John Adams to John Jay, May 8, 1785, *Founders Online.*

32 For a detailed discussion of Adams's views about the nexus between economic and foreign policy, see Clarfield, "John Adams."

33 Benjamin Franklin to Congress, August 9, 1780, in Lopez et al., *The Papers of Benjamin Franklin*, 23:117.

34 John Adams to John Quincy Adams, May 14, 1781, *Founders Online*.

35 John Adams to John Quincy Adams, May 18, 1781, *Founders Online*.

36 For a detailed analysis of the views of Adams and Jefferson about the conflict between the Prussians and Dutch Patriots in the Netherlands in the late 1780s, see Peter Nicolaisen, "John Adams, Thomas Jefferson, and the Dutch Patriots," in Sadosky et al., *Old World, New World*, 105–29.

37 R. R. Palmer, "Two Americans in Two Dutch Republics."

38 James C. Riley, "Financial and Economic Ties," 441, 444–55.

39 Duyverman, "An Historic Friendship."

40 John Adams to Abigail Adams, September 4, 1780, and December 18, 1780, *Adams Family Correspondence*, 3:485, 4:35.

41 *Diary and Autobiography of John Adams*, September 14, 1783, 3:8.

42 Hutson, *John Adams and the Diplomacy of the French Revolution*, 82–87.

43 Kaplan, "The Founding Fathers and the Two Confederations," 423.

44 John Adams to John Quincy Adams, December 14, 1781, *Founders Online*.

45 Nordholt, "John Adams Is Still with Us," 272.

46 John Adams to Robert R. Livingston, February 21, 1782, *Papers of John Adams*, 12:250–59.

47 Ryerson, *John Adams's Republic*, 268–69.

48 John Adams to Abigail Adams, October 9, 1781, *Adams Family Papers: An Electronic Archive*.

49 John Adams to Benjamin Franklin, October 22, 1781, in Lopez et al., *Papers of Benjamin Franklin*, 35:630, 632.

50 John Adams to Robert R. Livingston, September 17, 1782, *Papers of John Adams*, 13:473–75.

51 John Adams to Benjamin Rush, April 22, 1782, *Papers of John Adams*, 12:443–45.

52 John Adams to James Warren, September 7, 1782, *Papers of John Adams*, 13:439–40.

53 John Adams to Benjamin Rush, April 22, 1782, *Papers of John Adams*, 12:443–45.

54 John Adams to Robert R. Livingston, May 16, 1782, *Papers of John Adams*, 13:48–52.

55 John Adams to James Warren, August 19, 1782, *Papers of John Adams*, 13:255–56.

56 Although most scholars have emphasized Adams's key role in obtaining the critical Dutch loans, at least one historian has maintained that John's efforts have been exaggerated and that credit for the Dutch recognition of the American republic and the critical loans belong primarily to the French ambassador, Vauguyon, and his work with the Dutch Patriot party as well as Foreign Minister

Vergennes and his agitation for the much-needed loans. See Hutson, "John Adams and the Birth of Dutch American Friendship."

57 *Diary and Autobiography of John Adams*, October 8, 1782, 3:16.

58 *Diary and Autobiography of John Adams*, November 11, 1782, 3:51.

59 John Adams to John Quincy Adams, December 14, 1781, *Founders Online*.

60 Nabby Adams to John Quincy Adams, May 1783, in De Windt, *Journal and Correspondence of Miss Adams*, 25.

61 Abigail Adams to Elizabeth Smith Shaw, February–March 1782, *Founders Online*.

62 John Adams to Nabby Adams, September 26, 1782, in De Windt, *Journal and Correspondence of Miss Adams*, 18.

63 John Adams to Nabby Adams, September 25, 1782, in De Windt, *Journal and Correspondence of Miss Adams*, 19.

64 John Adams to Nabby Adams, September 25, 1782, in De Windt, *Journal and Correspondence of Miss Adams*, 23–24.

65 Lewis, "The Republican Wife," 708.

66 Edith B. Gelles, "The Marriage of Abigail and John Adams," in Yalom and Carstensen, *Inside the American Couple*, 6.

67 *Diary and Autobiography of John Adams*, October 9, 1782, 3:17.

68 *Diary and Autobiography of John Adams*, October 26 and 27, 1782, 3:37.

69 John Adams to Arthur Lee, January 31, 1785, *Founders Online*.

70 David N. Gellman, "Abbe's Ghost: Negotiating Slavery in Paris, 1783–1784," in Griffin, *Experiencing Empire*, 195–97.

71 *Diary and Autobiography of John Adams*, November 30, 1782, 3:85.

72 Stahr, *John Jay*, 162–70.

73 John Adams to Thomas Barclay, May 24, 1784, as cited in Morris, *John Jay*, 16.

74 *Diary and Autobiography of John Adams*, November 30, 1782, 3:85.

75 *Diary and Autobiography of John Adams*, November 11, 1782, 3:51–53.

76 *Diary and Autobiography of John Adams*, December 3, 1782, 3:86.

77 *Diary and Autobiography of John Adams*, January 11, 1783, 3:103

78 John Adams to Abigail Adams, January 22, 1783, *The Adams Papers: An Electronic Archive*.

79 *Diary and Autobiography of John Adams*, January 1, 1783, 3:101.

80 *Diary and Autobiography of John Adams*, January 21, 1783, 3:107.

81 *Diary and Autobiography of John Adams*, March 9, 1783, 3:111.

82 *Diary and Autobiography of John Adams*, April 30, 1783, 3:116.

83 James H. Hutson, "The American Negotiators; The Diplomacy of Jealousy," in Hoffman and Albert, *Peace and the Peacemakers*, 52–69. Hutson argues that both Jay and Adams were suspicious of their French and British counterparts because their jealously was a product of republican ideology.

84 Morris, "The Great Peace of 1783," 29.

85 Morris, "The Great Peace of 1783," 45–46.

86 John Adams to James Warren, April 16, 1783, *Founders Online*.

87 *Diary and Autobiography of John Adams*, March 9, 1783, 3:112.

88 John Adams to Thomas Jefferson, December 6, 1787, *Founders Online*.

89 See Lint, "Preparing for Peace."

90 *Diary and Autobiography of John Adams*, November 18, 1782, 3:61.

91 Kaplan, "The Treaty of Paris, 1783," 441.

92 Benjamin Franklin to Robert Livingston, July 22 [–26], 1783, *Founders Online*.

93 Abigail Adams to John Adams, December 23, 1782, in Abigail Adams, *The Letters of Mrs. Adams*, 137.

94 Abigail Adams to John Adams, June 20, 1783, in Abigail Adams, *The Letters of Mrs. Adams*, 142–44.

95 John Adams to Abigail Adams, August 13, 1783, in De Windt, *Journal and Correspondence of Miss Adams*, 203.

96 Abigail Adams to John Adams, November 19, 1783, in Abigail Adams, *The Letters of Mrs. Adams*, 145.

97 Abigail Adams to John Quincy Adams, November 20, 1783, in Abigail Adams, *The Letters of Mrs. Adams*, 146–49.

98 Abigail Adams to John Quincy Adams, December 26, 1783, in Abigail Adams, *The Letters of Mrs. Adams*, 154.

99 Abigail Adams to John Adams, October 19, 1783, *Adams Family Correspondence*, 5:257.

100 On February 17, 1812, the *Boston Patriot* published a fascinating autobiographical letter written by John Adams. Although composed nearly thirty years after the actual events, and therefore perhaps colored by nostalgia and the passage of time, it is a valuable insight into Adams's experience, personality, and world outlook. A copy is included in *Diary and Autobiography of John Adams*, 3:149–54.

101 John Jay to Sarah Jay, November 14, 1783, in Morris, *John Jay*, 2:642.

102 *Diary and Autobiography of John Adams*, Autobiographical Communication to the *Boston Patriot*, 3:151–53.

103 *Diary and Autobiography of John Adams*, Autobiographical Communication to the *Boston Patriot*, 3:153–54.

CHAPTER 3. ABIGAIL IN FRANCE

1 Abigail Adams to John Adams, December 15, 1783, *Adams Family Papers: An Electronic Archive*.

2 John Adams to Nabby (Abigail) Adams, April 14, 1783, in De Windt, *Journal and Correspondence of Miss Adams*, 22–23.

3 John Jay to Egbert Benson, May 19, 1781, as cited in Morris, *John Jay*, 15.

4 The only major biography of Jay remains Stahr, *John Jay*. For more details about the Jays' time in Europe, see 122–95.

5 John Adams to Abigail Adams, April 8, 1783–June 9, 1783, *Adams Family Papers: An Electronic Archive*.

6 Abigail Adams to John Adams, May 25, 1784, *Adams Family Correspondence*, 5:292.

7 Abigail Adams to John Adams, May 25, 1784, *Adams Family Correspondence*, 5:292.

8 Rice, *The Adams Family in Auteuil*, 3.

9 Thomas Jefferson to John Adams, June 19, 1784, in Cappon, *The Adams-Jefferson Letters*, 16.

10 "Abigail Adams' Diary of Her Voyage," July 4, 1784, *Diary and Autobiography of John Adams*, 3:162–63.

11 "Abigail Adams' Diary of Her Voyage," June 20–July 20, 1784, *Diary and Autobiography of John Adams*, 155.

12 Abigail Adams to Mary Cranch, July 6–20, 1784, in Abigail Adams, *The Letters of Mrs. Adams*, 157–60.

13 "Abigail Adams' Diary of Her Voyage," July 8 and 9, 1784, *Diary and Autobiography of John Adams*, 162–65. Abigail had been reading *A Political Survey of Britain* by John Campbell, published in 1774.

14 Abigail Adams to Mary Cranch, July 6–20, 1784, in Abigail Adams, *The Letters of Mrs. Adams*, 161–72.

15 John Jay to Robert Morris, October 2, 1782, quoted in Stahr, *John Jay*, 185.

16 Abigail Adams to Mary Cranch, July 6–20, 1784, in Abigail Adams, *The Letters of Mrs. Adams*, 161–72.

17 *Diary and Autobiography of John Adams*, June 22, 1784, 3:167.

18 John Adams to Abigail Adams, July 26, 1784, *Founders Online*.

19 Abigail Adams to Mary Cranch, July 20, 1784, in Abigail Adams, *The Letters of Mrs. Adams*, 173.

20 Abigail Adams to Elizabeth Shaw, July 28–30, 1784, *Founders Online*.

21 Abigail Adams to Betsy Cranch, August 1, 1784, *Founders Online*.

22 Abigail Adams to Mary Cranch, August 2, 1784, *Founders Online*.

23 Abigail Adams to Mary Cranch, July 24, 1784, in Abigail Adams, *The Letters of Mrs. Adams*, 173–76.

24 John Adams to Abigail Adams, July 26, 1784, *Adams Family Papers: An Electronic Archive*.

25 Abigail Adams to Mary Cranch, December 12, 1784, *Adams Family Correspondence*, 6:18.

26 Abigail Adams to Cotton Tufts, March 8, 1785, *Adams Family Correspondence*, 6:76–78.

27 Thomas Jefferson to James Madison, May 25, 1788, in Boyd et al., *The Papers of Thomas Jefferson*, 13:202.

28 Abigail Adams to Mary Cranch, September 5, 1784, in Abigail Adams, *The Letters of Mrs. Adams*.

29 John Adams to John Jay, January 3, 1785, *Papers of John Adams*, 16:508.

30 *Diary and Autobiography of John Adams*, August 17, 1784, 3:171.

31 John Adams to John Jay, January 3, 1785, *Papers of John Adams*, 16:508.

32 Nabby (Abigail) Adams to Elizabeth Cranch, December 10, 1784, *Adams Family Correspondence*, 6:24–25.

33 Nabby (Abigail) Adams to Mercy Warren, September 5, 1784, in De Windt, *Journal and Correspondence of Miss Adams*, 31.

34 Abigail Adams to Mrs. Warren, September 5, 1784, in Abigail Adams, *The Letters of Mrs. Adams*, 201.

35 Abigail Adams to Miss E. Cranch, December 13, 1784, in Abigail Adams, *The Letters of Mrs. Adams*, 211.

36 Abigail Adams to Mary Cranch, December 9, 1784, in Abigail Adams, *The Letters of Mrs. Adams*, 213–14.

37 Abigail Adams to Mary Cranch, December 9, 1784, in Abigail Adams, *The Letters of Mrs. Adams*, 213–14.

38 Abigail Adams to Isaac Smith Sr., May 8, 1785, *Adams Family Correspondence*, 6:136.

39 Alberts, *The Golden Voyage*, 120–42.

40 Abigail Adams to Mercy Otis Warren, September 5, 1784, *Adams Family Correspondence*, 5:446–53.

41 Abigail Adams to Elizabeth Cranch, December 3, 1784, *Adams Family Correspondence*, 6:3–10.

42 Alberts, *The Golden Voyage*, 147.

43 Journal entry, January 12, 1785, in De Windt, *Journal and Correspondence of Miss Adams*, 47.

44 Anne Willing Bingham to Thomas Jefferson, June 1, 1787, and Thomas Jefferson to Anne Willing Bingham, May 11, 1788, in Boyd et al., *The Papers of Thomas Jefferson*, 12:392–93, 13:151–52.

45 Branson, *These Fiery Frenchified Dames*, 7, 133–35.

46 Abigail Adams to Mary Cranch, December 9, 1784, in Abigail Adams, *The Letters of Mrs. Adams*, 215.

47 Abigail Adams to Mary Cranch, December 9, 1784, in Abigail Adams, *The Letters of Mrs. Adams*, 215.

48 Abigail Adams to Mary Cranch, December 9, 1784, in Abigail Adams, *The Letters of Mrs. Adams*, 215.

49 Abigail Adams to Mrs. Storer, January 20, 1785, in Abigail Adams, *The Letters of Mrs. Adams*, 228–31.

50 Abigail Adams to Mrs. Warren, September 5, 1784, in Abigail Adams, *The Letters of Mrs. Adams*, 201.

51 Journal entry, September 19, 1784, in De Windt, *Journal and Correspondence of Miss Adams*, 18.

52 John Quincy Adams to Mary Cranch, December 12, 1784, *Adams Family Correspondence*, 6:26–28.

53 Abigail Adams to Charles Storer, January 3, 1785, *Adams Family Correspondence*, 6:40–41.

54 Abigail Adams to Mary Cranch, September 5, 1784, *Adams Family Correspondence*, 5:443.

55 John Adams to Nabby Adams, April 14, 1783, in De Windt, *Journal and Correspondence of Miss Adams*, 22–23.

56 Abigail Adams to Lucy Quincy Tufts, September 3, 1785, *Adams Family Correspondence*, 6:331–32.

57 Abigail Adams to Mercy Warren, September 5, 1784, in Abigail Adams, *The Letters of Mrs. Adams*, 200–206.

58 Abigail Adams to Mary Cranch, December 9, 1784, in Abigail Adams, *The Letters of Mrs. Adams*, 213–14.

59 John Adams to James Warren, August 27, 1784, *Founders Online*.

60 Abigail Adams to Mary Cranch, May 8, 1785, in Abigail Adams, *The Letters of Mrs. Adams*, 248.

61 Thomas Jefferson to John Adams, May 25, 1785, in Cappon, *The Adams-Jefferson Letters*, 23.

62 Abigail Adams to Thomas Jefferson, June 6, 1785, in Cappon, *The Adams-Jefferson Letters*, 28.

63 Steele, *Thomas Jefferson and American Nationhood*, 85.

64 Crews, "Thomas Jefferson: Culinary Revolutionary."

65 Journal entry, January 12, 1785, in De Windt, *Journal and Correspondence of Miss Adams*, 45.

66 Brodie, *Thomas Jefferson*, 190–92.

67 Abigail Adams to Thomas Jefferson, July 6, 1787, in Cappon, *The Adams-Jefferson Letters*, 183.

68 Abigail Adams to Mary Cranch, April 24, 1786, *Adams Family Correspondence*, 7:147.

69 Abigail Adams to Elizabeth Shaw, December 14, 1784, *Adams Family Correspondence*, 6:29.

70 Abigail Adams to Mary Cranch, December 9, 1784, *Adams Family Correspondence*, 6:20.

71 Abigail Adams to Elisabeth Storer Smith, August 29, 1785, *Adams Family Correspondence*, 6:315.

72 Abigail Adams to Mary Cranch, December 9, 1787, in Abigail Adams, *The Letters of Mrs. Adams*, 214.

73 Journal entry, January 1, 1785, in De Windt, *Journal and Correspondence of Miss Adams*, 38–39.

74 Journal entry, March 29, 1785, and March 30, 1785, in De Windt, *Journal and Correspondence of Miss Adams*, 65–68.

75 Journal entry, March 29, 1785, and March 30, 1785, in De Windt, *Journal and Correspondence of Miss Adams*, 65–68.

76 Abigail Adams to Mary Cranch, December 16, 1785, in Abigail Adams, *The Letters of Mrs. Adams*, 327.

77 Abigail Adams to Mary Cranch, February 20, 1785, in Abigail Adams, *The Letters of Mrs. Adams*, 233–34.

78 John Adams to Benjamin Franklin and Thomas Jefferson, March 20, 1785, in Cappon, *The Adams-Jefferson Letters*, 18–20.

79 *Diary and Autobiography of John Adams*, May 3, 1783, 3:176.

80 Abigail Adams to Mary Cranch, April 15, 1785, *Founders Online*.

81 Abigail Adams to Cotton Tufts, May 2, 1785, *Adams Family Correspondence*, 6:105.

82 Journal entry, May 10, 1785, in De Windt, *Journal and Correspondence of Miss Adams*, 71.

83 John Adams to Richard Cranch, April 27, 1785, *Adams Family Correspondence*, 6:109.

84 John Adams to John Jay, May 13, 1785, *Founders Online*.

85 Abigail Adams to Cotton Tufts, May 2, 1785, *Adams Family Correspondence*, 6:103.

86 Abigail Adams to Elizabeth Shaw, October 15, 1786, in *Adams Family Correspondence*, 7:373.

87 Abigail Adams to Elizabeth Shaw, May 8, 1785, in Rice, *The Adams Family in Auteuil*, 30.

88 Abigail Adams to Elizabeth Cranch, May 8, 1785, in Abigail Adams, *The Letters of Mrs. Adams*, 246.

89 Abigail Adams to Mary Cranch, May 8, 1785, *Founders Online*.

90 *Diary and Autobiography of John Adams*, May 3, 1785, 3:176.

CHAPTER 4. ABIGAIL AND JOHN IN LONDON

1 John Adams to John Jay, May 5, 1785, *Papers of John Adams*, 17:88–90.

2 John Adams to Thomas Jefferson, May 22, 1785, in Cappon, *The Adams-Jefferson Letters*, 21.

3 Abigail Adams to Mary Cranch, June 24, 1785, *Adams Family Correspondence*, 6:186–94.

4 See McConville, *The King's Three Faces*.

5 John Adams to John Jay, June 2, 1785, *Papers of John Adams*, 17:134–45.

6 John Adams to John Jay, June 2, 1785, *Papers of John Adams*, 17:134–45.

7 John Adams to John Jay, June 2, 1785, *Papers of John Adams*, 17:134–45.

8 John Adams to John Jay, June 2, 1785, *Papers of John Adams*, 17:134–45.

9 John Adams to John Jay, June 2, 1785, *Papers of John Adams*, 17:134–45.

10 John Adams to Thomas Jefferson, June 3, 1785, in Cappon, *The Adams-Jefferson Letters*, 27.

11 Abigail Adams to Mary Cranch, June 24, 1785, *Adams Family Correspondence*, 6:186–94.

12 Abigail Adams to Mary Cranch, June 24, 1785, *Adams Family Correspondence*, 6:186–94.

13 John Adams to John Thaxter Jr., June 2, 1786, *Adams Family Correspondence*, 7:209.

14 Abigail Adams to Mary Cranch, June 24, 1785, *Adams Family Correspondence*, 6:186–94.

15 Abigail Adams to Thomas Jefferson, June 6, 1785, in Cappon, *The Adams-Jefferson Letters*, 29.

16 *Times* (London), June 10, 1785, 2.

17 Thomas Jefferson to Abigail Adams, June 21, 1785, *Adams Family Correspondence*, 6:180.

18 Abigail Adams to Thomas Jefferson, August 12, 1785, *Adams Family Correspondence*, 6:262–63.

19 Abigail Adams to Mary Smith Cranch, August 15, 1785, *Founders Online*.

20 Journal entry, December 11, 1785, in De Windt, *Journal and Correspondence of Miss Adams*, 83.

21 Judith Sargent Murray to Epes Sargent, October 2, 1798, as cited in Skemp, *First Lady of Letters*, 290.

22 Fisher Ames to Rufus King, September 24, 1800, in King, *The Life and Correspondence of Rufus King*, 3:304.

23 Abigail Adams 2d to John Quincy Adams, July 26, 1785, *Adams Family Correspondence*, 6:216.

24 *Boston Patriot*, February 17, 1812, in *Diary and Autobiography of John Adams*, 150.

25 John Adams to John Jay, December 3, 1785, *Founders Online*.

26 Abigail Adams to Mary Cranch, October 1, 1785, *Adams Family Correspondence*, 6:395.

27 See Alberts, *The Golden Voyage*, particularly the chapter covering the Binghams' return from Europe.

28 For a lucid discussion of the inherent contradictions between the acquisition of luxury objects and republican ideals, see Yokota, *Unbecoming British*, particularly chapter 2 and 74–75.

29 Abigail Adams to Mary Cranch, June 24, 1785, *Adams Family Correspondence*, 6:186–94.

30 Abigail Adams to Charles Williamos, July 1, 1785, *Adams Family Correspondence*, 6:202.

31 For an informative look at how fashion influenced the Adamses and Jefferson in Europe, see Gaye Wilson, "Jefferson and the Creation of an American Image Abroad," in Sadosky et al., *Old World, New World*, 155–78.

32 Abigail Adams to Elizabeth Cranch, July 18, 1786, *Adams Family Correspondence*, 7:258.

33 Abigail Adams to Thomas Jefferson, February 11, 1786, in Cappon, *The Adams-Jefferson Letters*, 119.

34 Chalus, *Elite Women in English Political Life*, 77, 80.

35 Abigail Adams to Mary Smith Cranch, June 24, 1785, *Founders Online*.

36 Abigail Adams to John Quincy Adams, June 26, 1785, *Adams Family Correspondence*, 6:194–96.

37 Abigail Adams to Mary Smith Cranch, June 24, 1785, *Founders Online*.

38 Abigail Adams to Mary Smith Cranch, June 24, 1785, *Founders Online.*

39 Abigail Adams to Mary Smith Cranch, June 24, 1785, *Founders Online.*

40 Abigail Adams to Mary Smith Cranch, June 24, 1785, *Founders Online.*

41 Abigail Adams to Mary Smith Cranch, September 30, 1785, *Founders Online.*

42 John Adams to Thomas Jefferson, June 7, 1785, in Cappon, *The Adams-Jefferson Letters,* 31.

43 John Adams to Cotton Tufts, June 2, 1786, *Adams Family Correspondence,* 7:210.

44 Abigail Adams to Mary Smith Cranch, June 24, 1785, *Founders Online.*

45 Abigail Adams to Mary Smith Cranch, June 24, 1785, in Abigail Adams, *The Letters of Mrs. Adams,* 102–5.

46 See Waldstreicher, *In the Midst of Perpetual Fetes.*

47 John Adams to Abigail Adams, July 3, 1776, *Adams Family Correspondence,* 2:30.

48 Abigail Adams to Mary Cranch, June 24, 1785, *Adams Family Correspondence,* 6:186–94.

49 Abigail Adams to Mary Cranch, June 24, 1785, *Adams Family Correspondence,* 6:186–94.

50 Abigail Adams to Thomas Welch, August 25, 1785, *Adams Family Correspondence,* 6:297.

51 Abigail Adams to Thomas Welch, August 25, 1785, *Adams Family Correspondence,* 6:297.

52 Abigail Adams to John Adams, August 29, 1776, *Adams Family Papers: An Electronic Archive.*

53 John Adams to Richard Cranch, August 22, 1785, *Adams Family Correspondence,* 6:294–95.

54 Abigail Adams to Mary Cranch, June 24, 1785, *Adams Family Correspondence,* 6:186–94.

55 Abigail Adams to Mary Smith Cranch, ca. July–August 1785, *Adams Family Correspondence,* 6:240–42.

56 John Adams to Thomas Jefferson, September 4, 1785, in Cappon, *The Adams-Jefferson Letters,* 61.

57 John Adams to John Quincy Adams, September 9, 1785, *Adams Family Correspondence,* 6:355.

58 Abigail Adams to Cotton Tufts, August 1, 1786, *Adams Family Correspondence,* 7:306.

59 Dull, *A Diplomatic History of the American Revolution,* 53–54.

60 Gilje, "Commerce and Conquest," 747.

61 Chalus, *Elite Women in English Political Life,* 91, 94.

62 Journal entry, September 2, 1785, in De Windt, *Journal and Correspondence of Miss Adams,* 80.

63 Abigail Adams to Mary Cranch, August 15, 1785, in Abigail Adams, *The Letters of Mrs. Adams,* 269.

64 Abigail Adams to Mary Smith Cranch, August 15, 1785, *Adams Family Correspondence,* 6:278.

65 Abigail Adams to John Quincy Adams, September 6, 1785, in Abigail Adams, *The Letters of Mrs. Adams,* 268–69.

66 John Adams to John Jay, October 15, 1785, *Founders Online.*
67 Abigail Adams to Thomas Jefferson, November 24, 1785, in Cappon, *The Adams-Jefferson Letters,* 100.
68 John Adams to Thomas Jefferson, November 1, 1785, in Cappon, *The Adams-Jefferson Letters,* 88.
69 Abigail Adams to Mary Smith Cranch, October 1, 1785, *Founders Online.*
70 Abigail Adams to John Quincy Adams, September 6, 1785, *Adams Family Correspondence,* 6:342–46.
71 Mary Palmer to Abigail Adams, December 11, 1785, *Adams Family Correspondence,* 6:489–91.
72 Abigail Adams to John Quincy Adams, September 6, 1785, *Adams Family Correspondence,* 6:342–46.
73 Abigail Adams to Mary Smith Cranch, September 30, 1785, *Adams Family Correspondence,* 6:392.
74 Benjamin E. Park has stressed the centrality of religion in the formation of American nationalism in *American Nationalisms.*
75 Constitution of the Commonwealth of Massachusetts, Part the First, Article Three, https://malegislature.gov.
76 Alberts, *The Golden Voyage,* 153–55.
77 Abigail Adams to Mary Smith Cranch, September 30, 1785, *Adams Family Correspondence,* 6:392–95.
78 Abigail Adams to Mary Cranch, September 30, 1785, in Abigail Adams, *The Letters of Mrs. Adams,* 270.
79 Nabby Adams to John Quincy Adams, February 9, 1786, *Adams Family Correspondence,* 7:33–36.
80 Abigail Adams to Miss E. Cranch, April 2, 1786, in Abigail Adams, *The Letters of Mrs. Adams,* 278–82.
81 Abigail Adams to Miss Lucy Cranch, April 2, 1786, *Adams Family Correspondence,* 7:126–29.
82 Abigail Adams to Mary Cranch, April 24, 1786, *Founders Online.*
83 Abigail Adams to Mary Cranch, October 1, 1785, in Abigail Adams, *The Letters of Mrs. Adams,* 273.
84 Abigail Adams to Elizabeth Smith Shaw, August 15, 1785, in Abigail Adams, *The Letters of Mrs. Adams,* 269.
85 Abigail Adams to Miss E. Cranch, August 15, 1785, in Abigail Adams, *The Letters of Mrs. Adams,* 264–65.
86 Abigail Adams to Elizabeth Smith Shaw, July 19, 1787, *Adams Family Correspondence,* 7:264.
87 Abigail Adams to Mary Smith Cranch, May 21, 1786, *Founders Online.*
88 John Adams to Thomas Jefferson, February 21, 1786, in Cappon, *The Adams-Jefferson Letters,* 123.

89 John Adams to Richard Cranch, March 11, 1786, *Adams Family Correspondence*, 7:85–86.

90 Thomas Jefferson to John Page, May 4, 1787, *Founders Online*.

91 Wood, *Friends Divided*, 111–16.

92 Abigail Adams to Charles Storer, March 23, 1786, *Adams Family Correspondence*, 7:113–14.

93 For details about the paintings, see Meschutt, "The Adams-Jefferson Portrait Exchange."

94 Abigail Adams to Mary Cranch, October 1, 1785, in Abigail Adams, *The Letters of Mrs. Adams*, 274.

95 Abigail Adams to Mary Smith Cranch, April 6, 1786, *Adams Family Correspondence*, 7:134.

96 For a detailed description of Jefferson's and Adams's tour, see Shackelford, *Thomas Jefferson's Travels in Europe*, 51–62.

97 John Adams to Abigail Adams, April 5, 1786, *Founders Online*.

98 *Diary and Autobiography of John Adams*, April 4–10, 20, 1786, 3:186, 189–90.

99 Abigail Adams to Elizabeth Shaw, April 24, 1786, *Adams Family Correspondence*, 7:149; *Diary and Autobiography of John Adams*, April 20, 1/86, 3:189–90.

100 Abigail Adams to Elizabeth Cranch, July 18, 1786, *Adams Family Correspondence*, 7:256–57.

101 Thomas Jefferson to James Madison, April 25, 1786, *Founders Online*.

102 Thomas Jefferson to James Madison, January 30, 1787, in Boyd et al., *The Papers of Thomas Jefferson*, 11:94.

103 Abigail Adams to Cotton Tufts, August 18, 1785, *Adams Family Correspondence*, 6:286.

104 Levin, *Abigail Adams*, 207–11.

105 John Quincy Adams to Nabby Adams, May 18, 1786, *Adams Family Correspondence*, 7:166.

106 Abigail Adams to Mary Smith Cranch, June 13, 1786, *Founders Online*.

107 Abigail Adams to Elizabeth Shaw, October 15, 1786, *Founders Online*.

108 Abigail Adams to William Stephens Smith, September 18, 1785, *Adams Family Correspondence*, 6:366–68.

109 Abigail Adams to Lucy Cranch, April 26, 1787, *Adams Family Correspondence*, 8:25.

110 Abigail Adams to Lucy Cranch, July 20, 1786, in Abigail Adams, *The Letters of Mrs. Adams*, 297–98.

111 Abigail Adams to Abigail Adams Smith, August 8, 1786, *Adams Family Correspondence*, 7:315–17.

112 Abigail Adams to Abigail Adams Smith, August 23, 1786, in De Windt, *Journal and Correspondence of Miss Adams*, 58.

113 Abigail Adams to Mary Cranch, September 12, 1786, in Abigail Adams, *The Letters of Mrs. Adams*, 300–301.

114 Abigail Adams to John Quincy Adams, October 12, 1787, in Abigail Adams, *The Letters of Mrs. Adams*, 342.

115 *Diary and Autobiography of John Adams*, July 16, 1786, 3:194.

116 Abigail Adams to Miss E. Cranch, July 18, 1786, in Abigail Adams, *The Letters of Mrs. Adams*, 293.

117 Abigail Adams to Elizabeth Shaw, November 21, 1786, in Abigail Adams, *The Letters of Mrs. Adams*, 310–11.

118 See, for example, Cotton Tufts to Abigail Adams, July 6, 1786, and Mary Smith Cranch to Abigail Adams, July 10, 1786, *Adams Family Correspondence*, 7:244, 248.

119 For a discussion of Warren's early life, education, and longtime close friendship with both Abigail and John Adams, see Rosemarie Zaggari's fine biography, *A Woman's Dilemma*.

120 Zagarri, *A Woman's Dilemma*, 102–4, 119.

121 Abigail Adams to Thomas Jefferson, January 29, 1787, in Cappon, *The Adams-Jefferson Letters*, 168–69.

122 John Adams to Cotton Tufts, July 4, 1786, *Founders Online*.

123 Thomas Jefferson to Abigail Adams, February 22, 1787, in Cappon, *The Adams-Jefferson Letters*, 173.

124 Steele, *Thomas Jefferson and American Nationhood*, 6, 118.

125 Abigail Adams to Mary Smith Cranch, March 8, 1787, *Founders Online*.

126 Abigail Adams to Elizabeth Smith Shaw, May 2, 1787, *Founders Online*.

127 Steele, *Thomas Jefferson and American Nationhood*, 113.

128 Maier, "Popular Uprising and Civil Authority," 3–4, 18, 24–26.

129 John Jay to Thomas Jefferson, October 27, 1786, and December 14, 1786, in Boyd et al., *The Papers of Thomas Jefferson*, 10:488, 597.

130 Abigail Adams to John Cranch, March 7, 1787, *Adams Family Correspondence*, 8:1.

131 Abigail Adams to Mary Cranch, January 20, 1787, *Founders Online*.

132 Abigail Adams to Mary Cranch, January 20, 1787, in Abigail Adams, *The Letters of Mrs. Adams*, 166–67.

133 John Adams to Abigail Adams, June 1, 1787, *Adams Family Correspondence*, 8:73.

134 Abigail Adams to Mary Cranch, September 15, 1787, *Founders Online*.

135 Abigail Adams to Lucy Cranch, October 3, 1787, *Founders Online*.

136 Abigail Adams to Mary Cranch, September 15, 1787, *Founders Online*.

137 Abigail Adams to Elizabeth Shaw, October 10, 1787, *Founders Online*.

138 Abigail Adams to Elizabeth Shaw, October 10, 1787, *Founders Online*.

CHAPTER 5. THE FINAL YEARS ABROAD

1 Abigail Adams to Mary Cranch, May 21, 1786, in Abigail Adams, *The Letters of Mrs. Adams*, 288–89.

2 Abigail Adams to Mary Cranch, May 21, 1786, in Abigail Adams, *The Letters of Mrs. Adams*, 288–89.

3 Thomas Jefferson to John Adams, February 20, 1787, in Cappon, *The Adams-Jefferson Letters*, 172.

4 Gelles, *Abigail and John*, 200.

5 Abigail Adams to Mary Cranch, September 15, 1787, *Founders Online*.

6 Abigail Adams to Mary Cranch, September 15, 1787, *Founders Online*.

7 Abigail Adams to Mary Cranch, September 15, 1787, *Founders Online*.

8 Abigail Adams to Mary Cranch, September 15, 1787, *Founders Online*.

9 George, *London Life in the Eighteenth Century*, 3.

10 Abigail Adams to John Quincy Adams, July 18, 1787, *Adams Family Correspondence*, 8:428, 125.

11 Abigail Adams to Cotton Tufts, October 5, 1787, *Adams Family Correspondence*, 8:184.

12 John Adams to Charles Adams, January 10, 1787, and John Adams to John Quincy Adams, January 10, 1787, *Adams Family Correspondence*, 7:428, 429.

13 John Adams to John Quincy Adams, July 20, 1787, *Adams Family Correspondence*, 8:130.

14 Abigail Adams to Mary Smith Cranch, April 28, 1787, *Adams Family Correspondence*, 8:32.

15 John Adams to Massachusetts Delegates in Congress, January 25, 1787, and John Adams to John Jay, February 3, 1787, *Founders Online*.

16 John Jay to Samuel Huntington, April 21, 1781, as quoted in Stahr, *John Jay*, 139.

17 John Adams to Cotton Tufts, February 21, 1787, *Adams Family Correspondence*, 7:467.

18 John Adams to Thomas Jefferson, July 19, 1787, in Cappon, *The Adams-Jefferson Letters*, 187.

19 Abigail Adams to Elizabeth Shaw, March 10, 1787, *Founders Online*.

20 Abigail Adams to Mary Cranch, April 28, 1787, *Adams Family Correspondence*, 8:29.

21 Abigail Adams to Isaac Smith Sr., March 12, 1787, *Adams Family Correspondence*, 8:9.

22 Abigail Adams to John Quincy Adams, February 28, 1787, *Adams Family Correspondence*, 7:475.

23 Thomas Jefferson to John Adams, February 20, 1787, in Cappon, *The Adams-Jefferson Letters*, 172.

24 John Adams to Thomas Jefferson, March 1, 1787, in Cappon, *The Adams-Jefferson Letters*, 176–77.

25 Nabby Adams to John Quincy Adams, February 10, 1788, *Adams Family Correspondence*, 8:228.

26 For an in-depth, early seminal analysis of the fundamental changes in Adams's political outlook, see Appleby, "The New Republican Synthesis."

27 Mayville, *John Adams and the Fear of American Oligarchy*, 6–14. See also Miroff, "John Adams."

28 Abigail Adams to John Quincy Adams, January 17, 1787, *Adams Family Correspondence*, 7:443.

29 Mary Cranch to Abigail Adams, September 24, 1786, *Adams Family Correspondence*, 7:342.

30 Cotton Tufts to Abigail Adams, October 14, 1786, *Adams Family Correspondence*, 7:371.

31 Abigail Adams to John Quincy Adams, November 28, 1786, *Adams Family Correspondence*, 7:405.

32 Abigail Adams to Mary Smith Cranch, March 8, 1787, *Adams Family Correspondence*, 8:2.

33 Abigail Adams to Cotton Tufts, October 10, 1786, *Adams Family Correspondence*, 7:363.

34 Abigail Adams to John Quincy Adams, November 22, 1786, *Adams Family Correspondence*, 7:395–96.

35 John Jay to Thomas Jefferson, October 27, 1785, in Boyd et al., *The Papers of Thomas Jefferson*, 10:488–89.

36 Abigail Adams to John Adams, December 30, 1786, *Adams Family Correspondence*, 7:415.

37 Abigail Adams to Mary Smith Cranch, January 20, 1787, *Adams Family Correspondence*, 7:450.

38 See Ryerson, *John Adams's Republic*, 282–310.

39 Wood, *The Americanization of Benjamin Franklin*, 165–66.

40 Thompson, *John Adams and the Spirit of Liberty*, xiii.

41 Richard Cranch to John Adams, May 24, 1787, *Adams Family Correspondence*, 8:59–60.

42 Thompson, "John Adams and the Coming of the American Revolution," 361–71.

43 Gordon S. Wood makes a similar point in *Friends Divided*, 213.

44 For an in-depth discussion of the foundation of Adams's political thought, as well as his deep disagreement with Wollstonecraft's assessment of the French Revolution, based on his handwritten notes in the margins of his copy of her book, see Kitch, "The Roots of John Adams's Political Science"; and O'Neill, "John Adams versus Mary Wollstonecraft."

45 For a careful, highly detailed description of Adams's political thought, see Ryerson, *John Adams's Republic*.

46 John Adams to Abigail Adams, May 22, 1777, *Adams Family Papers: An Electronic Archive*.

47 For a perceptive analysis of Adams's political outlook as evidenced in the *Defence*, see Ellis, *Passionate Sage*, chapter 5.

48 Kitch, "The Roots of John Adams's Political Science," 300.

49 John Adams, *Defence of the Constitutions of Government*, in Charles Francis Adams, *The Works of John Adams*, 4:557–58.

50 Ellis, *Passionate Sage*, 173. Ellis made similar points in his recent book, *American Dialogue*.

51 John Adams, *Defence of the Constitutions of Government*, in Charles Francis Adams, *The Works of John Adams*, 4:346.

52 John Adams to Thomas Jefferson, October 9, 1787, in Cappon, *The Adams–Jefferson Letters*, 202–3.

53 Randall N. Riley, "Adams, Burke, and Eighteenth-Century Conservatism."

54 Cornish, "John Adams, Cicero and the Traditions of Republicanism," 28–30, 34–35.

55 Steele, *Thomas Jefferson and American Nationhood*, 124.

56 John Adams, *Defence of the Constitutions of Government*, in Charles Francis Adams, *The Works of John Adams*, 4:346.

57 Steele, *Thomas Jefferson and American Nationhood*, 7, 55.

58 John Adams, *Defence of the Constitutions of Government*, in Charles Francis Adams, *The Works of John Adams*, 4:346.

59 John Adams to Thomas Jefferson, March 1, 1787, in Cappon, *The Adams-Jefferson Letters*, 176.

60 Ellis, *Passionate Sage*, 228.

61 John Adams to Samuel Adams, September 12, 1790, in Charles Francis Adams, *Works of John Adams*, 6:411–12.

62 Abigail Adams to Lucy Cranch, April 2, 1786, *Adams Family Correspondence*, 7:126.

63 Abigail Adams to John Adams, July 5, 1780, *Adams Family Papers: An Electronic Archive*.

64 Abigail Adams to John Quincy Adams, March 20, 1787, *Founders Online*.

65 Cotton Tufts to Abigail Adams, September 20, 1787, *Adams Family Correspondence*, 8:164.

66 Warren, *History of the Rise, Progress, and Termination of the American Revolution*, 3:394–95.

67 Mercy Otis Warren to John Adams, July 28, 1807, in Charles Francis Adams, "Correspondence between John Adams and Mercy Warren," reprinted in *Collections of Massachusetts Historical Society* (Boston: Massachusetts Historical Society, 1878), 363.

68 Rosemarie Zagarri discusses the deteriorating relationship and the Warrens' position in detail in *A Woman's Dilemma*, 117–22.

69 Taylor's critique was published in 1814, but a reprint is available: Taylor, *An Inquiry into the Principles and Policy of the Government of the United States*.

70 Abigail Adams to Mary Cranch, February 27, 1787, in Abigail Adams, *The Letters of Mrs. Adams*, 320.

71 Abigail Adams to Cotton Tufts, March 10, 1787, *Adams Family Correspondence*, 8:6.

72 Abigail Adams to Elizabeth Shaw, May 2, 1787, *Founders Online*.

73 Abigail Adams to John Adams, June 7, 1787, *Adams Family Correspondence*, 8:79–81.

74 Abigail Adams to Mary Smith Cranch, October 8, 1787, *Founders Online*.

75 Thomas Jefferson to John Adams, February 23, 1787, in Cappon, *The Adams-Jefferson Letters*, 174.

76 John Adams to Thomas Jefferson, July 13, 1813, in Cappon, *The Adams-Jefferson Letters*, 356.

77 Appleby, "The Jefferson-Adams Rupture."

78 For a detailed discussion of Jefferson, Adams, and conflicts over the ideology of the French Revolution, see Thompson, "John Adams and the Coming of the French Revolution."

79 John Adams to John Taylor, April 15, 1815, in Charles Francis Adams, *The Works of John Adams*, 6:447.

80 Abigail Adams to Cotton Tufts, November 6, 1787, *Adams Family Correspondence*, 8:203.

81 Abigail Adams to Mrs. Warren, May 14, 1787, in Abigail Adams, *The Letters of Mrs. Adams*, 322–23.

82 Abigail Adams to Mrs. Warren, May 14, 1787, in Abigail Adams, *The Letters of Mrs. Adams*, 325.

83 Abigail Adams to John Quincy Adams, October 12, 1787, in Abigail Adams, *The Letters of Mrs. Adams*, 343.

84 In *Marie-Antoinette*, John Hardman argues that the queen was far from frivolous, was politically astute, and near the end of her life was willing to support a constitutional monarchy to save the country.

85 Abigail Adams to John Adams, March 23, 1788, *Adams Family Papers: An Electronic Archive*.

86 John Adams to John Jay, September 22, 1787, *Founders Online*.

87 John Adams to John Jay, November 30, 1787, *Founders Online*.

88 John Adams to Royall Tyler, December 12, 1785, *Adams Family Correspondence*, 6:492–93.

89 John Adams to John Jay, December 16, 1787, *Founders Online*.

90 John Adams to Cotton Tufts, January 23, 1788, *Adams Family Correspondence*, 8:220.

91 John Adams to John Jay, December 16, 1787, *Founders Online*.

92 John Adams to Hezekiah Niles, February 13, 1818, in Charles Francis Adams, *The Works of John Adams*, 10:28.

93 Benjamin E. Parks examines some of these local cultures in *American Nationalisms*.

94 John Adams to John Jay, December 16, 1787, *Founders Online*.

95 Thomas Jefferson to Abigail Adams, February 2, 1788, and Abigail Adams to Thomas Jefferson, February 21, 1788, *Adams Family Correspondence*, 8:224, 236.

96 Abigail Adams to Thomas Jefferson, February 26, 1788, *Adams Family Correspondence*, 8:238.

97 Abigail Adams to Abigail Adams Smith, April 9, 1788, *Adams Family Correspondence*, 8:254–55.

98 Abigail Adams to Abigail Adams Smith, May 29, 1788, *Adams Family Correspondence*, 8:266.

99 For the story of Abigail's stint as America's second First Lady, see Abrams, *First Ladies of the Republic*.

100 *Massachusetts Centinel*, June 18, 1788.

101 Rice, *The Adams Family in Auteuil*, 4.

102 Abigail Adams to Mrs. Warren, May 24, 1786, in Abigail Adams, *The Letters of Mrs. Adams*, 291.

103 "John Jay's Address to the City of New York, August, 1783," cited in Stahr, *John Jay*, 195.

104 "Inaugural Address of John Adams," March 4, 1797, *The Avalon Project*, http://avalon.law.yale.edu/18th_century/adams/asp.

CONCLUSION

1 Whittock, *Mayflower Lives*, xi, 21, 169, 270–71.

2 Ryerson, *John Adams's Republic*, 13–14. Ryerson argues that Adams's political thought was not radically changed by his residence in Europe as an American diplomat, but that it just became more clearly defined and nuanced.

3 Charles Francis Adams, *The Works of John Adams*, 4:194.

4 Appleby, "The New Republican Synthesis," 587.

5 *Diary and Autobiography of John Adams*, July 21, 1786, 3:195.

6 Ryerson, *John Adams's Republic*, 7–8, 8–12.

7 Steele, *Thomas Jefferson and American Nationhood*, 150, 312.

8 Cotton Tufts to Abigail Adams, December 1, 1784, *Adams Family Correspondence*, 6:1.

9 John Adams to James Warren, January 9, 1787, *Founders Online*.

10 Mercy Otis Warren to Abigail Adams, April 30, 1785, *Adams Family Correspondence*, 6:113.

11 For an earlier cogent discussion of Adams's evolving political outlook, see Howe, *The Changing Political Thought of John Adams*, particularly the introduction, xi-xv, and 102–32.

12 Abigail Adams to Mary Cranch, June 28, 1789, in Mitchell, *New Letters of Abigail Adams*, 13.

13 Richard A. Ryerson, "John Adams in Europe: A Provincial Cosmopolitan Confronts the Metropolitan World, 1778–1788," in Sadosky et al., *Old World, New World*, 133, 144, 148.

14 Historian Richard Adam Samuelson argued this in his PhD dissertation, "The Adams Family and the American Experiment," 11.

15 John Adams to Thomas Jefferson, December 6, 1787, *Founders Online*.

16 Ryerson, "John Adams in Europe," 138–40.

17 Wood, *Friends Divided*, 213–14.

18 John Adams to Thomas Jefferson, December 6, 1787, *Founders Online*.

19 John Adams to Cotton Tufts, December 9, 1789, *Adams Family Correspondence*, 7:29.

20 Abigail Adams to Elizabeth Smith Shaw, March 4, 1786, *Founders Online*.

21 Abigail Adams to Miss Lucy Cranch, April 2, 1786, in Abigail Adams, *The Letters of Mrs. Adams*, 282–83.

22 Abigail Adams to Miss Lucy Cranch, April 2, 1786, in Abigail Adams, *The Letters of Mrs. Adams,* 282–83.

23 James Davison Hunter, as quoted in *Wall Street Journal*, June 7, 2019, A13.

24 Abigail Adams to Thomas Jefferson, January 29, 1787, *Adams Family Correspondence*, 7:454.

25 Abigail Adams to Elizabeth Smith Shaw, July 19, 1786, *Adams Family Correspondence*, 7:265–65.

26 John Adams to James Warren, January 9, 1787, *Founders Online*.

27 Abigail Adams to Elizabeth Smith Shaw, July 19, 1786, *Founders Online*.

28 John Adams to Mercy Otis Warren, April 16, 1776, *Adams Family Correspondence*, 4:123–26.

29 "Diary of Abigail Adams," July 4, 1784, in *Diary and Autobiography of John Adams*, 3:163.

30 Abigail Adams to Elizabeth Smith Shaw, October 12, 1787, *Founders Online*.

31 John Adams to James Warren, January 9, 1787, *Founders Online*.

32 Shaw, *The Character of John Adams*, made a similar point and went so far as to claim that "the years in England left Adams a confirmed pessimist," 224. I believe that Adams exhibited a much more ambivalent, nuanced, and often-positive outlook that varied with particular times and specific circumstances, especially as he aged.

33 "Diary of Abigail Adams," March 30–May 1, 1788, in *Diary and Autobiography of John Adams*, 3:215.

34 John Adams to John Quincy Adams, August 21, 1785, *Adams Family Correspondence*, 6:327.

35 Isenberg and Burstein, *The Problem of Democracy*, 439.

36 Abigail Adams to Mary Smith Cranch, March 13, 1785, *Adams Family Correspondence*, 6:67–71.

BIBLIOGRAPHY

PRIMARY SOURCES

Adams, Abigail. *The Letters of Mrs. Adams, the Wife of John Adams. With an Introductory Memoir by Her Grandson Charles Francis Adams*. 4th ed. Boston: Wilkins, Carter, 1848.

Adams, Charles Francis, ed. "Correspondence between John Adams and Mercy Warren." Reprinted in *Collections of Massachusetts Historical Society*. Boston: Massachusetts Historical Society, 1878.

———, ed. *The Works of John Adams*. 10 vols. Boston: Little and Brown, 1850–1856.

Adams Family Papers: An Electronic Archive. Boston: Massachusetts Historical Society. www.masshist.org/digitaladams.

Boyd, Julian, et al., eds. *The Papers of Thomas Jefferson*. Princeton, NJ: Princeton University Press, 1950–.

Butterfield, Lyman H., ed. *Diary and Autobiography of John Adams*. 4 vols. Cambridge, MA: Harvard University Press, 1961.

Butterfield, L. H., et al., eds. *Adams Family Correspondence*. 14 vols. Cambridge, MA: Harvard University Press, 1963–2019.

Cappon, Lester J., ed. *The Adams-Jefferson Letters*. New York: Simon and Schuster, 1971.

De Windt, Caroline, ed. *Journal and Correspondence of Miss Adams, Daughter of John Adams, Second President of the United States: Written in France and England, in 1875*. New York: Wiley and Putnam, 1841–1842.

Ford, Worthington C., ed. *Warren-Adams Letters, Being Chiefly a Correspondence among John Adams, Samuel Adams, and James Warren*. Boston: Massachusetts Historical Society, 1917–1925.

Founders Online. Washington, DC: National Archives. www.founders.archives.gov.

Hogan, Martha, and C. James Taylor, eds. *My Dearest Friend: Letters of Abigail and John Adams*. Cambridge, MA: Harvard University Press, 2007.

Johnston, Henry P., ed. *The Correspondence and Public Papers of John Jay*. Reprint, New York: Lenox Hill, 1970.

King, Charles R., ed. *The Life and Correspondence of Rufus King*. New York, 1895.

Lopez, Claude, et al., eds. *The Papers of Benjamin Franklin*. New Haven, CT: Yale University Press, 1959–.

Mitchell, Steward, ed. *New Letters of Abigail Adams, 1788–1801*. New York: Houghton Mifflin, 1947.

Morris, Richard B., ed. *John Jay: The Winning of the Peace, Unpublished Papers, 1780–1784*. New York: Harper and Row, 1980.

Taylor, John. *An Inquiry into the Principles and Policy of the Government of the United States*. New Haven, CT: Yale University Press, 1814, reprint, 1950.

Taylor, Robert, et al., eds. *Papers of John Adams*. 20 vols. Cambridge, MA: Harvard University Press, 2003–.

SECONDARY SOURCES
Books

Abrams, Jeanne E. *First Ladies of the Republic: Martha Washington, Abigail Adams, and Dolley Madison, and the Creation of an Iconic American Role*. New York: New York University Press, 2018.

———. *Revolutionary Medicine: The Founding Fathers and Mothers in Sickness and in Health*. New York: New York University Press, 2013.

Alberts, Robert C. *The Golden Voyage: The Life and Times of William Bingham, 1752–1804*. Boston: Houghton Mifflin, 1969.

Alsop, Susan Mary. *Yankees at the Court: The First Americans in Paris*. Garden City, NJ: Doubleday, 1992.

Barker-Benfield, G. J. *Abigail and John Adams: The Americanization of Sensibility*. Chicago: University of Chicago Press, 2010.

Branson, Susan. *These Fiery Frenchified Dames: Women and Political Culture in Early National Philadelphia*. Philadelphia: University of Pennsylvania Press, 2001.

Brodie, Fawn. *Thomas Jefferson: An Intimate History*. New York: Norton, 1974.

Chalus, Elaine. *Elite Women in English Political Life, c. 1754–1790*. New York: Oxford University Press, 2005.

Dull, Jonathan R. *A Diplomatic History of the American Revolution*. New Haven, CT: Yale University Press, 1985.

Ekirch, A. Roger. *American Sanctuary: Mutiny, Martyrdom, and National Identity in the Age of Revolution*. New York: Pantheon, 2018.

Ellis, Joseph J. *American Dialogue: The Founders and Us*. New York: Knopf, 2018.

———. *First Family: Abigail and John*. New York: Knopf, 2010.

———. *Passionate Sage: The Character and Legacy of John Adams*. New York: Norton, 1993.

Ferling, John. *John Adams: A Bibliography*. Westport, CT: Greenwood, 1994.

———. *John Adams: A Life*. Knoxville: University of Tennessee Press, 1992.

Fiero, Gloria K. *The Humanistic Tradition*. Book 4, *Faith, Reason, and Power in the Early Modern World*. New York: McGraw-Hill, 1998.

Gelles, Edith B. *Abigail and John: Portrait of a Marriage*. New York: William Morrow, 2009.

———. *Portia: The World of Abigail Adams*. Bloomington: Indiana University Press, 1992.

George, M. Dorothy. *London Life in the Eighteenth Century*. London: Penguin, 1965.

Georgini, Sara. *Household Gods: The Religious Lives of the Adams Family.* New York: Oxford University Press, 2019.

Griffin, Patrick, ed. *Experiencing Empire: Power, People, and Revolution in Early America.* Charlottesville: University of Virginia Press, 2017.

Hardman, John. *Marie-Antoinette: The Making of a French Queen.* New Haven, CT: Yale University Press, 2019.

Haulman, Kate. *The Politics of Fashion in Eighteenth-Century America.* Chapel Hill: University of North Carolina Press, 2011.

Hoffman, Ronald, and Peter J. Albert, eds. *Peace and the Peacemakers: The Treaty of 1783.* Charlottesville: University of Virginia Press, 1986.

Holton, Woody. *Abigail Adams.* New York: Free Press, 2009.

Howe, John R. *The Changing Political Thought of John Adams.* Princeton, NJ: Princeton University Press, 1966.

Hutson, James H. *John Adams and the Diplomacy of the American Revolution.* Lexington: University Press of Kentucky, 1980.

Isenberg, Nancy, and Andrew Burstein. *The Problem of Democracy: The Presidents Adams Confront the Cult of Personality.* New York: Viking, 2019.

Kermes, Stephanie. *Creating an American Identity: New England, 1789–1825.* New York: Palgrave Macmillan, 2008.

Kerrison, Catherine. *Jefferson's Daughters: Three Sisters, White and Black, in a Young America.* New York: Ballantine, 2018.

Levin, Phyllis Lee. *Abigail Adams: A Biography.* New York: St. Martin's, 1987.

Lopez, Claude-Anne. *Mon Cher Papa: Franklin and the Ladies of Paris.* Reprint, New Haven, CT: Yale University Press, 1990.

———. *My Life with Benjamin Franklin.* New Haven, CT: Yale University Press, 2000.

Mayville, Luke. *John Adams and the Fear of American Oligarchy.* Princeton, NJ: Princeton University Press, 2016.

McConville, Brendan. *The King's Three Faces: The Rise and Fall of Royal America, 1688–1776.* Chapel Hill: University of North Carolina Press, 2006.

McCullough, David. *John Adams.* New York: Simon and Schuster, 2001.

Morris, Richard B. *Seven Who Shaped Our Destiny: The Founding Fathers as Revolutionaries.* New York: Harper and Row, 1973.

Park, Benjamin E. *American Nationalisms: Imagining Union in the Age of Revolutions, 1783–1833.* New York: Cambridge University Press, 2018.

Rice, Howard C., Jr. *The Adams Family in Auteuil, 1784–1785.* Boston: Massachusetts Historical Society, 1956.

Rossiter, Clinton. *The American Quest, 1790–1860: An Emerging Nation in Search of Identity, Unity, and Modernity.* New York: Harcourt Brace Jovanovich, 1971.

Ryerson, Richard Alan. *John Adams's Republic: The One, the Few, and the Many.* Baltimore: Johns Hopkins University Press, 2016.

Sadosky, Leonard, Peter Nicolaisen, Peter S. Onuf, and Andrew J. O'Shaughnessy, eds. *Old World, New World: America and Europe in the Age of Jefferson.* Charlottesville: University of Virginia Press, 2010.

Samuelson, Richard Adam. "The Adams Family and the American Experiment." PhD diss., University of Virginia, 2000.

Saxton, Martha. *The Widow Washington: The Life of Mary Washington.* New York: Farrar, Straus and Giroux, 2019.

Shackelford, George Green. *Thomas Jefferson's Travels in Europe, 1784–1789.* Baltimore: Johns Hopkins University Press, 1995.

Shaw, Peter. *The Character of John Adams.* Chapel Hill: University of North Carolina Press, 1976.

Skemp, Sheila L. *First Lady of Letters: Judith Sargent Murray and the Struggle for Female Independence.* Philadelphia: University of Pennsylvania Press, 2009.

Smith, Page. *John Adams.* Westport, CT: Greenwood, 1962.

Stahr, Walter. *John Jay: Founding Father.* New York: Hambledon and London, 2005.

Steele, Brian. *Thomas Jefferson and American Nationhood.* New York: Cambridge University Press, 2012.

Thompson, C. Bradley. *John Adams and the Spirit of Liberty.* Lawrence: University Press of Kansas, 1998.

Waldstreicher, David. *In the Midst of Perpetual Fetes: The Making of American Nationalism, 1776–1820.* Chapel Hill: University of North Carolina Press, 1997.

Warren, Mercy Otis. *History of the Rise, Progress, and Termination of the American Revolution.* Boston: Murray and Long, 1805.

Whittock, Martyn. *Mayflower Lives: Pilgrims in a New World and the Early American Experience.* New York: Pegasus, 2019.

Wilkinson, Josephine. *Louis XIV: The Power and the Glory.* New York: Pegasus, 2019.

Withey, Lynne. *Dearest Friend: A Life of Abigail Adams.* New York: Free Press, 1981.

Wood, Gordon S. *The Americanization of Benjamin Franklin.* New York: Penguin, 2004.

———. *Friends Divided: John Adams and Thomas Jefferson.* New York: Penguin, 2017.

Yalom, Marilyn, and Laura Carstensen, eds. *Inside the American Couple.* Berkeley: University of California Press, 2002.

Yokota, Kariann Akemi. *Unbecoming British: How Revolutionary America Became a Postcolonial Nation.* New York: Oxford University Press, 2011.

Zagarri, Rosemarie. *A Woman's Dilemma: Mercy Otis Warren and the American Revolution.* 2nd ed. West Sussex, UK: John Wiley and Sons, 2015.

Articles

Allen, Brooke. "John Adams: Innocent Sage." *Hudson Review* 64 (July 2011): 259–69.

Appleby, Joyce. "The Jefferson-Adams Rupture and the First French Translation of John Adams' *Defence.*" *American Historical Review* 73 (April 1968): 1084–91.

———. "The New Republican Synthesis and the Changing Political Ideas of John Adams." *American Quarterly* 25 (December 1973): 578–95.

Aring, Charles D. "Adams and Jefferson: A Correspondence." *History Today* 21 (September 1971): 609–18.

Bauer, Jean. "With Friends Like These: John Adams and the Comte de Vergennes on Franco-American Relations." *Diplomatic History* 37 (2013): 664–92.

Clarfield, Gerald. "John Adams: The Marketplace and American Foreign Policy." *New England Quarterly* 32 (September 1979): 345–57.

Cornish, Paul Joseph. "John Adams, Cicero and the Traditions of Republicanism." *Michigan Academician* 41 (2012): 22–37.

Crews, Ed. "Thomas Jefferson: Culinary Revolutionary." *Colonial Williamsburg Journal* 35 (Summer 2013): 56–63.

Duyverman, J. P. "An Historic Friendship." *De Halve Maen* 40 (1965): 11–13.

Evans, William B. "John Adams' Opinion of Benjamin Franklin." *Pennsylvania Magazine of History and Biography* 92 (April 1968): 220–38.

Ferling, John. "John Adams, Diplomat." *William and Mary Quarterly* 52 (April 1994): 227–52.

Ferling, John, and Lewis E. Braverman. "John Adams's Health Reconsidered." *William and Mary Quarterly* 55 (January 1998): 83–104.

Fleming, Thomas. "Franklin Charms Paris." *American Heritage* 60 (Spring 2010).

Foster, Timothy. "'Bienvenido, Mister Adams!': Anti-Catholicism, the Black Legend, and Racial Politics in the Founding of American–Spanish Relations." *Dieciocho* 40 (Fall 2017): 269–84.

Gilje, Paul A. "Commerce and Conquest in Early American Foreign Relations, 1750–1850." *Journal of the Early Republic* 37 (Winter 2017): 747–70.

Hester, Jay. "Puritanism and the Rights of Man: John Adams and His Views on Human Nature." *New England Journal of History* 53 (Fall 1996): 53–68.

Hutson, James H. "John Adams and the Birth of Dutch American Friendship, 1780–1782." *BMGN: Low Countries Historical Review* 77 (January 1982): 409–22.

Kaplan, Lawrence S. "The Founding Fathers and the Two Confederations: The United States of America and the United Provinces of the Netherlands, 1783–89." *BMGN: Low Countries Historical Review* 77 (January 1982): 423–37.

———. "The Treaty of Paris, 1783: A Historiographical Challenge." *International History Review* 5 (August 1983): 431–42.

Kitch, Sarah Beth Vosburg. "The Roots of John Adams's Political Science." *Journal of Church and State* 58 (May 2015): 283–306.

Levy, H. Phillip. "John Adams Presents His Credentials." *History Today* 9 (January 1959): 59–63.

Lewis, Jan. "The Republican Wife: Virtue and Seduction in the Early Republic." *William and Mary Quarterly* 44 (October 1987): 689–721.

Lint, Gregg L. "Preparing for Peace: The Objectives of the United States, France, and Spain in the War of the American Revolution." In *Peace and the Peacemakers: The Treaty of 1783*, edited by Ronald Hoffman and Peter J. Albert, 30–51. Charlottesville: University Press of Virginia, 1986.

Maier, Pauline. "Popular Uprising and Civil Authority in Eighteenth-Century
    America." *William and Mary Quarterly* 27 (January 1970): 3–35.
Meschutt, David. "The Adams-Jefferson Portrait Exchange." *American Art Journal* 14
    (Spring 1982): 47–54.
Miroff, Bruce. "John Adams: Merit, Fame, and Political Leadership." *Journal of Politics*
    478 (February 1986): 116–32.
Morgan, Edmund S. "John Adams and the Puritan Tradition." *New England Quarterly*
    34 (December 1961): 518–29.
Morris, Richard B. "The Great Peace of 1783." *Proceedings of the Massachusetts Historical
    Society* 95 (1983): 29–51.
Nordholt, Jan Willen Schulte. "John Adams Is Still with Us." *New England Quarterly*
    66 (June 1993): 269–74.
O'Neill, Daniel I. "John Adams versus Mary Wollstonecraft on the French Revolution
    and Democracy." *Journal of the History of Ideas* 68 (July 2007): 451–76.
Palmer, Beverly Wilson. "Abigail Adams and the Apple of Europe." *New England
    Historical and Genealogical Register* 135 (April 1981): 109–20.
Palmer, R. R. "Two Americans in Two Dutch Republics." *BMGN: Low Countries
    Historical Review* 77 (January 1982): 393–407.
Riley, James C. "Financial and Economic Ties: The First Century." *BMGN: Low
    Countries Historical Review* 77 (January 1982): 439–55.
Riley, Randall N. "Adams, Burke, and Eighteenth-Century Conservatism." *Political
    Science Quarterly* 80 (June 1965): 216–35.
Rosenfeld, Sophia. "'Europe,' Women, and the American Political Imaginary: The
    1790s and the 1990s." *Journal of the Early Republic* 35 (Summer 2015): 272–77.
Rowen, Herbert H. "John Adams's Vision of the Dutch Republic." *Consortium on
    Revolutionary Europe, 1750–1850* 8 (1979): 3–14.
Slauter, Will. "Constructive Misreadings: Adams, Turgot, and the American State
    Constitutions." *Papers of the Biographical Society of America* 105 (March 2011): 33–67.
Storch, Neal T. "Adams, Franklin and the Origin of Consular Representation." *Foreign
    Service Journal* 52 (October 1975): 11–13.
Taylor, John M. "Adams and Jefferson in the Middle East." *Manuscripts* 33 (Summer
    1981): 237–40.
Thompson, C. Bradley. "John Adams and the Coming of the French Revolution."
    Journal of the Early Republic 16 (Autumn 1996): 361–87.
Wood, Gordon S. "Friends Divided." *Trend and Tradition*, Spring 2019.

INDEX

Pages numbers in *italics* denote images and associated captions.

ABOUT THE AUTHOR

JEANNE E. ABRAMS is Professor at the University Libraries and the Center for Judaic Studies at the University of Denver. She received her PhD in American history from the University of Colorado at Boulder with a specialization in archival management. She is the author of *Jewish Women Pioneering the Frontier Trail: A History in the American West*, *Dr. Charles David Spivak: A Jewish Immigrant and the American Tuberculosis Movement*, and *Revolutionary Medicine: The Founding Fathers and Mothers in Sickness and in Health*, as well as numerous articles in the fields of American, Jewish, and medical history that have appeared in scholarly journals and popular magazines. *Revolutionary Medicine* was reviewed widely in scholarly journals and the popular media, including the *Wall Street Journal*, and was named one of the "Top Books for Docs" by *Medscape*. Her latest book is *First Ladies of the Republic: Martha Washington, Abigail Adams, and Dolley Madison, and the Creation of an Iconic American Role*.